Hiking Yoho, Kootenay, Glacier, and Mt. Revelstoke National Parks

Help Us Keep This Guide Up to Date

Every effort has been made by the author and editors to make this guide as accurate and useful as possible. However, many things can change after a guide is published—trails are rerouted, regulations change, techniques evolve, facilities come under new management, and so on.

We would love to hear from you concerning your experiences with this guide and how you feel it could be improved and kept up to date. While we may not be able to respond to all comments and suggestions, we'll take them to heart and we'll also make certain to share them with the author. Please send your comments and suggestions to the following address:

The Globe Pequot Press
Reader Response/Editorial Department
P.O. Box 480
Guilford, CT 06437

Or you may e-mail us at:

editorial@globe-pequot.com

Thanks for your input, and happy trails!

Hiking Yoho, Kootenay, Glacier, and Mt. Revelstoke National Parks

by **Michelle Gurney**
and Kathy Howe

FALCON®
GUILFORD, CONNECTICUT

An imprint of The Globe Pequot Press

A FALCONGUIDE®

Copyright © 2002 by The Globe Pequot Press

Falcon and FalconGuide are registered trademarks of The Globe Pequot Press.

Cover photo: Courtesy of the authors, Michelle Gurney and Kathy Howe.
Photo credits: All photos courtesy of the authors.

Library of Congress Cataloging-in-Publication Data is available.
ISBN: 0-7627-1170-1

Text pages printed on recycled paper
Manufactured in the United States of America
First Edition/First Printing

To my mom and dad.
—Michelle Gurney

To mom, dad, and Allan.
—Kathy Howe

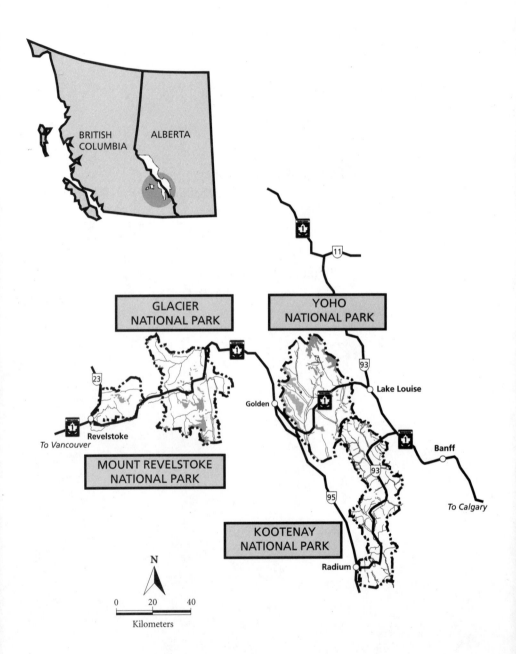

Contents

Acknowledgments

The following people helped make this book a reality:

The finest and most fearless hiking partners we could ever want: Jeff and Marci Humphrey, John Bereznicki and Claire Mitenko, Christi Cruz, Paul Choy, Russell Blown and Deborah Keene, and Sue Chenier, Lynda Yoisten, Bena Patel, and George Haeh, who helped us overcome our fear of grizzlies and return to Duchesnay Basin.

We are especially grateful to Adam Mills, Megan Jamison, and Pete Gurney who ventured out with us on some of the most remote trails, followed steaming bear scat, forged rivers and at times, even plucked us out of them—we appreciate your enthusiasm and the fact that you never once complained—even in the most dire circumstances.

Donna Nelson and GemTrek Publishing, who allowed us to trace their maps.

Dennis Blumenthal, who provided us with tickets for the Lake O'Hara bus.

Kim Baines, and Ingrid Boaz, the reviewers who scoured our manuscript for accuracy.

Robin Borstmayer, who from day one, has been completely supportive of this adventure. Thank you for bushwhacking through those overgrown trails, for not getting caught by that black bear, and for drawing and coloring maps on your days off. You're the best buddy.

Pat Gurney, who made sure our kitchen was always well stocked.

Morgan Neff, for lending us his beloved altimeter.

Kathy Janssens, our hobbyist cartographer.

Allan Maksymec, who was wifeless for three months while Kathy pursued her dream. Thanks for your support from afar, for loaning us assorted camping gear, and for assisting with those dreaded elevation charts.

Jay Nichols and Shelley Wolf, our editors, who seemed to drop everything to respond to our panicked e-mails and phone calls.

Valhalla Pure Outfitters in Edmonton, who sent new hiking boots on an overnight bus when our blisters took over our hiking schedule.

The great staff at the Parks Canada information centers in Kootenay, Rogers Pass, and Yoho, especially Rose, Roger, Jackie, Paul and Larry.

A very special thank you to Lorraine Zirke. Not only did she review our book for accuracy, but she also accompanied us on many of the trails, provided a wealth of information and a network of contacts, and showed us some of the parks' best-kept secrets. Most important, she became a great friend who kept us positive and enthusiastic even on the days we didn't feel like hiking.

Trail Map Legend

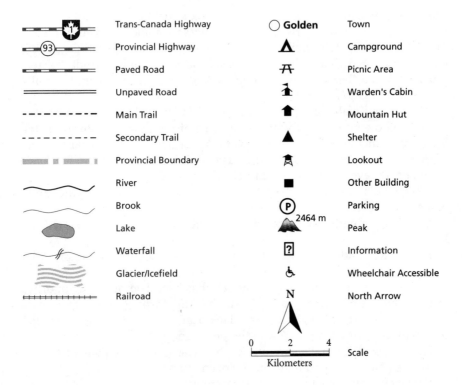

Trans-Canada Highway	
Provincial Highway	
Paved Road	
Unpaved Road	
Main Trail	
Secondary Trail	
Provincial Boundary	
River	
Brook	
Lake	
Waterfall	
Glacier/Icefield	
Railroad	

Golden — Town

Campground

Picnic Area

Warden's Cabin

Mountain Hut

Shelter

Lookout

Other Building

Parking

2464 m — Peak

Information

Wheelchair Accessible

N — North Arrow

0   2   4
Kilometers

Scale

Using This Guide

Canada's best-kept secrets. That's a good way to describe the four national parks we cover in this book: Yoho, Kootenay, Glacier, and Mount Revelstoke. Although these parks don't offer the immediate name recognition of Banff and Jasper, they do offer an off-the-beaten-path hiking experience—especially in the shoulder season.

Over the years we've spent many weekends exploring trails in these parks, along with all their enticing offerings—including the well-known Radium hot springs in Kootenay (hiked-out legs can't resist their calling at the end of a long day), the historic Burgess Shale site in Yoho, and the abandoned rails in Glacier. We researched this book during the summer of 2000 while hiking each trail with family and friends.

This guide is designed to help you choose hikes or backcountry trips that suit your ability and the amount of time you want to spend in the parks. Because we've hiked many of these trails more than once over the years, we can provide sound advice so that you can determine which trails you'd like to hike. Our trail accounts are candid and clear and are intended to provide all the information you need before heading off into the woods—including whether we spotted bears, where we gained the greatest views, and whether we felt the trail was worth the time spent. Keep in mind that trail conditions are constantly changing in the mountain parks: Check with park information centers (see Appendix A) for current trail reports and trail closures.

MAPS AND ELEVATION PROFILES

Although we've provided maps and elevation profiles for the hikes in this guide, we would suggest using them in conjunction with recreational topographical maps. You can purchase these maps at any sporting goods or map store, as well as area gift shops and information centers. We personally found the GemTrek Mountain Parks series to be one of the best—the maps are easy to read, durable, and weatherproof—a great advantage when it's wet.

TRAIL DESCRIPTIONS, LEVEL OF DIFFICULTY, AND RATINGS

Each trail description in this guide begins with a quick and easy reference section that includes a general description of the trail, the level of difficulty, directions for finding the trailhead, and our opinion on whether the trail was worthwhile.

The level of difficulty ratings are designed as follows: *Easy* trails can be completed without difficulty by any hiker; *moderate* trails will challenge novices; and *strenuous* trails will challenge even fit and experienced hikers.

For a quick overview of all the hikes on this book, refer to the Appendixes toward the back of the book. If you're interested in our picks for hikes with the best views, see the Top Ten Hikes in Appendix C. To compare the level of difficulty among all trails, consult the Trail Finder Table in Appendix D.

This short, flat loop around Balsam Lake in Mount Revelstoke National Park is rated as easy.

Following the quick reference section is a thorough breakdown of the trail, including landmarks, trail junctions, ecological and geological features, campsites, elevation charts, and other tidbits of important information.

BEFORE YOU HIT THE TRAILS

Before you hit the trails, look through the Preparing for the Backcountry section of this guide, where you'll find information on clothing, weather, park passes, and permits.

Due to the high elevation of these parks, and the amount of snow that falls during the winter months, the hiking season is quite short unless you have specific backcountry training and expertise. You can begin hiking in Kootenay and Yoho in June; however, we would recommend waiting until July to ensure that you can hike the higher elevation trails. In Glacier and Mount Revelstoke the season starts much later, beginning in late July, and the season can come to an abrupt end in September should the snow fall early. Also, in some areas, like Lake O'Hara in Yoho, reservations are required up to three months in advance, and the number of hikers allowed on the trails is limited by a daily quota to protect the ecology and wildlife. (See page 26.)

Happy hiking!
Michelle Gurney and Kathy Howe

2

Preparing for the Backcountry

Whether you're planning a leisurely two-hour walk in the woods or an extended backcountry excursion, you'll enjoy your trip much more thoroughly if you're well prepared. The following information is intended as a guideline only—based on our own mishaps (like winding up without any shelter or rain gear in golf-ball-sized hail) and lessons learned.

If you're planning numerous hiking or backpacking trips, consider picking up a copy of Falcon reference guides like *Wild Country Companion* and *Wilderness First Aid* or taking wilderness survival or first aid courses. And just to ensure that you don't forget anything, refer to A Hiker's Checklist in Appendix E.

PASSES, PERMITS, AND RESERVATIONS

When entering any Canadian national park by bus, car, bicycle, or on foot (unless you're part of a tour group), you will need to buy a Parks Pass, with fees starting at CDN $7.00 (one-person daily pass, including one vehicle). Fees vary based on the number of people in your party and the number of days you'll spend in the parks. If you plan to be in the parks for more than ten days or are traveling with a large group of people, it's most economical to buy an annual pass (CDN $72).

A Wilderness Pass is also required to camp in backcountry areas of all four parks in this book. You can purchase Wilderness Passes at park visitor centers for CDN $6.00 per person, per night, up to a maximum of CDN $30 per person per trip. If you're planning several backcountry camping trips, consider buying a one-year pass for CDN $42 per person.

During the peak summer months of July and August, it's a good idea to have your accommodations (whether camping, hostel, or hotel) booked in advance whenever possible. You can generally reserve backcountry sites in all four parks up to three months before your trip. Most frontcountry campgrounds operate on a first-come, first-served basis. During peak season the more popular sites are full by early afternoon—so arrive early, or you may be out of luck.

CLOTHING

The weather in Yoho, Kootenay, Glacier, and Mount Revelstoke National Parks is highly localized and changes rapidly. To stay comfortable during your hike, always carry a hat, gloves, and rain gear; and dress in layers.

Layer one, closest to your skin, is your comfort layer. Long underwear or underwear and T-shirts made of synthetics such as polypropylene and polyester are great choices for this layer since they absorb very little water and dry quickly.

Your middle layer is your insulation layer, which helps you retain warmth. Wool (as long as it doesn't get wet) and fleece/pile vests or jackets are logical choices. Your outer layer helps protect you from rain, snow, and wind. A wind shell may be all you need if conditions are dry; however, a waterproof/breathable fabric like Gore-Tex™ is ideal for many of the conditions you'll experience in Yoho, Kootenay, Glacier, or Revelstoke.

Up to 50 percent of your total body heat loss occurs through your head, so don't forget to carry a hat—even in summer. Besides helping to protect you against sun and rain, taking off or putting on your hat is one of the quickest ways to cool down or warm up.

FOOD AND WATER

You should always carry a little extra food and water and most important, toilet paper—even if you're out only for a few hours. If you get lost, despite what your grumbling stomach may signal, water is much more important than food. The average adult requires a minimum of two liters of water per day to stay hydrated. When hiking, you should drink at least three to four liters of water each day.

No matter how tempting those crystal-clear freshwater rivers and glacial lakes might appear, never drink directly from them. Giardia, a one-cell organism transmitted through the animal and human waste that is often present in these water sources, will give you flu-like symptoms during or soon after your trip (and we can tell you from personal experience that this is not something you want to learn about while on a backcountry trip).

As ironic as it sounds, all water gathered from natural sources should be purified. You can either boil your water for ten minutes (add one minute for each 300 meters of elevation) or use a water-filtration system, purification tablets, or iodine. Some purification methods cause a slightly unpleasant taste, so you may want to pack flavored drink crystals.

The amount of food you require depends on many factors, including your age (younger people burn food faster), the intensity and length of your hike, and the temperature (in cold weather your body requires more food to stay warm). On average, burning up the trails will burn 3,200 to 4,500 calories per day, or approximately two pounds of food.

The longer the trip, the more important the weight of your food becomes. Consider packing freeze-dried foods if weight is an issue or if you're traveling in bear country (freeze-dried foods remain odorless until opened). To reduce odors, it's also a good idea to double- and even triple-bag foods using sealable plastic bags.

NAVIGATION

When heading into the backcountry, consider registering at a warden's office or at a Parks Canada information center before your trip. Registration will initiate a search and rescue should you fail to return by your due date. If you register out, you must, by law, also register your return.

It's always a good idea to carry flares and a signaling mirror in your pack in case of emergency. You should also be prepared for all types of weather and pack a little extra food and water just in case.

HYPOTHERMIA

One of the most common hiking health hazards in the mountain parks is hypothermia. A significant decrease in body temperature, hypothermia is most prevalent in cold, wet, windy conditions with temperatures between 5 and 10 degrees Celsius (41 and 50 degrees Fahrenheit). It's characterized by complaints of cold, shivering, and slurring words in the early stages and sleepiness, muscle stiffness, and slow respiration and pulse in its more advanced stages.

You can protect yourself against hypothermia by wearing waterproof and windproof clothing and carrying a large plastic sheet in your pack so that you can build an emergency shelter if necessary.

If symptoms of hypothermia occur, act quickly to remove cold, wet clothing. Add extra layers of insulation, bundle up in a sleeping bag, or take shelter against cold, wet conditions.

Be prepared for all types of unexpected medical situations by carrying a small emergency first aid kit. You may also want to pick up a copy of Falcon's *Wilderness First Aid* or take a few wilderness survival or first aid courses.

Metric Conversions

Metric measurements are used throughout
this book; U.S. conversions are as follows:
1 meter = 3.28 feet
1 kilometer = 0.62 mile
1 hectare = 2.47 acres
1 liter = 0.26 gallon

Money

All prices in this book are in Canadian dollars (CDN $).
At press time:
CDN $1.00 = $0.66 US

Animal Hazards

BLACK BEARS AND GRIZZLY BEARS

Nothing will get your adrenaline pumping more than the unexpected sight of a bear. Most bears encountered in the backcountry will run at the sight of humans; others could follow you curiously or even attack if they feel threatened or are hungry. Bears in the frontcountry are more accustomed to humans and often visit campgrounds and other human-inhabited areas in search of food. Both black bears and grizzlies are unpredictable and may act aggressively.

There are many schools of thought on what to do when you encounter a bear; these range from "Play dead" to "Don't play dead." The best thing you can do is educate yourself (see Appendix B) and discuss your bear strategy with your hiking group before leaving home.

To protect yourself, take the following precautions:

- Travel in groups, and make noise while you hike so that bears are aware of your approach.

- Watch for bear signs, such as fresh tracks, droppings, or digging. If you see a bear, leave the area. Report all bear sightings to park officials.

- Sleep in a tent, not in the open, and always use a flashlight or headlamp at night.

- Cook downwind from your tent (500 meters if possible); hang stored food and other scented items like toothpaste between two trees (at least 6 meters off the ground and away from your campsite).

- Carry bear spray or bear bangers, loud flares you can shoot at a bear to momentarily stun them so that you can get away. Both items are available in sporting goods stores, but be sure you've tested them in advance and know how to use them correctly. Do not carry these items in your pack. Keep them handy—just in case.

There are no black-and-white rules on what to do if you encounter a bear. Generally you should stop and try to remain calm while assessing the situation (easier said than done). You will never outrun a bear, so don't even try. Instead, talk quietly and slowly as you back up to give the bear time to leave. Or act aggressively; yell out "hello, bear" and clap your hands. We learned firsthand that bears are extremely unpredictable and that every encounter is different. The best advice is to follow your instincts; do what you believe is the best thing in your specific situation.

If there's no tree to climb or the bear does attack, spray bear spray in the animal's eyes to give you enough time to escape. Try to get behind a tree to do this. If no escape is possible and the bear has knocked you to the ground, get face down, protect the back of your neck with your hands, and spread

A cheeky golden-mantled ground squirrel peeks out curiously from beneath a rock near Paget Lookout in Yoho National Park.

your legs so that the bear can't turn you over. If the bear continues to attack or attacks at night, fight back with everything at your disposal. More information on what to do if you encounter a bear is available in the *You are in Bear Country* publication available from park information centers.

OTHER WILDLIFE

Other wildlife you might encounter in the mountain parks include elk, deer, bison, wolverines, and cougars. Bison and elk can be dangerous and unpredictable and may charge without warning (especially elk during fall mating season, August to September, and spring calving season, May to June). Cougar attacks on humans are rare. If you encounter a cougar, pick up small children, and back away slowly. Do not stare into a cougar's eyes (a sign of aggression), and never run or crouch down.

Here are some general guidelines for dealing with all wildlife:

- DO NOT feed or approach any animal.

- Never come between two animals, particularly females and their young.

- Avoid bringing dogs on the trail, since they've been known to rile up the wildlife. If you don't want to leave them behind, keep them on a leash.

- Be alert for wildlife while driving; slow down when going through the parks. Report any collisions with animals to the closest park office or Royal Canadian Mounted Police (RCMP) detachment.

Environmental Hazards

AVALANCHES

Heavy snowfall, rain, drifting snow, or warming toward 0 degrees Celsius (32 degrees Fahrenheit) may be signs of increasing avalanche danger. Although the vast majority of avalanche accidents occur between December and April, avalanches also can happen during the warmer spring and summer months.

To reduce your risk of being caught in an avalanche in the mountain parks:

- Prepare adequately for your trip; obtain information from park information centers.

- Access information on snow stability at park information centers, take an avalanche awareness course, or travel with experienced persons.

- Learn basic search and rescue techniques for an avalanche situation.

The Canadian Avalanche Association, located in British Columbia, provides avalanche awareness and training courses. See Appendix A for the association's contact information. For voice bulletins on current avalanche hazard information, call (800) 667–1105.

ZERO IMPACT

Nowadays most wilderness users want to walk softly, but some aren't aware that they have poor manners. Often their actions are dictated by the outdated habits of a past generation of campers who cut green boughs for evening shelters, built campfires with fire rings, and dug trenches around tents. In the 1950s, these practices may have been acceptable. But they leave long-lasting scars, and today such behavior is absolutely unacceptable.

Because wild places are becoming rare and the number of users is mushrooming, a new code of ethics must be employed by the unending waves of people seeking a perfect backcountry experience. Today, we all must leave no clues of our passage. Enjoy the wild, but leave no trace of your visit.

THREE FALCON PRINCIPLES OF ZERO IMPACT

- Leave with everything you brought in.

- Leave no sign of your visit.

- Leave the landscape as you found it.

Most of us know better than to litter—in or out of the backcountry. Be sure you leave nothing, regardless of how small it is, along the trail or at your campsite. This means you should pack out everything, including orange peels, flip tops, cigarette butts, and gum wrappers. Also, pick up any trash that others leave behind.

Follow the main trail. Avoid cutting switchbacks and walking on vegetation beside the trail. Don't pick up "souvenirs," such as rocks, antlers, or wildflowers. The next person wants to see them, too, and collecting such souvenirs violates many regulations.

Avoid making loud noises on the trail (unless you are in bear country) or in camp. Be courteous—remember, sound travels easily in the backcountry, especially across water.

Carry a lightweight trowel to bury human waste six to eight inches deep and at least 200 feet away from any water source. Pack out used toilet paper.

Go without a campfire if you can't find an established fire pit. Carry a stove for cooking and a flashlight, candle lantern, or headlamp for light. For emergencies, learn how to build a no-trace fire.

Camp in obviously used sites when they are available. Otherwise, camp and cook on durable surfaces such as bedrock, sand, gravel bars, or bare ground.

Details on these guidelines and recommendations of Zero Impact principles for specific outdoor activities can be found in the Falcon Guide *Official Leave No Trace Handbook.* Visit your local bookstore, or call The Globe Pequot Press at (800) 243–0495 for a copy.

A lone brown-eyed susan greets hikers on the often-traveled Juniper Trail in Kootenay National Park.

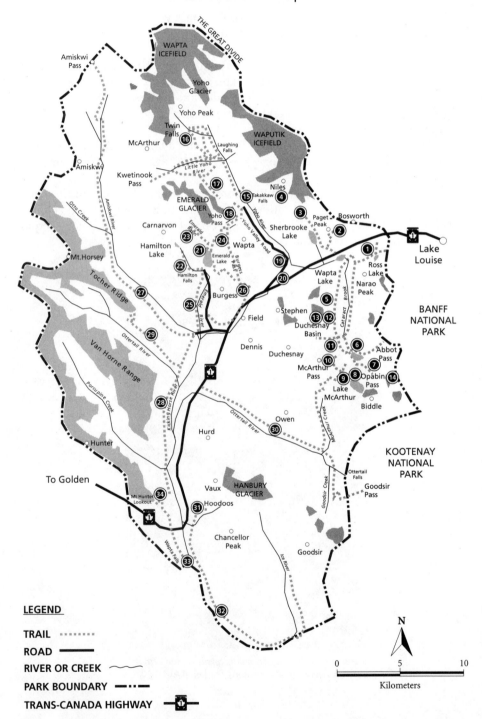

Yoho National Park
Trail Locator Map

THE GREAT DIVIDE

WAPTA ICEFIELD

Amiskwi Pass

Yoho Glacier

Yoho Peak

Twin Falls

McArthur

Laughing Falls

WAPUTIK ICEFIELD

Amiskwi

Kwetinook Pass

Little Yoho River

Niles

Takakkaw Falls

EMERALD GLACIER

Carnarvon

Emerald Glacier

Hamilton Lake

Mt. Horsey

Tocher Ridge

Hamilton Falls

Burgess

Paget Peak

Bosworth

Sherbrooke Lake

Yoho Pass

Wapta

Emerald Lake

Yoho Valley Road

Wapta Lake

Ross Lake

Narao Peak

Lake Louise

BANFF NATIONAL PARK

Stephen

Duchesnay Basin

Field

Dennis

Duchesnay

McArthur Pass

Abbot Pass

Owen

Opabin Pass

Lake McArthur

Biddle

Otter Creek

Amiskwi River

Pipestone River

Kicking Horse River

Ottertail River

Van Horne Range

Porcupine Creek

Hunter

To Golden

Mt Hunter Lookout

Vaux

Hoodoos

HANBURY GLACIER

Chancellor Peak

Hurd

Ottertail River

Goodsir Creek

Ottertail Falls

Goodsir Pass

KOOTENAY NATIONAL PARK

Ice River

Goodsir

Cataract Brook

McArthur Creek

Wapta Falls

LEGEND

TRAIL ....

ROAD ————

RIVER OR CREEK

PARK BOUNDARY — ·· —

TRANS-CANADA HIGHWAY

N

0   5   10
Kilometers

Yoho National Park

With one of Canada's highest waterfalls, the world's most complete Cambrian fossils, and twenty-eight peaks over 3,000 meters tall, Yoho National Park offers plenty to explore. Best of all, with 1,310 square kilometers of wilderness—but fewer than one million visitors annually—you will have some trails all to yourself.

Established in 1886 as Canada's second national park, Yoho is located in British Columbia along the Great Divide. Banff National Park borders Yoho to the east and Kootenay National Park to the south. Yoho is easily accessible on TransCanada Highway 1. It's just a one-hour drive west of the Banff townsite and approximately thirty minutes east of Golden, British Columbia.

The park offers more than 400 kilometers of hiking trails, providing the opportunity to see and experience all types of terrain, including alpine lakes, sparkling glaciers, and steep mountain peaks. That's why it's only fitting that the word "Yoho" means awe or wonder in Cree. Best of all, many of these spectacular sights are within a close walk from the road.

Native peoples were the first humans to visit the area now known as Yoho National Park. They used the Kicking Horse River as a summer hunting ground but migrated to warmer territory during Yoho's severe winters.

Between 1857 and 1860 Yoho saw some of its first European visitors, a British expedition studying the geography and geology of the area to determine its mineral composition and its potential for agriculture. Roughly twenty years later, more-permanent settlements were established as engineers and surveyors began work on the section of the Canadian Pacific Railway that would pass through the park. The area's steep terrain caused an enormous engineering challenge, but the rail route over the Great Divide was eventually completed in 1884.

UNESCO named Yoho as a World Heritage site in 1984.

SEASONS AND WEATHER

Weather in Yoho is localized and unpredictable, so be sure to dress in layers. The summer hiking season generally runs from mid-June to mid-September; however, you'll find snow at the higher elevations (above 1,500 meters) well into July and possibly all season. Unless you really like hiking and sleeping in snow, plan your high-elevation hikes for August and September.

Mean summer temperature: 12.5°C (54°F)
Average high: 20°C (68°F)
Average low: 5°C (41°F)

Daily weather forecasts are available at the visitor center located on the south side of TransCanada Highway 1 in Field, British Columbia. They're also posted daily at many campgrounds. You might also want to pick up a copy of Falcon's *Reading Weather* at your local bookstore.

BASIC SERVICES

The town of Field, located in the park, provides basic services including a post office, restaurants (Yoho Brothers Trading Post, Kicking Horse Cafe, Truffle Pigs Cafe, and CP Rail Bunkhouse Cafe), a general/liquor store (in Truffle Pigs Cafe), a lodge and several guest houses, as well as voluntary ambulance and fire-fighting services. Field is also home to the main visitor center in Yoho National Park, which provides year-round park information, maps, passes, permits, and information on area attractions, sites, and accommodations.

Note: There is no gas station in Field. The closest places to fuel up are Lake Louise (27 km east of Field) and Golden, British Columbia. (55.0 km west of Field). Accommodations, restaurants, grocery stores, and other basic services are also available in both Lake Louise and Golden.

FRONTCOUNTRY CAMPGROUNDS

Yoho has five road-accessible campgrounds, all of which accommodate tents, trailers, and motor homes and operate on a first-come, first-served basis.

- **Chancellor Peak,** 8 kilometers east of the park's west gate, operates from mid-May through mid-September; 64 sites with kitchen shelters, pump water, pit toilets, picnic tables, and fire rings.

- **Hoodoo Creek,** 6.5 kilometers east of the park's west gate, operates from late June through early September; 106 sites with kitchen shelters, flush toilets, hot and cold running water, a playground, picnic tables, and fire rings.

- **Kicking Horse,** Yoho Valley Road, 31.7 kilometers east of the park's west gate, operates from mid-May through early October; 86 sites with kitchen shelters, flush toilets, hot and cold running water, wheelchair-accessible washrooms with hot showers (CDN $1.00, coin-operated), a playground, picnic tables, and fire rings.

- **Monarch,** Yoho Valley Road, 31 kilometers east of the park's west gate, operates from late June through early September; 46 sites with kitchen shelters, pit toilets, pump water, and picnic tables.

- **Takakkaw Falls,** Yoho Valley Road, 44 kilometers east of the park's west gate, operates from late June through mid-September; 35 sites with kitchen shelters, bear-proof food and garbage storage, pump water, pit toilets, and fire rings.

You can stay at any one frontcountry campground for a maximum of fourteen nights. If you're visiting Yoho during its busiest tourist months, July or August, it pays to plan ahead; the most popular campgrounds often fill up by early afternoon.

BACKCOUNTRY CAMPGROUNDS

There are seven backcountry campgrounds in Yoho National Park—four in the Yoho Valley, two in the Ottertail Valley, and one at Lake O'Hara. It's a good idea to reserve these sites in advance, although some last-minute sites are available. The visitor center in Field provides information on campground opening and closing dates and conditions, as well as backcountry rules and regulations. Backcountry campgrounds include:

- McArthur Creek (10 sites)

- Float Creek (4 sites)

- Yoho Lake (8 sites)

- Laughing Falls (8 sites)

- Twin Falls (8 sites)

- Little Yoho (10 sites)
  Bear poles and outhouses are available at each site.

- Lake O'Hara (30 sites). Food storage, outhouses, and drinking water are available at this site.

Random camping is also permitted at Amiskwi, Ice River, and Otterhead River valley campgrounds. Check with the Field Visitor Centre for more information.

Note: Permits are required to camp in Yoho's backcountry. You can purchase your Wilderness Pass at the Field Visitor Centre for $6.00 per person per night, to a maximum of CDN $30 per trip. If you're planning several backcountry camping trips in Canadian national parks, it's more economical to buy a season pass (valid for one year from the date of purchase) for CDN $42 per person.

Approximately 75 percent of sites at each backcountry campground may be reserved up to three months before your trip by calling (250) 343–6783. The remaining sites are assigned in person only, on a first-come, first-served basis, at the Field Visitor Centre up to twenty-four hours before your first night of camping.

ALPINE HUTS AND HOSTELS
The Alpine Club of Canada maintains three backcountry huts in Yoho:

- The Stanley Mitchell hut in the Yoho Valley

- The Elizabeth Parker and Abbott Pass huts at Lake O'Hara

For information and reservations call (403) 678–3200, or e-mail alpclub@telusplanet.net.

The Whiskey Jack Hostel is located in the Yoho Valley near Takakkaw Falls. Call (403) 762–4122 for more information.

1 Ross Lake

Highlights:	This short stroll through the woods ends at picturesque Ross Lake, which is nestled among Narao Peak, Pope's Peak, and Mount Whyte.
Type of hike:	Day hike; out-and-back.
Total distance:	6.4 kilometers.
Difficulty:	Easy.
Hiking time:	1½–2 hours.
Elevation at trailhead:	1,610 meters.
Elevation gain:	Minimal.
Topo maps:	Lake Louise & Yoho (GemTrek Publishing); Lake Louise, 82 N/7.

Finding the trailhead: To get to the Ross Lake trailhead, follow the Lake O'Hara turnoff on the south side of TransCanada Highway 1, approximately 41.5 kilometers east of Yoho National Park's west gate and 2.5 kilometers west of the park's east boundary. Turn south off the highway, and stay to the left (northeast) at the fork in the road. Park in the gravel lot to your left (east) just before the railroad tracks. From here it's a 1.8- kilometer hike to your left (east) along Highway 1A to reach the trailhead.

Key points:
- 0.0 Parking lot.
- 1.8 Ross Lake trailhead; head right (south).
- 3.2 Ross Lake.
- 6.4 Parking lot.

The hike: It's flat, quick, and picturesque. Ross Lake is also a bit off the beaten path—especially now that Highway 1A is closed to vehicles. When we hiked this trail in early June, we didn't meet a single person—a pleasant surprise after experiencing some of Yoho's busier trails.

The only drawback is the 1.8-kilometer trudge along Highway 1A. Although you'll enjoy views of both Mount Bosworth (2,771 m) and Sink Lake to your left (north), the highway noise is an unpleasant distraction, as are the thundering trains on nearby tracks.

At 1.7 kilometers, you'll reach a directional sign for Ross Lake to your right (south), which appears to be pointing into the woods. Resist the temptation to duck into the forest just yet, even though there are several beaten paths, and continue along the road an extra 100 meters to the Ross Lake trailhead on your right (south). From the trailhead you can see Narao Peak (2,974 m) straight ahead (south).

The early part of the trail leads you through a forest of lodgepole pine, Douglas fir, and spruce. You may spot black, hairy-looking moss draped across the branches of some of these trees. This is called horsehair lichen and does not harm the trees. Goosefoot violets and northern anemones line the very gradual ascent to the lake.

Ross Lake

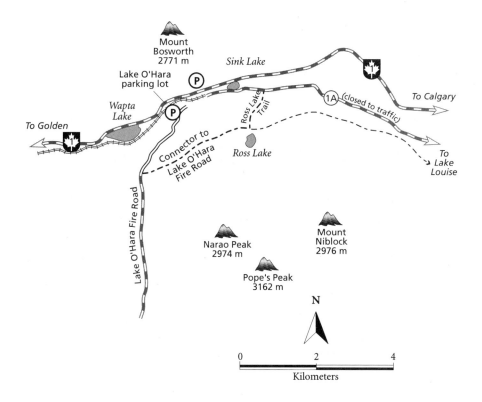

At 2.3 kilometers the moss-carpeted trail briefly skirts a small creek to your right (east). You'll still hear highway noise at this point, but you'll also begin to hear the chirping of various local birds.

When you arrive at the lake just 900 meters later, continue along the wooden boardwalk, which covers the more swampy sections of the trail, for a panoramic view of the lake and the three mountains framing it. Pope's Peak (3,162 m) stands straight ahead of you (south), Narao Peak (2,974 m) lies slightly to your right (south), and Mount Niblock (2,976 m) in Banff National Park stands to your left (southeast).

Option:
Lake O'Hara Fire Road Loop—5.7 kilometers. After enjoying the lake, you can either return the way you came or loop back on the connecting road to the Lake O'Hara Fire Road—the option we chose. The trail connecting Ross Lake with the Lake O'Hara Fire Road lies approximately 25 meters before the lake to your left (west). Look for the red and yellow directional sign, which is a bit buried in the woods. This flat path travels 3.6 kilometers through

Ross Lake lies just west of the Great Divide. In June, western anemones dot its lakeshore.

both forest and willow-filled marsh and offers scenic views of Mount Bosworth before arriving at the Lake O'Hara Fire Road. Follow the fire road to your right (north) 2.1 kilometers along Cataract Brook back to the parking lot.

2 Paget Peak

Highlights: A short, steep climb to the lookout on Paget Peak.
Type of hike: Day hike; out-and-back.
Total distance: 7 kilometers.
Hiking time: 2–3 hours.
Elevation at trailhead: 1,520 meters.
Elevation gain: 605 meters.
Difficulty: Moderate.
Topo maps: Lake Louise & Yoho (GemTrek Publishing);
Lake Louise, 82 N/8.

Finding the trailhead: Follow TransCanada Highway 1 to the Wapta Lake picnic area on the north side of the highway, 5 kilometers west of Yoho's east boundary and 39 kilometers east of Yoho's west gate. The trailhead sign is just left (north) of the sheltered picnic area.

Key points:

0.0 Trailhead.
1.4 Trail junction right (east) to Paget Lookout.
3.5 Paget Lookout.

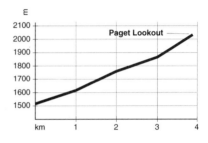

The hike: This trail, while steep, is certainly worth the climb, particularly early in the season when other high-elevation hikes are still beneath 1.5 meters of snow. Once you reach Paget Lookout, you'll gain panoramic views of the Kicking Horse Pass and its valley, as well as Cataract Valley and the Bow Valley and Slate Range in Banff National Park. If it's windy, the shelter offers a warm respite from the cold; it's even more enjoyable if you remembered to bring a thermos of hot chocolate.

The hike begins with an ascent along a root-filled trail up the southern flank of Paget Peak. The forest is filled primarily with Engelmann spruce and alpine fir. In mid-June, just after the snow has cleared, masses of yellow glacier lilies with anthers that range from white to yellow, red, and purple line the trail. Approximately 100 meters into the trail, you will cross over a small brook and will likely notice that you can still hear the hum from the highway, but as you head a little farther into the forest, the noise will disappear. About 200 meters into the hike, the switchbacks will start, and the trail will change from being root-filled to rocky. Gain another 100 meters, and you will cross a stream on wooden boards; here you may spot a few bright-yellow goosefoot violets. Continue on, and catch a great view of Cathedral Mountain (3,189 m) through the trees to your left (south). You will also have a clear view of the sheer gray slopes of Mount Ogden (2,695 m) to the west.

Paget Peak

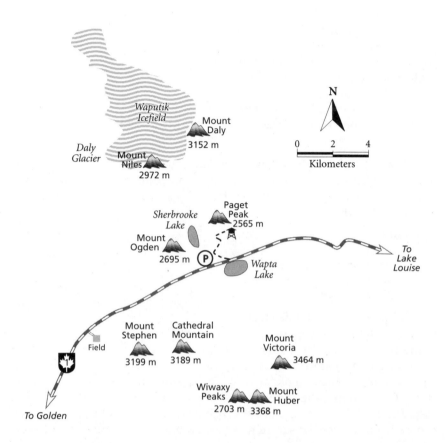

After a gradual 1.4-kilometer climb, you will reach the trail junction for Paget Lookout and Sherbrooke Lake. Head right (east) toward Paget. If you're a strong hiker, you can easily climb to Paget Lookout then come back down to the junction and walk the 1.6 kilometers to Sherbrooke Lake. Although the trail to Paget becomes noticeably more difficult from this point, the walk to the lake follows a gradual incline for about a kilometer, then levels off.

As you head upward you will likely see Sherbrooke Lake through the trees at the base of Mount Ogden. At 2.2 kilometers, the trail takes a sharp right-hand turn and you gain a spectacular view of Cathedral Mountain, Mount Victoria (3,464 m), and the Cataract Valley above Lake O'Hara. The odd juniper bush appears alongside the trail as you pass across loose shale. From here the ascent is quite steep and rocky; however, the scenic views of Mt. Stephen (3,199 m) and the Kicking Horse Valley below, including the town of Field—which sits at the top of an alluvial fan nearly 11 kilometers to the west—make the trip worthwhile.

At 3.5 kilometers, you will reach the lookout. Once there, you can easily see why this spot was chosen for a fire lookout. Although it's no longer used, it is swept clean and affords panoramic views of the valley below. To the east you'll see the Bow Valley and Slate Range; below you'll see Wapta Lake. Across the highway stand Cathedral Mountain and Mount Victoria; to the west sit Mount Odgen and the Van Horne Range. And if you didn't see one on the way up, you'll likely meet a few gold-mantled ground squirrels scampering from rock to rock. They are easily mistaken for giant chipmunks; however, you can tell them apart by their back stripes—the squirrel's extend only as far as its neck, whereas a chipmunk's stripes continue through its eyes and face. These squirrels, like chipmunks and Columbian ground squirrels or marmots, love the rocky, open country, particularly when there are a few trees in the area. They eat leaves and grasses, flowers, seeds, and roots; late in the summer they cache their food, helping fungi and flowering plants to spread and regenerate themselves. The squirrels are prey for hawks, weasels, and coyotes.

3 Sherbrooke Lake

Highlights:	A short trail that climbs moderately to the steep slopes of Mount Ogden and Sherbrooke Lake. If you're looking for a longer day hike, you can follow an unmaintained trail along the lake's east shore for approximately 1.4 kilometers and another 3 kilometers to reach Niles Meadows.
Type of hike:	Day hike; out-and-back.
Total distance:	6 kilometers.
Difficulty:	Easy.
Hiking time:	2–3 hours.
Elevation at trailhead:	1,520 meters.
Elevation gain:	280 meters.
Topo maps:	Lake Louise & Yoho (GemTrek Publishing); Lake Louise, 82 N/8.

Finding the trailhead: Follow TransCanada Highway 1 to the Wapta Lake picnic area on the north side of the highway, 5 kilometers west of Yoho's east boundary and 39 kilometers east of Yoho's west gate. The trailhead sign is just left of the sheltered picnic area.

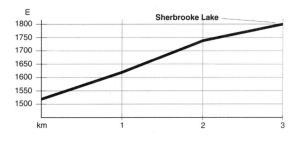

Sherbrooke Lake

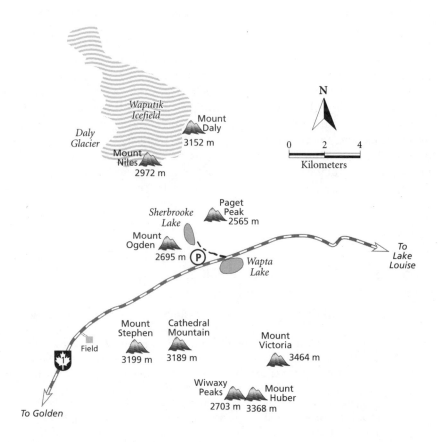

Key points:

0.0   Trailhead.
1.4   Trail junction; left (northwest) to Sherbrooke Lake.
3.0   Sherbrooke Lake.

The hike: This easy day hike to the turquoise waters of Sherbrooke Lake is perfect for families and hikers of all fitness levels. Strong hikers climbing to the Paget Lookout can enjoy the lake as a short side trip.

The hike begins with an ascent along a root-filled trail up the southern flank of Paget Peak. The forest is filled primarily with Engelmann spruce and alpine fir. In mid-June, just after the snow has cleared, hundreds of yellow glacier lilies, Indian paintbrush, and arnica line the trail. Approximately 100 meters into the hike, you will cross a small brook before you encounter a few soft switchbacks where the trail will change from being root filled to rocky. Gain another 100 meters and you will cross a stream on wooden boards; here you may spot a few goosefoot violets or globeflowers. At 1.0 kilometer, off to your left (west) you will have a clear view of Mount Ogden (2,695 m).

Mount Ogden provides the backdrop for the turquoise waters of Sherbrooke Lake.

After a gradual 1.4 kilometer climb, you'll reach the trail junction for Sherbrooke Lake and Paget Lookout. Head left (northwest) toward Sherbrooke Lake. If you're a strong hiker, you can easily climb to Paget Lookout, then come back down to the junction and walk the flat, sidewalk-smooth trail 1.6 kilometers to Sherbrooke Lake. Beyond this point, the trail begins a soft climb toward the lake. You'll know you're getting closer to Sherbrooke as you see more and more globeflowers, which thrive in wet woods near streams and lakes. These, like the glacier lily, appear soon after the snow has melted. If you're hiking early in the season, you will also see many tiny white buttercuplike flowers, northern anemones, on your approach.

As you reach the south end of the lake, you will pass through a marshy area filled with deadfall. This beautiful turquoise lake, which can be milky-blue in May, is a settling pond for glacial silt. Mount Ogden provides a spectacular backdrop for Sherbrooke Lake, particularly on a clear summer day.

At this point most hikers turn and head back to the Wapta picnic area. If you're looking for more of a challenge, you can follow the trail approximately 1.4 kilometers along Sherbrooke Lake's east side, then another 4.3 kilometers to the head of the valley in Niles Meadows. We would highly recommend forging on; the views of the meadows are breathtaking, and the trail is seldom traveled. It can be extremely muddy, depending on the weather, and you may have to ford a creek (the bridge was out the day we went up; bring your hiking poles for extra balance), but it will be worth it. (See Hike 4 for a full description of this hike.)

4 Niles Meadows

Highlights: A nice climb past Sherbrooke Lake to Niles Meadows. If you wish, you can scramble to the ridge just 500 meters below Mount Niles Peak—the view from here is breathtaking.
Type of hike: Day hike; out-and-back.
Total distance: 17.4 kilometers (2 kilometers if you complete the scramble).
Difficulty: Moderate.
Hiking time: 6–8 hours.
Elevation at trailhead: 1,520 meters.
Elevation gain: 660 meters (1055 meters if you complete the scramble).
Topo maps: Lake Louise & Yoho (GemTrek Publishing); Lake Louise, 82 N/8.

Finding the trailhead: Follow TransCanada Highway 1 to the Wapta Lake picnic area on the north side of the highway, 5 kilometers west of Yoho's east boundary and 39 kilometers east of Yoho's west gate. The trailhead sign is just left of the sheltered picnic area.

Key points:
0.0   Trailhead.
1.4   Trail junction; left (northwest) to Sherbrooke Lake.
3.0   Sherbrooke Lake.
4.4   North shore of Sherbrooke Lake.
5.9   Cross a footbridge over Sherbrooke Creek.
7.7   Cross Sherbrooke Creek over a stable old log.
8.1   Cross Sherbrooke Creek via a washed-out bridge.
8.7   Niles Meadows.

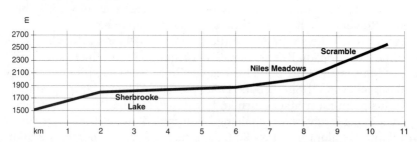

The hike: This hike to Niles Meadows is fantastic. Pass by popular Sherbrooke Lake, and follow the trail along Sherbrooke Creek, its falls, and through a spectacular meadow with large boulders that invite you to enjoy this perfect lunch spot. From here continue to Niles Meadows, where we would highly recommend completing the easy scramble to the ridge below Mount Niles (2,972 m); the 360-degree view of mountains and snowfields is jaw-dropping. You can see the ranges of Lake O'Hara—Wiwaxy Peaks (2,703 m),

Niles Meadows

Mount Huber (3,368 m), and Mount Victoria (3,464 m)—as well as Cathedral Mountain (3,189 m) and Vanguard Peak (2,464 m) to the south. Mount Ogden (2,695 m) sits to the west, and the Bath Glacier, Mount Daly (3,152 m), Paget Peak (2,565 m), and the Great Divide lie to the east.

The hike begins with an ascent along a root-filled trail up the southern flank of Paget Peak. The forest is filled primarily with Engelmann spruce and alpine fir. In mid-June, just after the snow has cleared, yellow glacier lilies, Indian paintbrush, and arnica add a little color to the trail—even more are in view after the junction to Sherbrooke Lake. At 1.0 kilometer you'll catch a great view of Cathedral Mountain behind you (south); off to your left (west), you'll see the looming Mount Ogden (2,695 m).

After a gradual 1.4-kilometer climb, you'll reach the trail junction for Sherbrooke Lake and Paget Lookout. Head left (northwest) toward Sherbrooke Lake. Follow the trail along the east side of the lake for approximately 1.4 kilometers. Depending on the weather, you may be in for some mud;

Hikers pose for a quick shot just 500 meters below the summit of Niles Peak. In the distance from left to right are Paget Peak, Mount Victoria, Mount Huber, and the flank of Mount Ogden.

otherwise the trail is well trodden. From here you'll follow Sherbrooke Creek and meet up with its spectacular falls before entering an alpine meadow at 5.7 kilometers. At 5.9 kilometers you'll cross a small footbridge over the creek. The view of Cathedral Mountain, Mount Huber, and Mount Victoria behind you (south) is absolutely breathtaking, and it only gets better from here. In front of you is Mount Niles, to the east is Paget Peak, and to the west is Mount Ogden.

Follow the buttercup-lined trail out of the meadow, crossing Niles Creek at 6.2 kilometers. In July the glacier lilies were in full bloom, as were the globeflowers and western anemones. At 7.1 kilometers you'll pass another set of falls before meeting Sherbrooke Creek once again at 7.5 kilometers. The views of the back of Mount Ogden are great, and from here you'll glimpse Niles Peak as it waits in the distance. At 7.7 kilometers, cross Sherbrooke Creek over a stable old log, and cross it once again at 8.1 kilometers. The bridge here is partly washed out so use care—and two hiking poles for extra stability. At 8.2 kilometers you'll see another set of waterfalls spilling down the side of Mount Odgen. Hike on for 300 meters to enjoy the last misty waterfall on the trail.

At 8.7 kilometers, enter Niles Meadows. The view to the south down the valley you just hiked through is incredible, with snow-capped mountains as far as you can see. You can end your hike here or look for the trail to the right (east) that will lead you part way up the flank of Mount Niles. The vista from the top is worth the scramble; however, the shale stone can be quite loose in places, so use care. From here you'll gain those 360-degree views mentioned earlier and a great glimpse of the turquoise waters of Sherbrooke Lake, 5 kilometers to the south. Bath Glacier and its huge snowfield are to your immediate right (east). This is a great spot to enjoy an afternoon snack.

Lake O'Hara

GETTING THERE—RESERVATIONS REQUIRED

The hikes at Lake O'Hara (Hikes 5 through 14) are in a protected area, with access controlled by a daily quota system. To get there, you may either reserve a seat on the Lake O'Hara bus system, or walk the 12.2-kilometer Cataract Brook Trail (or the Lake O'Hara Fire Road, which is slightly shorter) to the lake. The fire road is closed to cyclists and private vehicles.

The Lake O'Hara bus runs several times daily from June 19 through September 30. You may make reservations up to three months before your trip by calling (250) 343–6433 (March through September). A limited number of last-minute bus tickets are also available twenty-four hours in advance of each trip on a first-come, first-served basis at the Field Information Centre, which is located just south of TransCanada Highway 1, in Field, British Columbia.

AMENITIES

Le Relais, Lake O'Hara's day shelter, serves hot and cold beverages and snacks and provides basic maps and trail information. It's also a great place to warm up on a chilly day. You can use the tables inside and out to eat your lunch. Le Relais usually offers sandwiches in the peak season, but it's wise to bring your own lunch just in case. Outhouses are located just north of Le Relais.

Lake O'Hara Lodge offers an afternoon tea, but don't plan on buying your lunch or dinner there. The Lodge is often full and caters primarily to its overnight guests.

WHAT TO BRING

- Your lunch. Le Relais offers limited sandwiches, and Lake O'Hara Lodge seldom has space available for anyone other than its overnight guests.

- Plenty of warm clothes. Because of its high elevation, you can expect snow and cooler temperatures well into July at Lake O'Hara. Dress in layers and bring gloves and a hat.

- Waterproof boots. They are a necessity for your comfort in June and the first part of July, when you may still be trudging through snow on some trails.

5 Cataract Brook

Highlights:	A scenic hike through the woods and along Cataract Brook from the Lake O'Hara Campground to the Lake O'Hara Parking Lot.
Type of hike:	Day hike; shuttle.
Total distance:	12.2 kilometers.
Difficulty:	Easy.
Hiking time:	3–4 hours.
Elevation at trailhead:	2,020 meters.
Elevation loss:	420 meters.
Recreational Topo maps:	Lake Louise & Yoho, (GemTrek Publishing); Lake Louise, 82 N/8.

Finding the trailhead: Follow TransCanada Highway 12.5 kilometers west of Yoho's east boundary, and turn left (south) at the Lake O'Hara turnoff. If you're heading in via Yoho's west gate, turn right after approximately 41.5 kilometers; the turn is marked on both sides of the highway. Follow the short road toward the Lake O'Hara parking area. Because this is a shuttle hike, you have two options to complete it: Begin at the parking area and hike up the trail toward Lake O'Hara, or begin at the Lake O'Hara Campground and hike down the trail to the parking area. There are washrooms in the parking area.

Special considerations: Lake O'Hara has a daily quota system. To hike this trail you need to make reservations for the bus to Lake O'Hara as early as three months in advance. You can also hike the 12.2-kilometer Cataract Brook Trail to the lake. (See Hike 5 for more information.)

Key points:
0.0	Lake O'Hara Campground.
1.5	Trail junction; head left (east).
1.8	Cross Morning Glory Creek.
2.3	Four-way trail junction; continue straight ahead (north).
2.8	Cross Duchesnay Creek.
10.3	Cross Cataract Brook.
11.8	Lake O'Hara parking area.

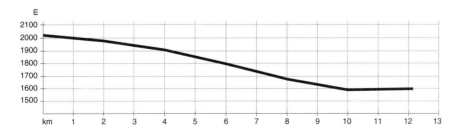

Cataract Brook

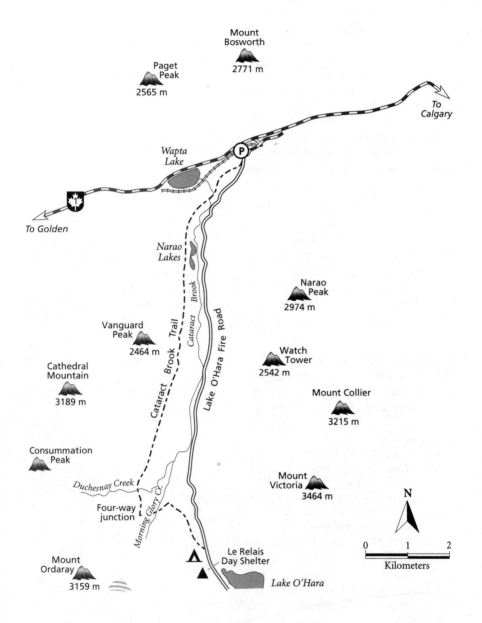

Mount Bosworth
2771 m

Paget Peak
2565 m

To Calgary

Wapta Lake

To Golden

Narao Lakes

Narao Peak
2974 m

Cataract Brook Trail

Cataract Brook

Lake O'Hara Fire Road

Vanguard Peak
2464 m

Watch Tower
2542 m

Cathedral Mountain
3189 m

Mount Collier
3215 m

Consummation Peak

Mount Victoria
3464 m

Duchesnay Creek

Morning Glory Cr.

Four-way junction

Mount Ordaray
3159 m

Le Relais Day Shelter

Lake O'Hara

N

0   1   2
Kilometers

The hike: Unlike most round-trip day hikes, here you have a choice—walk uphill or down. Either way, there are three spectacular viewpoints on this leisurely wooded trail.

Begin this downhill hike at the northern end of the Lake O'Hara Campground. You'll see a small trail sign where you should head left (east). This lush, forested trail filled with lodgepole pine is lined with moss and mint-green pixie cup lichens. You'll hear the creek as soon as you begin the hike and will lose the sound only a few times along the way. At 1.5 kilometers, you'll reach your first junction; head left (east). If you head right (west) you'll walk 600 meters before reaching the Lake O'Hara Fire Road. At approximately 1.8 kilometers, you'll pass over Morning Glory Creek. From here you'll have an impressive view of Odaray Mountain (3,159 m) and its glacier.

At 2.3 kilometers, you'll reach a four-way junction; continue straight ahead (north). Approximately 500 meters farther down the trail, you'll pass over the rock-bottomed Duchesnay Creek, where your view of Cathedral Mountain (3,189 m), Cathedral Prospect, and Consummation Peak is quite nice. From here you'll pass through several old quartzite rockfalls covered in crust lichens; it's quite rocky in places, so be sure to watch your footing. Approximately 3.5 kilometers into the hike, the trail will begin to open up and you'll have an awesome view. To the right (east) are Mount Victoria (3,464 m) and Mount Collier (3,215 m); to the northeast is the Watch Tower (2,542 m).

Follow the trail down a few soft switchbacks and you'll see both Vanguard Peak (2,464 m) and Mount Bosworth (2,771 m) straight ahead of you (north). The trail is quite moist at times due to the number of underground springs in the area. Approximately 7 kilometers into the trail, you'll catch a glimpse of the Lake O'Hara Fire Road off to your right (east). You'll then enter an open meadow filled with bright-yellow goosefoot violets, the occasional Canadian toad, and the swampy-looking Narao Lakes. Off to the right (east) is Narao Peak (2,974 m). Continue on to reach the last trail junction before you return to the parking lot. You'll pass over an unused fire road, where you'll reacquaint yourself with the familiar roar of the TransCanada Highway. Mount Bosworth is in clear view to the north.

At 10 kilometers you'll finally meet up with Cataract Brook, which in early June is raging. You'll cross it on a footbridge at approximately 10.3 kilometers. From here the brook enters a canyon before it falls to fill Wapta Lake. If you look north, you can easily spot Paget Peak (2,565 m) and its old fire lookout from the trail. Follow the well-trodden path through the trees to the parking area. Here you may notice a few more signs of bears; many of the trees have rather large scratch marks.

If you're planning on skipping this trail entirely to take the return bus trip to Lake O'Hara, consider arriving about an hour earlier than your departure time so that you can at least walk from the parking area to Cataract Brook. This short stroll will be well worth the trip—and it will get you limbered up to conquer the tough hikes that await you up at the lake.

6 Lake O'Hara Shoreline Trail

Highlights: This gentle stroll loops around Lake O'Hara, offering fantastic views of surrounding mountains and Seven Veils Falls.

Type of hike: Day hike; loop.

Total distance: 3 kilometers.

Difficulty: Easy.

Hiking time: 1 hour.

Elevation at trailhead: 2,035 meters.

Elevation gain: Minimal.

Topo maps: Lake Louise & Yoho, (GemTrek Publishing); Lake Louise, 82 N/8.

Finding the trailhead: The turnoff to Lake O'Hara is located on the south side of TransCanada Highway 1, approximately 2.5 kilometers west of Yoho National Park's east boundary and 41.5 kilometers east of the park's west gate. Turn right (west) immediately after the train tracks, and park in the large lot. An outhouse is available in the parking lot.

You'll find the trailhead for the Lake O'Hara Shoreline Trail on the east side of the Lake O'Hara Fire Road, just to the right (south) of the warden's cabin and directly across the road (east) from the Le Relais day-use shelter.

Special considerations: Lake O'Hara has a daily quota system. To hike this trail you need to make reservations for the bus to Lake O'Hara as early as three months in advance. (See page 26 for more information.) You can also hike the 12.2- kilometer Cataract Brook Trail to the lake. (See hike 5 for more information.)

Key points:

- 0.0 Trailhead/Sargent's Point.
- 0.7 West Opabin Trail junction; continue straight ahead (southeast).
- 1.0 East Opabin Trail junction; continue straight ahead (east).
- 1.5 Seven Veils Falls.
- 1.8 Lake Oesa Trail junction; continue straight ahead (west).
- 2.3 Wiwaxy Gap Trail junction; continue straight ahead (west).
- 2.4 Campground Trail junction and stream crossing; continue straight ahead (west).
- 3.0 Sargent's Point.

The hike: If you skip Lake O'Hara, you'll miss some of the most breathtaking scenery in Yoho National Park. Perfect for all ages and fitness levels, the Lake O'Hara Shoreline Trail offers a gentle stroll, with fantastic views of surrounding mountain ranges as well as the exquisite Lake O'Hara. As a bonus, the daily quota system prevents the overwhelming crowds sometimes found at other popular Yoho destinations.

Start the trail directly across the fire road (east) from the Le Relais day-use shelter. Known as Sargent's Point, this area is named after American

Lake O'Hara Shoreline Trail

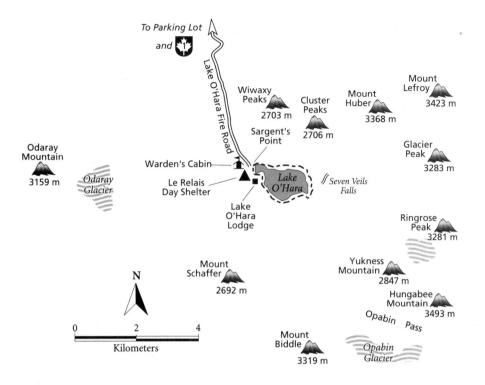

J. S. Sargent, an artist who painted many landscapes here. You'll find several interpretive signs at Sargent's Point to help familiarize you with the area.

From Sargent's Point you'll also have fabulous views of the Wiwaxy Peaks (3,703 m), Cluster Peaks (2,706 m), and Mount Huber (3,358 m) to your left (north and northeast); Mount Lefroy (3,436 m), Glacier Peak (3,294 m), Yukness Mountain (2,847 m), and Ringrose Peak (3,292 m) straight ahead (east); and Opabin Pass (2,590 m), and Mount Schaffer (2,693 m) to your right (southeast and south).

Follow the trail counterclockwise around the lake, passing several of Lake O'Hara's lakefront cabins before reaching the first trail junction at 0.7 kilometer. Continue straight ahead (southeast) on the Shoreline Trail. Almost immediately after the junction, you'll cross a wooden bridge over a small stream, which originates in Mary Lake.

At 1.0 kilometer you'll reach another trail junction; continue straight ahead (east) around the lake. Just a few meters later you'll find a natural viewpoint to your left (west) with great views of Mount Odaray (3,133 m) and the Odaray Glacier. Take advantage of the small bench here to stop for a rest or a picnic lunch.

The picturesque Lake O'Hara is named for Lieutenant Robert O'Hara, from Galway, Ireland, one of the first tourists to visit the area.

At 1.1 kilometers and 1.2 kilometers, respectively, you'll cross wooden bridges over two small streams originating in the Cascade Lakes and Moor Lakes. Look to your right (northeast) here for a fantastic view of Seven Veils Falls. At 1.5 kilometers, you'll see the falls directly above you (north), although the view as you approach the falls is considerably better.

At 1.8, 2.3, and 2.5 kilometers, you'll pass the trail junctions for Lake Oesa, Wiwaxy Gap, and the Lake O'Hara Campground, respectively. Continue straight ahead (west) around the lake. You'll cross a wooden bridge over Cataract Brook before returning to Sargent's Point.

7 Lake Oesa

Highlights:	A moderate, rocky climb from Lake O'Hara past Yukness Lake, Lake Victoria, and Lefroy Lake before meeting Lake Oesa. Stunning scenery.
Type of hike:	Day hike; loop.
Total distance:	7 kilometers.
Difficulty:	Easy.
Hiking time:	3–4 hours.
Elevation at trailhead:	2,035 meters.
Elevation gain:	298 meters.
Topo maps:	Lake Louise & Yoho (GemTrek Publishing); Lake Louise, 82 N/8.

Finding the trailhead: Follow TransCanada Highway 12.5 kilometers west of Yoho's east boundary and turn left at the Lake O'Hara turnoff. If you're heading in via Yoho's west gate, turn right after traveling approximately 41.5 kilometers. The turn is marked on both sides of the highway. Follow the secondary road toward the Lake O'Hara parking area. There is an outhouse in the parking area.

You'll find the trailhead for the Lake O'Hara Shoreline Trail on the east side of the Lake O'Hara Fire Road, just south of the warden's cabin and directly east of the Le Relais day-use shelter.

Special considerations: Lake O'Hara has a daily quota system. To hike this trail, you need to make reservations for the bus to Lake O'Hara as early as three months in advance. (See page 26 for more information.) You can also hike the 12.2-kilometer Cataract Brook Trail to the lake. (See hike 5 for more information.)

Key points:

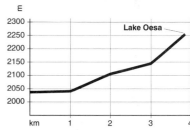

- 0.0 Sargent's Point.
- 1.8 Trail Junction on Lake O'Hara shoreline; turn left (north).
- 2.5 Yukness Lake.
- 3.2 Plaque paying tribute to Lawrence Grassi.
- 3.5 Lake Victoria.
- 3.7 Lefroy Lake.
- 3.8 Lake Oesa.
- 5.8 Completed the Lake Oesa Loop; back at Lake O'Hara Shoreline Trail.
- 7.0 Sargent's Point.

The hike: Like many of the other trails in the Lake O'Hara area, you won't be disappointed by mediocre scenery. If you delight in visiting alpine lakes, you'll really enjoy this trip.

Start the trail at Sargent's Point directly across the fire road (east) of the Le Relais day-use shelter. From here you'll also have fabulous views of the Wiwaxy Peaks (3,703 m), Cluster Peaks (2,706 m), and Mount Huber (3,358 m)

Lake Oesa

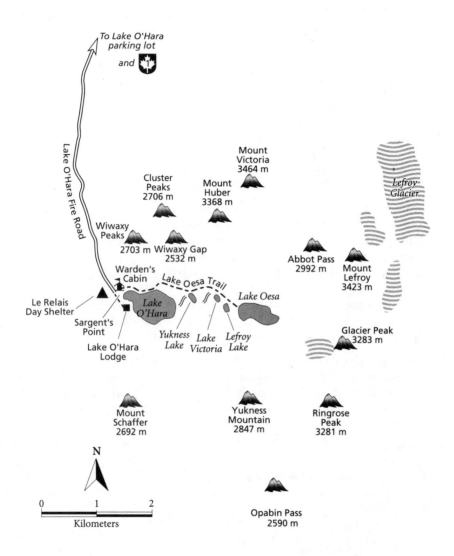

to your left (north); Mount Lefroy (3,436 m), Glacier Peak (3,294 m), Yukness Mountain (2,847 m), and Ringrose Peak (3,292 m) straight ahead (east); and Opabin Pass (2,590 m), and Mount Schaffer (2,693 m) to your right (southeast and south).

Follow the Lake O'Hara Shoreline Trail clockwise around the lake to the Lake Oesa junction at 1.8 kilometers and turn left (north). Begin a soft ascent through a series of switchbacks, with the peacock-blue waters of Lake O'Hara in constant view below you to the west. You'll notice a few small Douglas firs along the way, and at 300 meters you'll pass through a short stretch of subalpine forest as you head away from the lake. From here you'll step your way up through several rockfalls. Lawrence Grassi, who built many of the trails in the Banff–Lake Louise area, constructed these steps out of the rock to ease the trek for those who followed his footsteps.

As you hike along you'll have an awesome view of Wiwaxy Gap (2,532 m) and Mount Huber (3,368 m) to your left (north) and Yukness Mountain (2,847 m) to your right (southeast). At 2.5 kilometers, you'll come across a natural viewpoint of Lake O'Hara below. Climb across another shale slide and achieve panoramic views of the peaks that surround O'Hara and the beautifully sculpted Yukness Lake. Travel another 200 meters, and you'll see an unnamed creek that falls beside the trail to your right (south). Because the creek is fed by Lake Victoria, you could always refer to these as the Victoria Falls; they obviously don't hold the same grandeur as those found in Africa, but they're lovely nonetheless.

At 2.9 kilometers, you'll reach another small section of forest filled with spruce and Douglas fir. About 100 meters farther along the trail, you'll hear the rushing of Seven Veils Falls. If you reach them you've gone too far and will have to backtrack just a few feet to regain the trail; however, they're worth taking a look at. Follow the trail sharply to the left at the trail junction just before the falls. At this point you'll notice that the trail becomes a bit steeper. At 3.2 kilometers lies a plaque paying tribute to Lawrence Grassi and his commitment toward the exploration and creation of trails like this one. The tribute was erected by the Alpine Club of Canada.

Continue along past Lake Victoria toward Lake Oesa. At 3.5 kilometers you'll walk through a short valley. It's here that we met a very shy marmot on our trip. You'll also pass by Lefroy Lake as you complete the remaining 100-meter ascent to the sparkling glacial-blue waters of Lake Oesa (2,263m). The scenery here is inspirational. Several peaks surround the lake—to the north, Mount Victoria's South Peak (3,464 m); Abbot Pass (2,922 m) to the northeast; Mount Lefroy (3,423 m) to the east; and Glacier Peak (3,283 m), Ringrose Peak (3,281 m), Yukness Mountain (2,847 m), and the Oesa Glacier at the lake's basin to the south.

Once you've hiked back down to the Lake O'Hara Shoreline Trail, head west the remaining 1.2 kilometers to complete the Shoreline Circuit at Sargent's Point.

Don't forget that despite blue sky, the weather at the alpine level can change in a heartbeat; always bring extra clothing for layering. On this particular hike in late June, we were enjoying the sunshine in our T-shirts when, with no warning at all, it began to snow.

8 Opabin Circuit/Highline Trail

Highlights:	A moderate climb from Lake O'Hara to the natural lookout, Opabin Prospect, via the Opabin Circuit. Panoramic views throughout the hike.
Type of hike:	Day hike; loop.
Total distance:	5.2 kilometers.
Difficulty:	Moderate.
Hiking time:	3 hours.
Elevation at trailhead:	2,035 meters.
Elevation gain:	215 meters.
Topo maps:	Lake Louise & Yoho (GemTrek Publishing); Lake Louise, N/8.

Finding the trailhead: Follow TransCanada Highway 12.5 kilometers west of Yoho's east boundary and turn left (south) at the Lake O'Hara turnoff. If you're heading in via Yoho's west gate, turn right (south) after traveling approximately 41.5 kilometers. The turn is marked on both sides of the highway. Follow the road toward the Lake O'Hara parking area.

Leave the Le Relais day-use shelter, and follow the road northeast toward Lake O'Hara. Approximately 150 meters along the Lakeshore Trail, you'll reach the trailhead for Opabin Plateau.

Special considerations: Lake O'Hara has a daily quota system. To hike this trail you need to make reservations for the bus to Lake O'Hara as early as three months in advance. (See page 26 for more information.) You can also hike the 12.2- kilometer Cataract Brook Trail to the lake. (See Hike 5 for more information.)

Key points:

0.0	Le Relais day-use shelter.
0.25	Trail junction on Lake O'Hara Shoreline Trail.
0.5	Trail junction; head toward Opabin Lake.
0.7	Mary Lake.
2.0	Trail junction; follow Opabin Circuit.
2.5	Opabin Prospect natural lookout.
2.6	Trail junction; follow Opabin Plateau East Circuit.
3.35	Trail junction; continue straight ahead toward Opabin Plateau Circuit.
3.6	Trail junction, continue straight ahead toward Opabin Plateau Circuit.
4.2	Lake O'Hara Shoreline Trail.
5.2	Le Relais day-use shelter.

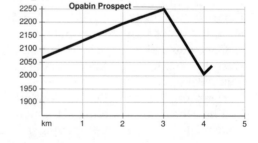

The hike: Overwhelming. That's the only way to describe the view from Opabin Prospect. Once you arrive at the top of this plateau, it's as though you've attained some sort of sensory overload; there's so much to look at,

Opabin Circuit/Highline Trail

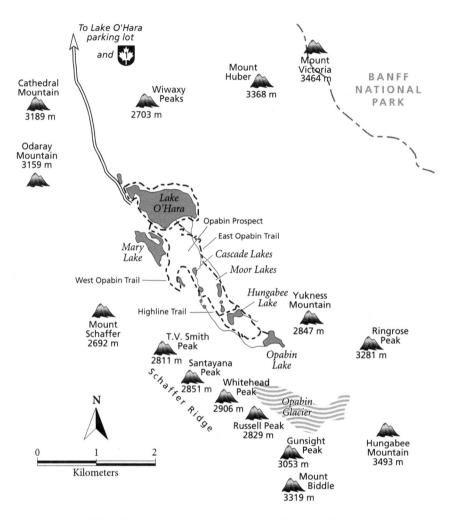

you can't possibly fix your vision to one spot. You just have to stop, take a deep breath, and slowly take it all in.

To begin the hike, leave the Le Relais day-use shelter, heading southeast along the road toward Lake O'Hara. After walking approximately 150 meters, you'll reach a wooden trail junction that will direct you to Opabin Plateau. Pass by the Lake O'Hara Lodge staff quarters on your right (south). Once you reach the Shoreline Trail, take another right (southeast) and meet a second junction approximately 250 meters into the trail. From here you'll gain your first vista of Yukness Mountain (2,847 m) and Opabin Prospect straight ahead (southeast), as well as Wiwaxy Peaks (2,703 m), Mount Huber (3,368 m), and the tip of Mount Victoria (3,464 m) to the left (north) and Mount Schaffer (2,692 m) to the right (southeast). Follow the flat Shoreline Trail southbound until you reach another trail junction at 0.5 kilometer. Take a right (southeast) toward Opabin Lake, where you'll begin a soft climb toward Mary Lake. The trees along the trail are primarily Douglas fir. At approximately 0.7 kilometer you'll arrive at Mary Lake. From here you have a prime view of the All Souls Alpine Route and Mount Schaffer, both to your left (south).

Continue through the rocky slope up West Opabin; the Prospect is on your left (north). At approximately 1.3 kilometers, you'll come out of the trees; you may glimpse a few pikas here, and if you turn around, you'll have a nice view looking back down (southwest) on Mary Lake. To the right (southwest) you'll also see Mount Odaray (3,159 m) and Mount Schaffer. You'll then have to climb through a short series of rocky switchbacks. At 1.8 kilometers you'll finish off the steep section. About 100 meters farther along, you'll have a great view of Lake O'Hara to your left (north) and Mary Lake to your right (south).

At 2 kilometers you'll meet a trail junction—follow the Opabin Plateau Circuit to the left (north). In minutes you'll reach one of the natural lookouts from Opabin Prospect; the fantastic Mount Schaffer sits off to your left (south), and you'll see Mary Lake below (south) as well. Just beyond this point you'll reach another junction. Turn left (north) toward Opabin Prospect, and you'll head back to Lake O'Hara via the Prospect to complete your loop. At 2.5 kilometers you'll reach one of the greatest viewpoints in all of Yoho National Park—the Prospect. From here you're engulfed by the natural beauty of Lake O'Hara. Wiwaxy Peaks, Wiwaxy Gap, and Mount Huber lie straight ahead (north), creating a scenic backdrop for the lake. Mount Victoria is off to the northeast, Yukness is beside you to the east, and Mount Schaffer, Mount Odaray, and Little Odaray sit to your left (west), as does the back side of Cathedral Mountain. Once you've taken the time to enjoy the view from the Prospect, continue along the trail heading east.

When you reach another junction, follow the Opabin Plateau East Circuit to your left (east). Here you will gain another awesome view. The Opabin Glacier and Hungabee Mountain (3,493 m), the highest peak in this area, are ahead of you (southeast) as you pass the lovely Cascade Lakes. At approximately 3 kilometers you'll reach an unnamed creek as you head northeast toward Lake O'Hara. If you look closely to your right (east), you can see the Yukness Ledge Alpine Route.

At 3.3 kilometers you'll reach another trail junction; stay straight ahead (west) on Opabin Plateau East Circuit. About 50 meters farther down the trail, you'll begin to head northwest to Lake O'Hara. At 3.6 kilometers you'll reach yet another trail junction; continue straight ahead (northwest). Here you may spot a few alpine buttercups. As you enter the treed trail, you'll have one more view of the lake. At 4 kilometers you'll cross a small suspension bridge over the creek before entering into an old rock slide. Here you can see the alpine route markers—blue and yellow squares painted on rocks. At 4.2 kilometers you'll reach the Lake O'Hara Shoreline Trail, where you can take your choice of directions. Head right (northwest) 1.0 kilometer or left (east) for 2 kilometers to reach the Le Relais shelter.

Strong hikers can easily complete the out-and-back trip to Lake Oesa as well. Head east 800 meters along the Shoreline Trail to your right (northeast) before meeting the Oesa Trail junction. (See Hike 7 for a description of the hike.)

Option:
Highline Trail—2.5 kilometers—easy. At 2 kilometers, at the junction of West Opabin and the Opabin Prospect, you can also continue straight ahead (south) on the Highline Trail toward Hungabee Lake and Opabin Lake. This picturesque trail is well worth the extra 2.5 kilometers.

At 2.4 kilometers you'll cross a small stream that connects the Cascade Lakes to your left (north) and right (south). Immediately after the stream crossing, you'll reach a trail junction; turn right (south) here. Western spring beauty, alpine buttercups, and western anemones add a splash of color to this section of trail. At 2.7 kilometers, after passing the Moor Lakes to your left (east), you'll reach another trail junction; continue straight ahead (south) here. You'll travel 600 meters and pass Hungabee Lake before arriving at Opabin Lake. At the Opabin Lake Trail junction, head left (north) 1.2 kilometers to connect with the East Opabin Trail.

9 Lake McArthur/Big Larches Loop

Highlights:	This trail skirts Schaffer Lake and offers fantastic views of Mount Odaray, Mount Schaffer, Lake McArthur, and the Big Larch Forest.
Type of hike:	Day hike; loop.
Total distance:	7.3 kilometers.
Difficulty:	Easy.
Hiking time:	3 hours.
Elevation at trailhead:	2,035 meters.
Elevation gain/loss:	230 meters.
Topo maps:	Lake Louise & Yoho (GemTrek Publishing); Lake Louise, 82 N/8.

Finding the trailhead: The turnoff to Lake O'Hara is located on the south side of TransCanada Highway 1, approximately 2.5 kilometers west of Yoho National Park's east boundary and 41.5 kilometers east of the park's west gate. Turn right (west) immediately after the train tracks, and park in the large lot. An outhouse is available in the parking lot.

This loop begins and ends just behind (southwest of) the Le Relais dayuse shelter, which is located on the west side of the Lake O'Hara fire road.

Special considerations: Lake O'Hara has a daily quota system. To hike this trail you need to make reservations for the bus to Lake O'Hara as early as three months in advance. (See page 26 for more information.) You can also hike the 12.2-kilometer Cataract Brook Trail to the lake. (See Hike 5 for more information.)

Key points:
- 0.0   Trailhead.
- 0.1   Trail junction; continue straight ahead (west).
- 0.3   Trail junction; bear right (west).
- 0.4   Schaffer Creek crossing.
- 0.5   Trail junction; continue straight ahead (southwest).
- 0.6   Schaffer Creek crossing.
- 1.4   Schaffer Lake/trail junction; continue straight ahead (west).
- 1.5   Trail junction; continue straight ahead (west).
- 2.2   Trail junction; turn left (southeast).
- 2.3   Trail junction; continue left (southeast).
- 2.6   Trail junction; continue left (southeast).
- 2.7   Trail junction; continue left (southeast).
- 3.9   Trail junction; turn right (northwest).
- 4.1   McArthur Pool.
- 4.9   Trail junction; continue straight ahead (northeast).
- 5.2   Trail junction; continue straight ahead (northeast).
- 6.1   Schaffer Lake/trail junction; turn right (east).
- 6.2   Trail junction; continue left (northeast).
- 7.2   Trail junction; continue left (east).
- 7.6   Trail junction; turn left (north).
- 7.8   Trail junction; turn left (northwest).
- 8.5   Return to trailhead.

The hike: At 84 meters, Lake McArthur is the deepest lake in Yoho National Park. Framed by Park Mountain, Mount Biddle, Mount Schaffer, and the Biddle Glacier, this ice-blue lake is also one of the most beautiful.

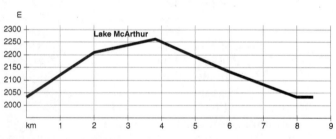

This trail begins just behind (southwest of) the Le Relais day-use shelter.

Just 100 meters into the trail, you'll reach the first trail junction; continue straight ahead (west) toward the Elizabeth Parker alpine hut. At 300 meters you'll hit another trail junction; bear right (west) following signs for the hut. The trail parallels Schaffer Creek, crossing it at 400 meters, and offers great views of Mount Odaray (3,133 m) and the Odaray Glacier before arriving at the hut.

Just before the hut you'll reach the Lake McArthur Trail junction; continue straight ahead (southwest). At 0.6 kilometer you'll cross Schaffer Creek a second time. Here's where you'll start your steady ascent to the lake on a mossy trail lined primarily with Douglas fir.

At 1.4 kilometers you'll reach Schaffer Lake and another trail junction; continue straight ahead (west) and cross Schaffer Creek for the third time. While you're enjoying the lake, look to your left (southeast) for a great view

Lake McArthur/Big Larches Loop

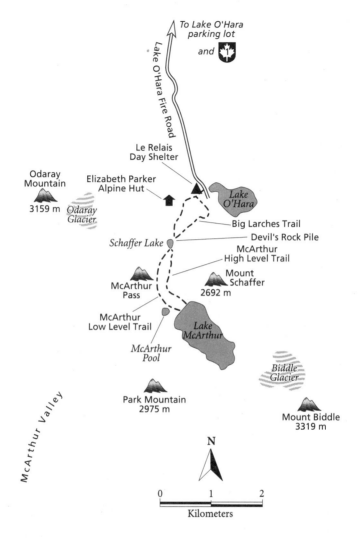

of Mount Schaffer (2,693 m) and to your right (northwest) for views of Mount Odaray.

Just 100 meters later you'll hit another trail junction. From here you can choose one of two routes to Lake McArthur. Continue straight ahead (west) to reach the lake via the Low Level Circuit (like we did), or take a left (south) to reach Lake McArthur via the High Level Circuit.

Just after Schaffer Lake you'll pass meadows sprinkled with alpine buttercups and western anemones. At 2.2 kilometers you'll reach another trail junction; head left (southeast) to reach Lake McArthur via the High Level

Lake McArthur, with its icy blue water, is the deepest lake in Yoho National Park.

Circuit or right (southwest) to reach the lake via McArthur Pass and the Low Level Circuit. We turned left (southeast) here—opting for optimal views from the higher elevation trail. Just 100 meters later you'll reach another trail junction; continue left (southeast) to follow the High Level Circuit.

At 2.6 and 2.7 kilometers respectively, you'll reach two additional trail junctions. Continue left (southeast) toward Lake McArthur via the High Level Circuit. On this section of trail, you'll enjoy views of Park Mountain (2,952 m) straight ahead (south), Mount Biddle (3,319 m) to your left (southeast), and McArthur Valley to your right (southwest). You may also spot pikas, marmots, and mountain goats among the rocks here.

At 3.7 kilometers you'll arrive at a ridge overlooking the ice-blue lake, which is nestled among three mountain peaks—Park Mountain, Mount Biddle, and Mount Schaffer. Depending on the time of year, you may hear the powerful roar of avalanches in this area. You'll also enjoy a fantastic view of the Biddle Glacier straight ahead (southeast).

Continue 200 meters to your right (southwest) along the trail to reach the trail junction at the edge of Lake McArthur. You can either return to Schaffer Lake the way you came (northeast) or loop back on the Low Level Circuit to your right (northwest), as we did.

Continuing on the Low Level Circuit, you'll pass McArthur Pool on your left (south) at 4.1 kilometers. Enjoy the views of McArthur Valley to your left (southwest) as well as the alpine buttercups and western anemones along this section of trail. At 4.9 and 5.2 kilometers respectively, you'll reach two more trail junctions; continue straight ahead (northeast), then head left (northeast) to return to Schaffer Lake.

At 6 kilometers you'll return to Schaffer Lake. Just 100 meters later, you'll reach a trail junction. From here you can either return to Lake O'Hara the way you came (north) or take a right (east) to return to Lake O'Hara via the Big Larches Loop. If you've never seen a larch tree before, you're in for a treat. These wispy, kelly-green trees are soft to the touch and create an almost mystical, fairy-tale feeling.

At 6.2 kilometers you'll reach another trail junction; continue left (northeast). Just 600 meters later you'll start your descent to Lake O'Hara as you pass through a series of rocky switchbacks on Devil's Rock Pile.

At 7.2 kilometers you'll hit another trail junction; continue right (east) and return to Le Relais via Big Larch Forest and Mary Lake. You'll reach another trail junction at 7.6 kilometers; turn left (north) and follow the trail to Lake O'Hara, where you'll head left (northwest) along the shoreline back to Le Relais.

10 Odaray Highline Trail

Highlights:	This tough climb offers fantastic views of Lake O'Hara, McArthur Lake, the Odaray Glacier, and Mount Goodsir's two towers.
Type of hike:	Day hike; out-and-back.
Total distance:	5.4 kilometers.
Difficulty:	Moderate (with some strenuous sections).
Hiking time:	2 hours (Odaray Highline) plus 30 minutes to get to the trailhead from Lake O'Hara.
Elevation at trailhead:	2,135 meters.
Elevation gain:	390 meters.
Topo maps:	Lake Louise & Yoho, (GemTrek Publishing); Lake Louise, 82 N/8.

Finding the trailhead: The turnoff to Lake O'Hara is located on the south side of TransCanada Highway 1, approximately 2.5 kilometers west of Yoho National Park's east boundary and 41.5 kilometers east of the park's west gate. Turn right (west) immediately after the train tracks, and park in the large lot. An outhouse is available in the parking lot.

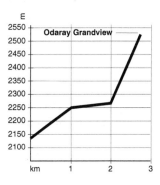

From the Le Relais day shelter (where the bus drops you off), you'll walk 1.4 kilometers to the trailhead at Schaffer Lake. To get to Schaffer Lake, head west directly behind Le Relais to the Elizabeth Parker alpine hut; turn left (southwest) at the hut, and follow the trail 900 meters to Schaffer Lake.

Odaray Highline Trail

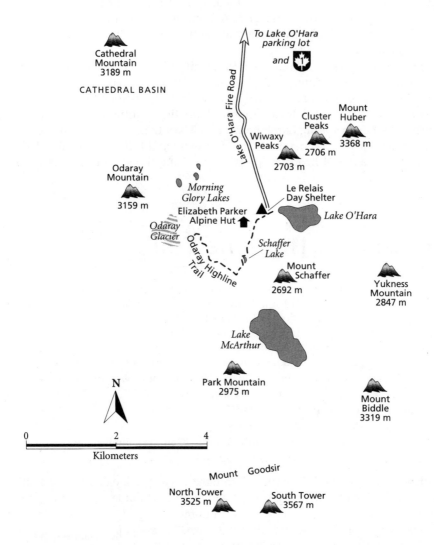

Special considerations: Lake O'Hara has a daily quota system. To hike this trail you need to make reservations for the bus to Lake O'Hara as early as three months in advance. (See page 26 for more information.) You can also hike the 12.2-kilometer Cataract Brook Trail to the lake. (See Hike 5 for more information.)

Because the Odaray Highline is an important wildlife corridor, Parks Canada has recently implemented programs to reduce human traffic on the trail. Check with Parks Canada staff before venturing onto this trail. In 2000, hikers were asked to voluntarily limit their use of the Odaray Highline to

These hikers trek up the rock path to Odaray Grandview, leaving Mount Schaffer (left), Lake McArthur, and Mount Biddle (right) behind them.

four groups of hikers per day before August 15 and two groups per day from August 15 to September 15. Traffic was monitored via a log book at Schaffer Lake, as well as through warden patrols and trail cameras.

Key points:
- 0.0 Schaffer Lake; continue straight ahead (southwest).
- 0.5 Trail junction; head right (southwest).
- 1.8 Trail junction; turn right (northwest).
- 2.6 Trail junction; head left (northwest).
- 2.7 Odaray Grandview.
- 5.4 Schaffer Lake.

The hike: The Odaray Highline is also known as the Odaray Grandview— a fitting name for this trail, which offers spectacular panoramic views of area mountain peaks, lakes, and glaciers.

From Schaffer Lake you'll head southwest through meadows sprinkled with alpine buttercups, Indian paintbrush, and western anemones. Just 500 meters into the trail, you'll hit a trail junction; continue straight ahead (southwest) toward the Odaray Plateau Circuit. The closer you get to Mount Odaray (3,159 m), the rockier the trail becomes. You'll head through a forest of Douglas fir and larch, where you'll spot various wildflowers, including valerian, mountain avens, heather, and moss campion, before trekking through a rocky slide area.

At 1.0 kilometer look to your left (south) for fantastic views of Mount Goodsir's North Tower (3,525 m) and South Tower (3,562 m), as well as Park Mountain (2,975 m). You'll also catch a glimpse behind you (southeast and east) of Mount Biddle (3,319 m) and Mount Schaffer (2,692 m).

The trail becomes a bit sketchy in sections as you follow switchbacks through the rocky slide; look for the cairns and the blue and yellow Alpine Route markers. At 1.4 kilometers you'll enjoy high-elevation views of Lake O'Hara and midnight-blue Lake McArthur to your right (east and southeast), as well as the mountains framing Lake O'Hara. Just 400 meters later you'll hit a trail junction; head right (northwest) toward the Odaray Grandview Alpine Route. The trail climbs steeply from the trail junction, becoming more like a scramble in sections as you clamber up the rock using both hands and feet. As you continue toward Odaray Grandview, beneath you to your right (east) you'll see the old Odaray Plateau Trail, which is now permanently closed to protect wildlife movement through this corridor.

At 2.6 kilometers you'll reach an unmarked trail; head left (northwest), following the blue Alpine Route markers to Odaray Grandview. From here you'll enjoy close-up views of the Odaray Glacier to your right (north), as well as prime views of Morning Glory Lakes and Cathedral Basin, also to your right (north), and Lake O'Hara and McArthur Lake behind you (east).

11 Linda Lake Circuit/ Morning Glory Lakes

Highlights: This pleasant walk in the woods circles Linda Lake and skirts Morning Glory Lakes and offers prime views of Cathedral Mountain, Mount Odaray, and the Odaray Glacier.

Type of hike: Day hike; loop or shuttle.
Total distance: 6.2 kilometers.
Difficulty: Easy.
Hiking time: 2½–3 hours.
Elevation at trailhead: 1,920 meters.
Elevation gain: 130 meters.
Topo maps: Lake Louise & Yoho (GemTrek Publishing); Lake Louise, 82 N/8.

Finding the trailhead: The turnoff to Lake O'Hara is located on the south side of TransCanada Highway 1, approximately 2.5 kilometers west of Yoho National Park's east boundary and 41.5 kilometers east of the park's west gate. Turn right (west) immediately after the train tracks, and park in the large lot. An outhouse is available in the parking lot.

You can start the loop to Linda Lake and Morning Glory Lakes in one of three locations: just behind (west of) the Le Relais day shelter via the trail to the Elizabeth Parker alpine hut; on the west side of the Lake O'Hara Fire Road, 2.3 kilometers north of Le Relais; or on the Cataract Brook Trail, 9.5 kilometers south of the Lake O'Hara bus stop. We chose to start on the Lake O'Hara Fire Road, and headed west to Linda Lake and then southeast to Morning Glory Lakes before ending at Le Relais via the Lower Morning Glory Trail.

Special considerations: Lake O'Hara has a daily quota system. To hike this trail you need to make reservations for the bus to Lake O'Hara as early as three months in advance. (See page 26 for more information.) You can also hike the 12.2-kilometer Cataract Brook Trail to the lake. (See Hike 5 for more information.)

Key points:

0.0	Trailhead.
0.6	Campground trail junction; continue straight ahead (southwest).
1.0	Creek crossing.
1.4	Four-way junction; continue straight ahead (west).
1.8	Linda Lake.

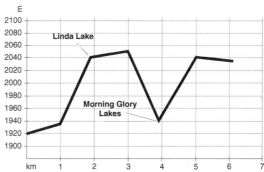

Linda Lake Circuit/Morning Glory Lakes

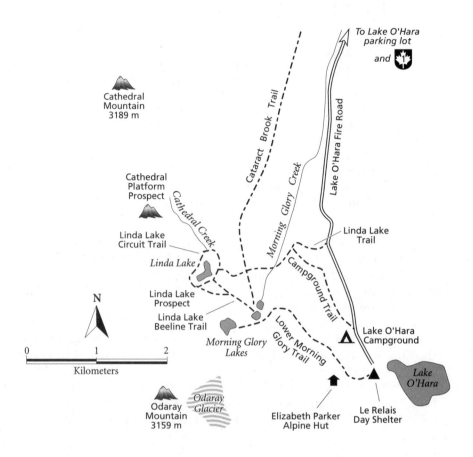

2.5 Duchesnay Basin Ttrail junction; continue left (south).

2.9 Morning Glory Lakes/Linda Lake Beeline Trail junction; turn right (southeast).

3.7 Morning Glory Lakes/Lake O'Hara via Alpine Meadows Trail junction; turn right (south).

5.7 Elizabeth Parker Alpine Hut Trail junction; turn left (east).

5.9 Mary Lake Loop Trail junction; continue left (east).

6.1 Trail junction; continue left (east).

6.2 Le Relais day-use shelter.

The hike: This quiet, relatively easy walk in the woods is perfect if you're seeking a bit of solitude. We encountered very few hikers on this trail—probably because we chose to complete it in the opposite direction that most follow. If you ask the Lake O'Hara bus driver politely, he will drop you off just shy of the Lake O'Hara Campground on the west side of the Lake O'Hara

Fire Road. From there you'll head west toward Linda Lake, then southeast to Morning Glory Lakes via the Linda Lakes Beeline Trail, before ending at Le Relais via the Lower Morning Glory/Alpine Meadows Trail.

The single-file trail starts with a gradual climb through a mossy forest lined with Douglas fir and sunny globeflowers. Just 600 meters into the trail, you'll reach the Lake O'Hara Campground Trail junction; continue straight ahead (southwest) toward the Linda Lake/Morning Glory Circuit. At 1.0 kilometer you'll cross Morning Glory Creek, which originates in Morning Glory Lakes. Look to your left (south) here to soak up fantastic views of Mount Odaray (3,159 m) and the Odaray Glacier.

At 1.4 kilometers you'll reach a four-way trail junction; continue straight ahead (west) toward Linda Lake. Just 400 meters later you'll get your first look at the brilliant, aquamarine-colored lake. Before proceeding around the Linda Lake Circuit, follow the beaten path straight ahead (southwest) past the trail junction for a fabulous view of Linda Lake Prospect straight ahead (southwest), Mount Odaray (3,133 m) to your left (south), and Cathedral Platform Prospect and Cathedral Mountain (3,189 m) to your right (north). Continue counterclockwise around the lake on the Linda Lake Circuit.

We heard several avalanches thundering near Linda Lake in mid-July, including a huge slide just before we crossed Cathedral Creek at 2.1 kilometers. Just 400 meters later you'll reach the trail junction for Duchesnay Basin; continue left (south) to complete the Linda Lake Circuit. The trail becomes a bit rocky here as you cross part of the Rutherford Moraine, and it's easy to lose your way. To stay on the trail stick close to the lake, rather than trying to scramble up the rocks.

At 2.9 kilometers you'll reach the junction for Morning Glory Lakes via Linda Lake Beeline. Take a right (southeast) here and enjoy the 300-meter descent to Morning Glory Lakes. At 3.7 kilometers you'll reach another trail junction just before Morning Glory Lakes; head right (south), skirting one of the lakes and crossing Morning Glory Creek before reaching an area near the base of the Odaray Prospect. Keep an eye out for lazy hoary marmots lounging on the rocks here; we saw several.

From here the heavily forested trail proceeds slightly northeast, skirting the Odaray Plateau and then heading southeast through a forest dominated by Douglas fir. You'll pass through a brief alpine meadow before arriving at the Elizabeth Parker alpine hut. Turn left (east) at the trail junction to head toward Lake O'Hara and Le Relais. From this point you'll briefly enjoy Schaffer Creek tumbling to your left (north). You'll reach two final trail junctions at 5.9 and 6.1 kilometers; stay to your left (east) at both to finish the trail at Le Relais.

12 Cathedral Basin

Highlights:	This short trail skirts Linda Lake and Cathedral Lakes and ends with panoramic views of Cathedral Basin, Monica Lake, and area mountain peaks.
Type of hike:	Day hike; out-and-back.
Total distance:	3.6 kilometers.
Difficulty:	Moderate.
Hiking time:	2 hours (Cathedral Basin) plus 2 hours to get to the trailhead from Lake O'Hara.
Elevation at trailhead:	2,125 meters.
Elevation gain:	185 meters.
Topo maps:	Lake Louise & Yoho (GemTrek Publishing); Lake Louise, 82 N/8.

Finding the trailhead: The turnoff to Lake O'Hara is located on the south side of TransCanada Highway 1, approximately 2.5 kilometers west of Yoho National Park's east boundary and 41.5 kilometers east of the park's west gate. Turn right (west) immediately after the train tracks, and park in the large lot. An outhouse is available in the parking lot.

To get to the Cathedral Basin trailhead, follow one of the three possible routes from Lake O'Hara to Linda Lake (see Hike 11), then follow the Duchesnay Basin Trail (located at the southwest corner of Linda Lake) 1.7 kilometers west. The trailhead for Cathedral Basin is located at a small unnamed lake.

Special considerations: Lake O'Hara has a daily quota system. To hike this trail you need to make reservations for the bus to Lake O'Hara as early as three months in advance. (For more information, see page 26.) You can also hike the 12.2- kilometer Cataract Brook Trail to the lake. (See Hike 5 for more information.)

Key points:

- 0.0 Cathedral Basin trailhead; turn right (north).
- 1.3 Cathedral Platform Prospect.
- 1.8 Monica Lake viewpoint/end of trail.
- 3.6 Back at trailhead.

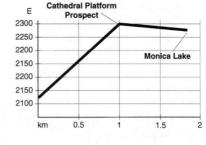

The hike: It may take you a full day to trek from Lake O'Hara to Cathedral Basin and back, but the solitude you'll gain as you venture farther away from the more popular hikes near the lake makes it all worthwhile. We didn't see any other hikers on this trail—even in mid-July—and the views from the end of the trail are absolutely spectacular.

Heading right (north) from the trail junction, you'll start climbing immediately on the single-file path lined primarily with Douglas fir. The trail opens

Cathedral Basin • Duchesnay Basin

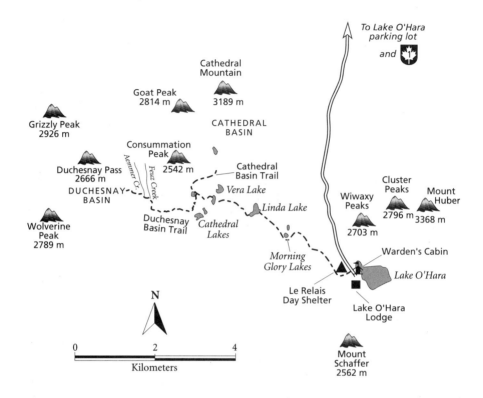

up quickly into a swampy meadow filled with a delightful array of globe-flowers, alpine buttercups, valerian, goosefoot violets, Indian paintbrush, and an occasional stray larch. Just 400 meters into the trail, you'll start walking next to a rocky slide area to your left (north). Watch your step as the trail heads north through the slide. This is a tough climb; it's steep, easy to loose your footing among all the rocks, and even easier to lose the trail as you concentrate on your feet. To stay on the trail follow the orange and red markers on the rock.

You may hear the high-pitched squeak of pikas on this section of trail or spot a lazy marmot sunning itself on a rock. You may also spot yellow and pink mountain heather poking up around the rocks. Depending on the time of year, you may even hear an avalanche or two thundering in the distance, as we did.

At the top of the rocky section, the trail continues to your right (northeast). At 900 meters you'll cross a small creek created by meltwater from nearby mountains. From here you'll enjoy a fantastic view of Mount Huber (3,358 m) and the Upper Victoria Glacier to your right (east). Just 100 me-

Tiny Monica Lake is nestled in this snowy basin.

ters later you'll cross another rocky section; follow the orange and red markers on the rock.

At 1.2 kilometers you'll enjoy a great view of Lake O'Hara and Linda Lake to your right (east), along with Mount Schaffer (2,693 m), Wiwaxy Peak (2,704 m), Cluster Peaks (2,706 m), Mount Huber, and other peaks too numerous to name also to your right (east). Just 300 meters later you'll arrive at Cathedral Platform Prospect, where you'll enjoy your first good glimpse of the rock and snow–filled Cathedral Basin and soak up the panoramic views of nearby mountain peaks, including Cathedral Mountain (3,189 m), Goat Peak (2,814 m), and Consummation Peak (2,542 m) straight ahead (north); Mount Huber and the Huber glaciers to your right (east); and Duchesnay Pass (2,666 m), Grizzly Peak (2,926 m), and Wolverine Peak (2,789 m) to your left (west).

At 1.8 kilometers you'll arrive at a small plateau overlooking tiny Monica Lake, which is nestled in the heart of the basin to your north. Although the trail stops just shy of the lake, you can scramble down the embankment to reach the shore.

13 Duchesnay Basin

Highlights: This easy trail skirts Linda Lake and Cathedral Lake and ends with panoramic views of area mountain peaks.

See Map on Page 51

Type of hike: Day hike; out-and-back.
Total distance: 7.4 kilometers.
Difficulty: Easy.
Hiking time: 3 hours (Duchesnay Basin) plus 2 hours to reach the trailhead.
Elevation at trailhead: 2,040 meters.
Elevation gain: 235 meters.
Topo maps: Lake Louise & Yoho (GemTrek Publishing); Lake Louise, 82 N/8.

Finding the trailhead: The turnoff to Lake O'Hara is located on the south side of TransCanada Highway 1, approximately 2.5 kilometers west of Yoho National Park's east boundary and 41.5 kilometers east of the park's west gate. Turn right (west) immediately after the train tracks, and park in the large lot. An outhouse is available in the parking lot.

The trailhead for Duchesnay Basin starts at the west end of Linda Lake. (See Hike 11 for three possible routes to Linda Lake.)

Special considerations: Lake O'Hara has a daily quota system. To hike this trail you need to make reservations for the bus to Lake O'Hara as early as three months in advance. (See page 26 for more information.) You can also hike the 12.2-kilometer Cataract Brook Trail to the lake. (See Hike 5 for more information.)

Key points:
- 0.0 Trailhead.
- 1.2 Cathedral Lakes Trail junction/creek crossing; continue left (south).
- 1.4 Consummation Creek crossing.
- 1.7 Cathedral Basin/Duchesnay Basin Trail junction; continue straight ahead (southwest).
- 2.6 Small unnamed lake.
- 3.1 Feuz Creek crossing.
- 3.2 Aenumer Creek crossing.
- 3.7 Last Larch Prospect.
- 7.4 Back at trailhead.

The hike: Two curious grizzly bears approached us the first time we hiked this trail. Because it's less traveled than other Lake O'Hara trails, consider hiking in groups of four or more for safety whenever possible. You should also carry a compass and topographic map, since the trail becomes a bit sketchy in sections.

The trail starts at the west end of Linda Lake; turn right (north) at the

Hikers stand on the edge of Duchesnay Basin scouring Deception Peak for a sign of the Swiss Guides Monument.

trail junction toward Cathedral Lakes and Duchesnay Basin. You'll take in prime views of Cathedral Mountain (3,189 m) and Goat Peak (2,814 m) straight ahead (north and northwest) on this part of the trail.

At 1.1 kilometers you'll catch the first glimpse of the Cathedral Lakes to your left (south). Just 100 meters later you'll reach the Cathedral Lakes Trail junction. You'll cross a tumbling creek, which connects Cathedral Lakes to your left (south) and Vera Lake to your right (north), before continuing along the trail to your left (south). At 1.4 kilometers you'll cross Consummation Creek, which originates in Cathedral Basin. A delightful array of wildflowers including Indian paintbrush, valerian, and pink and yellow mountain heather brighten this section of trail.

At 1.7 kilometers, at a tiny unnamed lake, you'll reach another trail junction; continue straight ahead (southwest) toward Duchesnay Basin. This lake, along with others in the area, is a "kettle pond," a small lake formed when glacial ice melted, leaving a poorly drained cavity behind.

At 2.6 kilometers the trail appears to end abruptly at a another small lake, but if you look closely you can actually see the trodden trail under 1 meter of water. You'll need to blaze your own trail around the right (north) side of the lake and join the trail in the swampy area immediately following the lake to your left (west). The trail becomes difficult to find here, so look for the cairns, and follow the path up the steep hill through the trees to your left (west). Keep an eye out for bears here as well.

You'll hear bubbling water as you approach the 3-kilometer mark. Look to your left (west) to enjoy the falls created as Aenumer Creek flows down a steep rocky embankment to join Feuz Creek. Just 100 meters later you'll literally jump across Feuz Creek and start climbing the embankment just right (north) of Aenumer Creek. At 3.2 kilometers you'll cross Aenumer Creek; from here on, the trail becomes slightly sketchy.

At 3.3 kilometers look for the steps on your left (west), and continue west toward a small unnamed lake. From here you'll skirt the right (north) side of the lake, climbing the steep grassy slope to your right (north) and skirting the ridge to your left (south). Continue northeast 400 meters to Last Larch Prospect, where the trail ends.

From the Prospect you'll feel like you're on top of the world as you soak up fantastic, panoramic views of area mountains, including Cathedral Mountain, Goat Peak, and Consummation Peak (2,542 m) to your right (northeast); Lynx Head (3,029 m), Deception Pass (3,139 m), and Grizzly Peak (2,926 m) also to your right (northwest); Duchesnay Pass (2,666 m) and Wolverine Peak (2,789 m) straight ahead (west); Marten Peak (2,641 m) and Odaray Mountain (3,133 m) to your left (south); and Mount Huber (3,358 m) and Wiwaxy Peaks (North Peak, 2,704 m; Cluster Peaks, 2,706 m) behind you (east).

14 Alpine Loop

Highlights:	This high-elevation trail offers bird's-eye views of Lake O'Hara, Lake Oesa, the Opabin Plateau, Schaffer Lake, and the many mountains surrounding Lake O'Hara.
Type of hike:	Day hike; loop.
Total distance:	5.2 kilometers.
Difficulty:	Moderate.
Hiking time:	5½–7 hours.
Elevation at trailhead:	2,035 meters.
Elevation gain:	495 meters to Wiwaxy Gap; 75 meters to Yukness Ledge; 274 meters to All Soul's Prospect.
Topo maps:	Lake Louise & Yoho (GemTrek Publishing); Lake Louise, 82 N/8.

Finding the trailhead: The turnoff to Lake O'Hara is located on the south side of TransCanada Highway 1, approximately 2.5 kilometers west of Yoho National Park's east boundary and 41.5 kilometers east of the park's west gate. Turn right (west) immediately after the train tracks and park in the large lot. An outhouse is available in the parking lot.

You'll find the trailhead for Wiwaxy Gap on the north side of Lake O'Hara. Follow the Lake O'Hara Shoreline Trail clockwise (northeast) from the Lake O'Hara warden's cabin approximately 700 meters to reach the trailhead.

Special considerations: Lake O'Hara has a daily quota system. To hike this trail you need to make reservations for the bus to Lake O'Hara as early as three months in advance. (See page 26 for more information.) You can also hike the 12.2-kilometer Cataract Brook Trail to the lake. (See Hike 5 for more information.)

Key points:

0.0	Trailhead/Sargent's Point.
0.7	Wiwaxy Gap trail junction; turn left (north).
1.4	Optional scramble to Baby Buttress.
2.2	Huber Ledges Trail junction; turn right (southeast).
3.9	Trail junction; turn left (southwest).
4.0	Lake Oesa Trail junction; continue straight ahead (south).
4.7	Yukness Ledge Trail junction; turn right (south).
6.1	Hungabee Lake Trail junction; turn right (west).
6.2	Trail junction; turn left (southwest).
6.5	Trail junction; turn right (north).
6.8	Trail junction; turn left (west).
7.2	Trail junction; turn left (west).
9.1	Trail junction; turn right (northeast).
10.9	Le Relais.

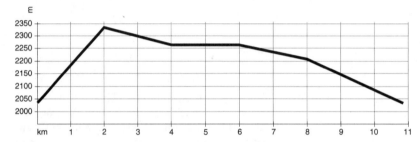

The hike: Looking up from Lake O'Hara, this hike appears much more treacherous than it actually is. Although some parts of the trail involve a steep climb, you won't want to miss Yoho National Park's most spectacular trail. We passed a woman well into her eighties and kids as young as seven on the Alpine Loop, which offers fantastic bird's-eye views of Lake O'Hara, Lake Oesa, Schaffer Lake, and area mountain peaks. If you only have a day or two to spend at Lake O'Hara, this hike provides an excellent overview of the entire area.

You'll need better-than-average route-finding skills on the Alpine Loop. Although it's well marked with cairns and blue and yellow Alpine Trail symbols, it can still be difficult to navigate in some sections. Be sure to carry a map and a compass, as well as gloves, a hat, and plenty of warm layers. The weather changes frequently at these high elevations; we ran into a light dusting of snow on this trail in mid-August. Before you head out, it's always wise to ask Parks Canada staff about potential avalanche hazards on the trail.

Starting at Sargent's Point, directly east of the Le Relais day-use shelter, follow the lakeshore trail approximately 700 meters clockwise (northeast) to the Wiwaxy trailhead. You'll start gaining elevation immediately on this rocky trail, which, along with its magnificent views, treats you to an array of colorful wildflowers. In mid-July we spotted valerian, alpine forget-me-

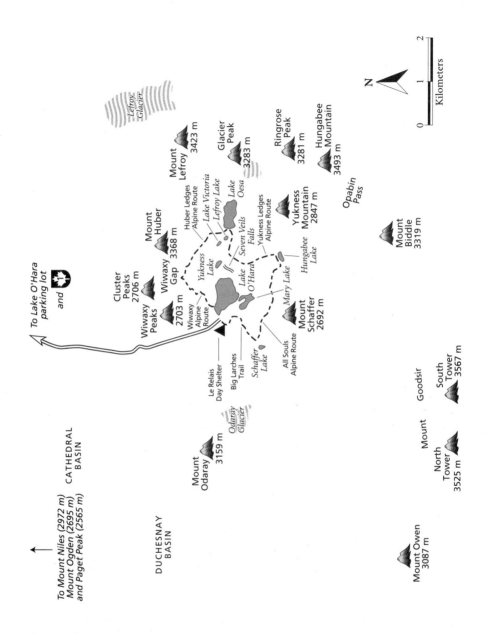

nots, yellow columbine, wild strawberries, white mountain heather, common blue violets, and others too numerous to name.

At 1.0 kilometer you'll enjoy a great view of Lake O'Hara beneath you (south); Mount Biddle (3,328 m) and Opabin Pass (2,590 m) to your right (southeast); and Mount Owen (3,087 m) and Mount Goodsir (North Tower, 3,525 m;

South Tower, 3,562 m) to the southwest. Approximately 300 meters later, watch your step as you walk on an exposed cliff with a steep drop to your left.

At 1.4 kilometers you can choose to leave Wiwaxy to scramble up Baby Buttress to your right (north). Proceed with caution; the trail is hard to find, and there are no signs to mark the route. The Wiwaxy route also becomes a bit more difficult to follow after the 1.6-kilometer point—look for the cairns and the blue and yellow alpine route markers painted on the rocks as your guide.

At 1.9 kilometers you'll have a prime view to your right of Lake O'Hara (south), as well as views of Mary Lake (south), Seven Veils Falls (east), and Glacier Peak (3,294 m), Ringrose Peak (3,292 m), and Hungabee Peak (northeast and east). If you're lucky, you may also spot a few white mountain goats in the area; however, we found only their hair and a lot of scat.

At 2.2 kilometers you'll reach the Huber Ledges Trail junction. Before continuing on the trail, take a left (west) and head for the large cairn atop Wiwaxy Gap. While you're enjoying spectacular views of Lake O'Hara and the surrounding mountains, don't forget to look behind you (north) to see Mount Niles (2,972 m), Mount Ogden (2,695 m), and Paget Peak (2,565 m). By the way, Wiwaxy is Stoney Indian for "windy," and you can definitely expect a bit of wind as you enjoy the view from here.

Head right (southeast) at the Huber Ledges Trail junction toward Lake Oesa. This is highest part of the alpine route, and although you're traveling along fairly wide ledges, take your time and watch your step. At 2.6 kilometers the trail becomes a bit sketchy; turn left, following the small cairn. Just 200 meters later you'll enjoy prime views straight ahead (southeast) of Lake Oesa, along with Mount Lefroy (3,423 m), Glacier Peak (3283 m), and their spectacular glaciers. You'll also spot the three tiny lakes—Yukness Lake, Lake Victoria, and Lefroy Lake—leading up to Lake Oesa.

At 3.5 kilometers you'll pass through an orange-and-gray-

striped rocky slide area to your left (north). Poking out amidst the rock are a surprising variety of stubborn wildflowers, including moss campion, fringed grass-of-parnassus, and yellow columbine. At 3.9 kilometers you'll reach a trail junction; head left (southwest) toward Lake Oesa. You'll arrive at picturesque Lake Oesa and the Lake Oesa Trail junction just 100 meters later. This is a great spot to relax and have lunch while you enjoy some of the same views of the lake and the surrounding mountains that you saw from Huber Ledges. If you're lucky, you may also spot mountain grouse waddling among the rocks here.

At the Lake Oesa Trail junction, continue straight ahead (south) toward Opabin Plateau via the Yukness Ledges Alpine Route. It becomes very difficult to spot the trail in the rocks near the lake; look for the cairns and continue heading south. At 4.6 kilometers you'll notice a small waterfall tumbling over the ledges to your left (east). On a scorching-hot day, dunking your head in this icy water will provide all the refreshment you need.

At 4.7 kilometers you'll reach another trail junction; turn right (south) toward Opabin Plateau via the Yukness Ledge Alpine Route. From the

The Alpine Loop offers a spectacular view of Lake O'Hara, as seen here from Yukness Ledge.

Yukness Ledges you'll enjoy tremendous views to your right (west) of Mount Odaray (3,159 m) and the Odaray Glacier, along with Lake O'Hara. Between 5 and 6 kilometers you'll also gain great views of Mount Biddle (3,328 m), Gunsight Peak (3,053 m), and Russell Peak (2,829 m) straight ahead (south) and Cathedral Basin and Duchesnay Basin to your right (northwest and west). Far down beneath you to your right (west), you'll catch a glimpse of Cascade Lakes and the Moor Lakes.

At 6.1 kilometers you'll reach the shores of Hungabee Lake and another trail junction; head right (west) here. Take a left (southwest) at the trail junction 100 meters later, skirting Hungabee Lake, which is speckled with fuzzy western anemones, to your left (south). At 6.5 kilometers you'll reach another trail junction; head right (north). Just 300 meters later you'll reach another trail junction; head left (west) past the Moor Lakes. At 7.2 kilometers you'll reach another trail junction; head left (west) toward the All Souls Alpine Route. This is a steep scramble up slopes of giant boulders and slippery scree. At 8.1 kilometers you'll enjoy prime views of Lake O'Hara, Mary Lake, and Schaffer Lake to your right (north). You'll also have fantastic views of Mount Huber (3,368 m), Wiwaxy Peak (2,703 m), and Yukness Mountain (2,847 m) to your right (east).

At 8.6 kilometers you'll reach the giant cairn at the summit of the All Souls Alpine Route (2,460 m). Your tired legs will hate you on the steep descent from here to Schaffer Lake. The rocky trail gives way to larch-lined forest at 8.9 kilometers. At 9.1 kilometers, just before Schaffer Lake, you'll reach the Big Larches Trail junction. Head right (northeast) 1.8 kilometers from here to the Le Relais day shelter.

15 Takakkaw Falls

Highlights:	A flat, paved trail that follows along the Yoho River before turning to take you to the base of Takakkaw Falls. Ideal for wheelchairs and strollers.
Type of hike:	Short walk; out-and-back.
Total distance:	1.0 kilometer.
Difficulty:	Easy.
Hiking time:	30 minutes.
Elevation at trailhead:	1,425 meters.
Elevation gain:	Minimal.
Topo maps:	Lake Louise & Yoho (GemTrek Publishing); Lake Louise, 82 N/8.

Finding the trailhead: Follow TransCanada Highway 1 approximately 2.5 kilometers northeast from the Field Information Centre, and turn left onto Yoho Valley Road. If you're heading in via Yoho's east boundary, turn right (north) after approximately 12.3 kilometers. Follow the Yoho Valley Road for 12.7 kilometers until you reach the Takakkaw Falls parking area on the right

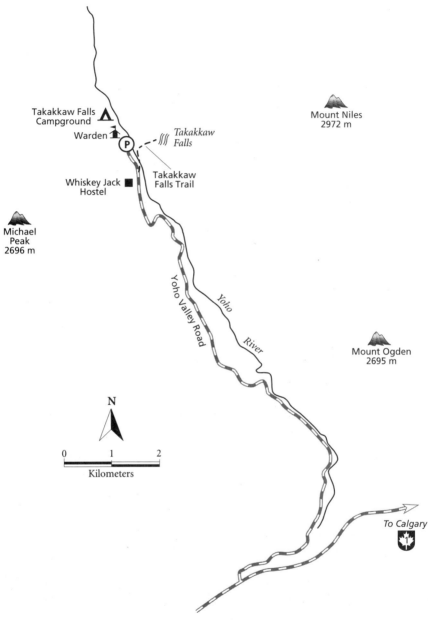

(east) side of the road. The paved trail begins at the southeast end of the parking area. There are washrooms and picnic tables around the parking area.

Key points:
0.0   Parking area.
0.5   Takakkaw Falls viewpoint.

The hike: Because this is a paved trail, it is ideal for anyone yearning for an up-close view of Takakkaw Falls. It's meaning in Cree—*magnificent*—provides a pretty good description of the view from the end of the trail. Although the sight from Yoho Valley Road is quite spectacular, the short walk to the base of the falls is worth the time spent—even if you're anxious to head off on a longer day hike to Laughing or Twin Falls.

From the southeast end of the parking area, follow the paved trail along the Yoho River. Approximately 150 meters along this well-trodden track, you'll reach a fork; stay left (northeast)—or follow the other camera-wielding tourists. They arrive here by the busload in the busy summer months. At about 0.25 kilometer you'll reach a trail junction. To walk to the base of the falls stay left (northeast) and cross the wooden footbridge over the Yoho River. There are a few log benches along the trail if you care to stop and enjoy the view. You'll see Mount Ogden (2,695 m) off to the right (east) and Mount Niles (2,972 m) (northeast). On a clear day you'll also see Cathedral Mountain (3,189 m) to the south and the Vice President (3,066 m), and Michael Peak (2,696 m) to the left (west). At 0.5 kilometer you'll reach the final viewpoint, where you can actually feel the force of the misty falls. Fed by the Daly Glacier (which is fed by the Waputik Icefields), these falls drop 254 meters, and are one of the highest waterfalls in Canada. You'll likely notice a few eager hikers on the rocks higher up by the base of the falls; however, it's not advisable to climb up there as the rock can be very slippery.

If you've enjoyed this short walk, you may want to hike to Point Lace Falls or the Angel's Staircase, just 2.7 kilometers north of the parking area.

16 Point Lace Falls/Laughing Falls/ Twin Falls

Highlights:	An easy loop through the YohoValley with views of four waterfalls.
Type of hike:	Day hike; out-and-back.
Total distance:	17.2 kilometers.
Difficulty:	Easy.
Hiking time:	4–6 hours.
Elevation at trailhead:	1,425 meters.
Elevation gain:	335 meters.
Topo maps:	Lake Louise & Yoho (GemTrek Publishing); Lake Louise, 82 N/8.

Finding the trailhead: Follow TransCanada Highway 1 approximately 2.5 kilometers northeast from the Field Information Centre, and turn left onto Yoho Valley Road. If you're heading in via Yoho's boundary, turn right (north) after approximately 12.3 kilometers. Follow Yoho Valley Road for 12.7 kilometers until you reach the Takakkaw Falls parking area on the right (east) side of the road. The trail begins at the north end of the parking area by the Warden's Cabin. There are washrooms and picnic tables around the parking area.

Key Points:
- 0.0 Trailhead.
- 0.6 Trail junction; straight ahead (north) toward the Twin Falls Campground.
- 2.7 Trail junction to Point Lace Falls and the Angel's Staircase; continue straight ahead (north).
- 4.8 Cross a footbridge over the Little Yoho River to reach the Laughing Falls Campground.
- 4.9 Trail junction; continue straight ahead (north).
- 5.3 Cross bridge over Twin Falls Creek.
- 6.8 Trail junction; turn left (west).
- 8.3 Trail junction; turn left (south).
- 9.0 Marpole Lake.
- 10.8 Trail junction; turn left (east) to Laughing Falls.
- 12.4 Trail junction; turn right (south) to head back toward the Takakkaw Falls parking area.
- 17.2 Parking area.

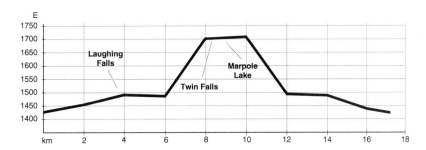

The hike: We refer to this day hike as the Waterfall Loop; you'll see four waterfalls in about four hours. This trail begins at the north end of the Takakkaw Falls parking area. Pass by the warden's cabin, and walk along the road toward Takakkaw Falls Campground. You may see a few northern anemones along the way, as well as Mount Gordon and Mount Balfour straight ahead (north). Follow the road through the campground as it winds to the left just past the cook shelter and washrooms. It is here that you will find the true trailhead before walking into the big, wide-open rocky flats of the Yoho Valley; you can see the Yoho River off to your right (east). Approximately 1.5 kilometers into the wide-open trail you'll reach the trees—lodgepole pine and some white spruce with old man's beard desperately hanging on the branches. You may also see some bright-yellow goosefoot violets before you glimpse the Waputik Range to your right (east).

At 2.7 kilometers you'll reach the junction for Point Lace Falls, about 150 meters off the main trail to the left (west), and Angel's Staircase Falls; the viewpoint is just a few meters to the right (east). Continue straight ahead (north) on the narrow trail toward Yoho Valley. The trail begins a short (150 meter), steep, rocky climb and then levels off again. At 3.2 kilometers you'll

Point Lace Falls/Laughing Falls/Twin Falls

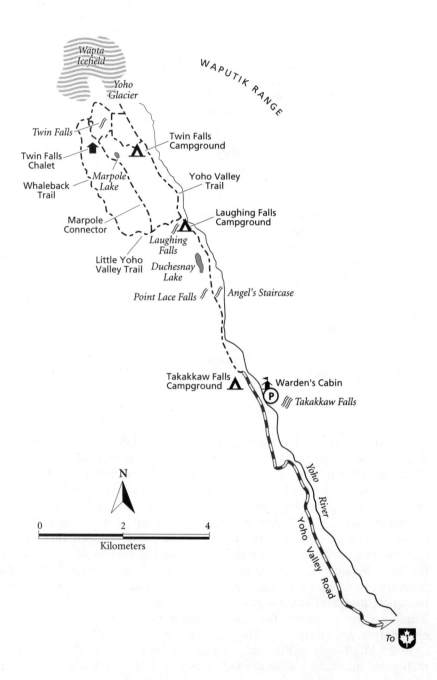

reach the trail junction to Duchesnay Lake (400 meters), and off to the right (east) you'll see a natural viewpoint for the Yoho River.

Just before the Laughing Falls Campground, you'll cross over the Little Yoho River on a footbridge. The campground sits at the base of the falls; in early summer they are quite spectacular. Just beyond the campground is the junction that can lead you to Twin Falls, whichever way you choose to go. We recommend staying on the main trail toward the Yoho Glacier Junction and the falls (north), coming back down the more westerly route to pass Marpole Lake before meeting this same junction one more time. You'll find the walk a little less scenic, but it isn't as steep. Follow the trail lined by hemlock as it parallels the Yoho River; you'll gain a fantastic view of Yoho Peak off in the distance. At 5.3 kilometers cross the bridge over Twin Falls Creek.

At 6.8 kilometers you will reach another junction. If you continue straight ahead (north), you'll reach the Yoho Glacier. The views here aren't that great; you'll have a better view of the Yoho Glacier if you complete the Whaleback Trail. Stay left (west) and head 200 meters toward the Twin Falls Campground. Walk through the campground (there will be no directional signage) and begin a moderate ascent to a junction at 8.3 kilometers.

You can hear the roaring falls as you walk toward the Twin Falls Chalet, which is approximately 100 meters to your left. You'll have a great view of the falls from the porch of this two-story log cabin, built in 1923 (open July to August; for lodge reservations call 403–228–7079). From here you can either hike back the way you came or continue down the trail toward a bridge, which provides a great viewpoint for the carved canyon below the falls, as well as Whaleback Mountain straight ahead (west).

Follow the trail down through a meadow with views of the Waputik Range and its glacier; at 9 kilometers you'll meet up with the clear waters of Marpole Lake. Leaving the lake, the trail changes from soft, dirt-pack to rocky limestone. You'll climb the Marpole Connector Trail, heading through an old rock slide for approximately 1.8 kilometers before heading back into the forest and down the trail the remaining 1.6 kilometers to reach the trail junction at 12.4 kilometers. Laughing Falls Campground is approximately 100 meters down the trail; from here you follow the path 4.8 kilometers back to the Takakkaw Falls parking area.

Options:
Yoho Glacier—4.8 kilometers. From the Yoho Valley Trail/Twin Falls Trail junction at 6.8 kilometers, take a right (north) to head to the Yoho Glacier. This gentle trail leads you through a forest of Douglas fir, along with fireweed, arnica, and fleabane, before emerging on the lip of a rocky moraine with the Yoho River to your right (east). In some spots the trail becomes a bit more difficult to find; look for the cairns. We found the views from the end of the trail disappointing, since we expected to get close to the glacier—not just see it from across the valley. If you really want to see glaciers, skip this trail in favor of the Iceline Trail, where you'll enjoy fantastic, close-up views of the Emerald Glacier.

Whaleback Trail to Twin Falls—6.2 kilometers. The Whaleback Trail is named for the shape of nearby Whaleback Mountain, which, as its name implies, is similar to a whale's curved gray posterior. It's on this trail that you'll gain the best views of the Yoho Glacier. From the Twin Falls Chalet turn right (north). Following a series of steep switchbacks, the Whaleback Trail skirts Whaleback Mountain to the right (west), leading you along a ridge above Twin Falls before descending to the Little Yoho Valley Trail. From here you can either return to Takakkaw Falls via the Little Yoho Valley Trail/Yoho Valley Trail or follow the Celeste Lake Connector/Iceline Trail back to Takakkaw Falls.

17 Iceline Trail/Little Yoho/ Yoho Valley Loop

Highlights:	This hike offers some of the most fantastic scenery in Yoho National Park, including close-up views of the Emerald Glacier.
Type of hike:	Backpack or day hike; loop.
Total distance:	20.7 kilometers.
Difficulty:	Moderate.
Hiking time:	2 days.
Elevation at trailhead:	1,475 meters.
Maximum elevation:	2,200 meters.
Elevation gain:	725 meters.
Topo maps:	Lake Louise & Yoho (GemTrek Publishing); Lake Louise, 82 N/8; Blaeberry, 82 N/10.

Finding the trailhead: Follow TransCanada Highway 1 approximately 2.7 kilometers east of the town of Field, and turn left (west) onto Yoho Valley Road. The road heads northwest toward Takakkaw Falls, approximately 13 kilometers. You'll find the Iceline trailhead near the Whiskey Jack Hostel on the left (west) side of Yoho Valley Road.

If you're not staying at the hostel, park in the Takakkaw Falls parking lot at the end of Yoho Valley Road on your right (east). From there follow the 500-meter connector trail southwest from the Takakkaw Falls Trail junction, and cross Yoho Valley Road to reach the trailhead. You'll find washrooms, picnic tables, and a campground near the Takakkaw Falls parking lot.

Key points:
 0.0 Trailhead.
 1.1 Hidden Lake Trail junction; continue straight ahead (northwest).
 1.3 Iceline Trail junction; turn right (northwest).
 2.4 Trail junction; continue straight ahead (northwest).
 3.9 Stream crossing.
 5.6 Celeste Lake Trail junction; continue straight ahead (northwest).
 7.1 Stream crossing.
 10.4 Trail junction; turn right (northeast).
 10.7 Little Yoho Valley Trail junction; turn right (east).

11.3	Little Yoho River crossing.
13.7	Celeste Lake Trail junction; continue straight ahead (east).
13.8	Whaleback Trail junction; continue straight ahead (east).
15.4	Laughing Falls Trail junction; turn right (southwest).
20.7	Takakkaw Falls parking lot.

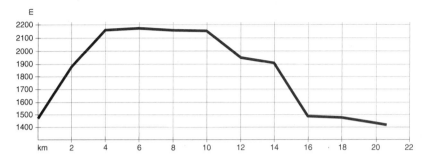

The hike: From close-up views of glaciers to crystal-clear mountain lakes and rivers, golf-course green forests, and a sea of rocky morraines, this hike has it all. On a sunny day you'll enjoy absolutely spectacular views of area glaciers and mountain peaks, which contrast sharply with the blue sky.

The trail starts north of the Whiskey Jack Hostel with 1.0 kilometer of densely forested switchbacks. At 1.1 kilometers you'll reach the Hidden Lake Trail junction; continue straight ahead (northwest) 200 meters to reach the Iceline Trail junction. Turn right (northwest) at the junction and continue through the overgrown meadows, which frequent avalanches have cleared of larger trees.

A colorful array of flowers, including fleabane, yellow columbine, white mountain rhododendron, leather leaf saxifrage, and valerian, line this section of trail. At 1.4 kilometers you'll catch a glimpse of Whiskey Jack Falls to your right (northeast). You'll also enjoy an incredible view of Takakkaw Falls across the valley to your right (northeast), along with Mount Niles (2,972 m) and Mount Odgen (2,695 m).

From here the trail ascends steeply through 200 meters of switchbacks. At 1.6 kilometers look behind you (south) for views of Cathedral Mountain (3,189 m), Mount Stephen (3,199 m), Wapta Mountain (2,778 m), and Mount Burgess (2,599 m). You'll also catch a glimpse of the Yoho River far beneath you in the valley to your right (east) before you enter a brief Douglas fir forest. As you emerge from the woods, you'll enjoy a fantastic view of the Wapta Icefield straight ahead (north).

At 2.4 kilometers you'll reach a trail junction; continue straight ahead (northwest). Just past this junction you'll find a TRAIL CLOSED sign for the abandoned Highline Trail; continue straight ahead (northwest). For the next 5 kilometers the trail leads you through rolling hills and ridges of rocky moraine formed by receding glaciers. It almost resembles a scene from *Star Wars*—with the finely crushed rock appearing like sand dunes from a distance. The views on this part of the trail are fantastic—especially views to your right (east) of the Daly Glacier, which feeds Takakkaw Falls, along with the Waputik Icefield, Mount Niles, Mount Daly (3,152 m), and Mount Ogden.

Iceline Trail/Little Yoho/Yoho Valley Loop

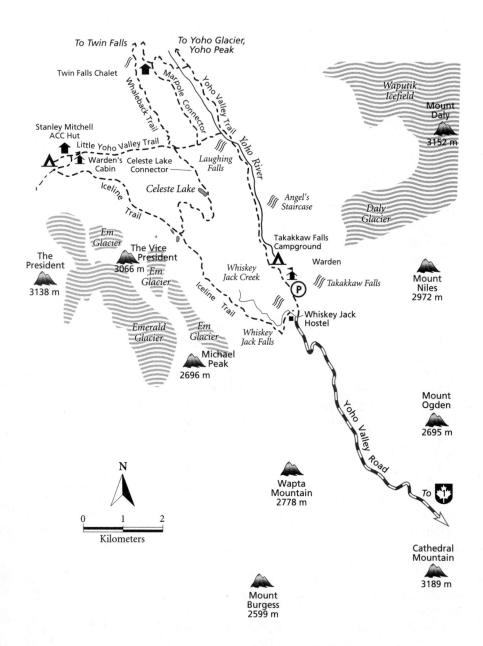

To Twin Falls

To Yoho Glacier,
Yoho Peak

Twin Falls Chalet

Waputik
Icefield

Mount
Daly
3152 m

Stanley Mitchell
ACC Hut

Little Yoho Valley Trail

Warden's
Cabin

Celeste Lake
Connector

Laughing
Falls

Daly
Glacier

Celeste Lake

Iceline
Trail

Angel's
Staircase

Em
Glacier

The Vice
President
3066 m

Em
Glacier

Takakkaw Falls
Campground

Warden

The
President

3138 m

Emerald
Glacier

Em
Glacier

Iceline Trail

Whiskey
Jack Creek

Takakkaw Falls

Mount
Niles
2972 m

Michael
Peak
2696 m

Whiskey
Jack Falls

Whiskey Jack
Hostel

Mount
Ogden
2695 m

N

0   1   2
Kilometers

Wapta
Mountain
2778 m

Yoho Valley Road

To

Cathedral
Mountain
3189 m

Mount
Burgess
2599 m

At 3.3 kilometers you'll reach the first part of the multifaceted Emerald Glacier to your left (west), along with Michael Peak (2,696 m) also to your left (west). Cascading over the striated ledges of the President Range to your left (west) are several small waterfalls. If you've never seen a glacier close-up before, you're in for quite a treat. You'll also have great views of Wapta Mountain behind you and the Waputik Icefield to your right (east).

At 3.5 kilometers the trail becomes sketchy as it passes through a section of large rocks; follow the cairns and continue heading northwest. Approximately 300 meters later you'll pass a giant boulder to your left (west) that seems strangely out of place amidst the more finely ground rock beneath your feet. The glacial runoff creates a small stream, which you'll cross by picking your way across the rocks at 3.9 kilometers.

At 4 kilometers you'll pass the second of four components of the Emerald Glacier that you'll see from the Iceline Trail on your left (west). Meltwater from this part of the glacier creates its own aquamarine-colored lake, which you'll cross on small rocks as you continue along the trail. Past this point you'll enjoy fantastic views of the President (3,138 m) and the Vice President (3,066 m) to your left (west).

At 5.3 kilometers, off to your right you'll see a sparse forest so green and perfectly manicured it looks like a golf course, except instead of divots, you'll spot grizzly bear digs. Just 100 meters later you'll reach the third component of the Emerald Glacier, which generates two small robin's-egg-blue lakes. At 5.6 kilometers you'll reach a trail junction; continue straight ahead (northwest). Be prepared for small drifts of snow on this section of trail—even in early August.

At 6.9 kilometers you'll pass the fourth and final component of the Emerald Glacier as viewed from the Iceline to your left (west). This part of the glacier also creates a small lake. Just 200 meters later you'll cross a small stream originating from the lake. From here you'll enter an alpine heath lined with heather, mosses, shrubby penstemon, western spring beauty, Douglas fir, and the occasional pine.

At 8.6 kilometers you'll head past the rocky moraine into the trees. A grizzly bear roams this area, so stay alert and make lots of noise. You may also spot arnica, Indian paintbrush, and sharptooth angelica on this section of trail.

At 10.4 kilometers you'll reach a trail junction; head to your right (northeast) past the warden's cabin and the Stanley Mitchell alpine hut. You'll reach another trail junction at the base of the hut at 10.7 kilometers. Continue 3 kilometers to your right (east) along the densely forested Little Yoho Valley trail. This trail skirts the Little Yoho River to your right (south), which you'll cross at 11.3 kilometers. At 13.7 kilometers you'll arrive at the Celeste Lake and Whaleback Trail junctions. You'll have a number of choices there, as outlined below.

Options:
Return to Takakkaw Falls via Laughing Falls and Yoho Valley Trail. (Total loop: 20.7 kilometers; easy.) This is the most popular way to com-

On the Iceline Trail hikers get close-up views of a glacier.

plete the loop to Takakkaw Falls, and it's the option we've used to compute the total distance for this trail. From the Celeste Lake Trail junction, continue straight ahead (east) 2.2 kilometers to Laughing Falls. At the Laughing Falls Trail junction, turn right (southwest) and follow the Yoho Valley Trail 4.8 kilometers to the Takakkaw Falls parking lot. (See Hike 15 for a complete description of the Yoho Valley Trail.)

Return to Takakkaw Falls via Celeste Lake Connector/Iceline. (Total loop: 23.2 kilometers; moderate.) If you don't mind repeating a portion of the Iceline Trail, the Celeste Lake Connector is an excellent option. Take a right (southeast) at the Celeste Lake Trail junction and follow a series of forested switchbacks 4.2 kilometers to the Iceline Trail junction. Just 300 meters into the trail, you'll pass a small unnamed lake; at 1.3 kilometers you'll skirt the swimming-pool green Celeste Lake. At the Iceline Trail junction, turn left (southeast) and follow the trail back to the trailhead.

Extended trip: Whaleback Trail to Twin Falls. (Total distance: 6.2 kilometers.) The Whaleback Trail is named for the shape of nearby Whaleback Mountain, which, as its name implies, is similar to a whale's curved gray posterior. You'll reach the Whaleback Trail junction at 13.8 kilometers; turn right (north) here. Following a series of steep switchbacks, the Whaleback Trail skirts Whaleback Mountain to the left (west), leading you along a ridge above Twin Falls before descending to the base of the falls near Twin Falls Chalet. From here you can either return to Takakkaw Falls via the Marpole Connector and the Little Yoho Valley Trail/Yoho Valley Trail or follow the Yoho Valley Trail back to the Takakkaw Falls parking lot.

18 Yoho Lake

Highlights:	A series of forested switchbacks leads you to Yoho Lake and offers excellent views of Takakkaw Falls.
Type of hike:	Day hike; out-and-back or loop.
Total distance:	7.8 kilometers.
Difficulty:	Easy.
Hiking time:	2½–4 hours.
Elevation at trailhead:	1,480 meters.
Maximum elevation:	1,745 meters.
Elevation gain:	265 meters.
Topo maps:	Lake Louise & Yoho (GemTrek Publishing); Lake Louise, 82 N/8; Golden 82 N/7.

Finding the trailhead: Follow TransCanada Highway 1 approximately 2.7 kilometers east of the town of Field, and turn left (west) onto Yoho Valley Road. The road heads northwest toward Takakkaw Falls approximately 13 kilometers. You'll find the trailhead for Yoho Lake near the Whiskey Jack Hostel on the left (west) side of Yoho Valley Road.

If you're not staying at the hostel, park in the Takakkaw Falls parking lot at the end of Yoho Valley Road on your right (east). From there follow the 500-meter connector trail southwest from the Takakkaw Falls Trail junction, and cross Yoho Valley Road to reach the trailhead. You'll find washrooms, picnic tables, and a campground near the Takakkaw Falls parking lot.

Key points:

0.0	Trailhead.
1.0	Stream crossing.
1.1	Hidden Lake Trail junction; continue straight ahead (west).
1.3	Yoho Lake Trail junction; turn left (southeast).
3.1	Yoho Lake.
3.9	Yoho Pass Trail junction.

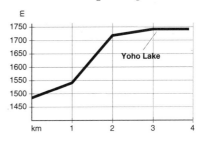

The hike: Keep an eye out for bears as you head through the densely forested switchbacks on the initial part of this trail. Grizzlies frequent the area; we saw one digging in an avalanche chute just south of this trailhead.

As you head up the narrow mossy trail, pink mountain heather, sunny globeflowers, and yellow glacier lilies add a splash of color. At 1.0 kilometer you'll cross Whiskey Jack Creek. Take a look to your left (northeast) at this point for an excellent view of Takakkaw Falls and Mount Ogden (2,695 m). Just 100 meters later you'll reach the junction for Hidden Lake. You can either take a detour to your left (southeast) here and trek 1.6 kilometers to Hidden Lake or continue straight ahead (west) toward Yoho Lake.

At 1.3 kilometers you'll reach another trail junction; turn left (southeast) toward Yoho Lake. You'll reach the lake at 3.1 kilometers. Similar to nearby Emerald Lake, Yoho Lake is also a brilliant aquamarine color—a result of

Yoho Lake

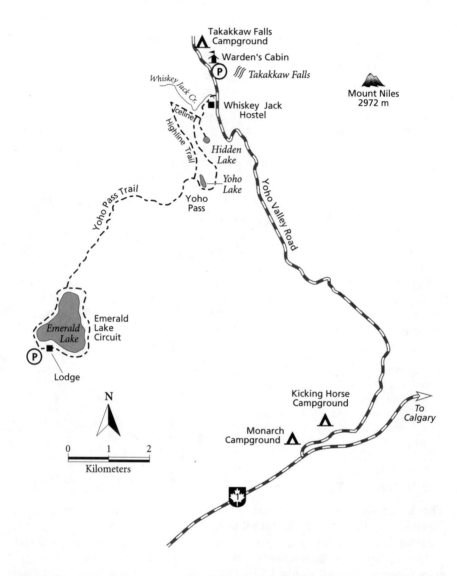

light reflecting off the glacial silt suspended in the water. Late in the summer the alpine meadows near the lake contain an abundance of colorful wildflowers. Yoho Lake Campground is located near the southwest corner of the lake.

Options:
Highline Loop to Takakkaw Falls (4.4 km, easy). Instead of returning to Takakkaw Falls the same way you came, consider looping back to the falls via the Highline Trail. Eventually linking with the Iceline Trail, the High-

Clouds are reflected in the clear waters of Yoho Lake.

line offers tremendous views of Takakkaw Falls, the Daly Glacier, and the Waputik Icefield.

The Highline Trail junction is located on the west side of Yoho Lake at Yoho Lake Campground. You'll turn right (north) at the junction. After briefly skirting the lake, you'll head up a series of forested switchbacks lined with Douglas fir, Englemann spruce, and a variety of wildflowers, including pink mountain heather, valerian, yellow columbine, and fleabane. Just 600 meters into the trail, you'll start to hear the rumbling of Takakkaw Falls; just 1.0 kilometer later you'll enjoy a great view of both the falls and the Daly Glacier.

At 2 kilometers you'll reach the Iceline Trail junction; head to your right (southeast). Enjoy the views of the Yoho River Valley straight ahead of you (east) before joining the same trail you traveled on your way to Yoho Lake at 3.1 kilometers. From here it's 1.3 kilometers through the trees back to Takakkaw Falls.

Emerald Triangle to Emerald Lake (6.6–13.2 kilometers, moderate). From Yoho Lake, we would strongly recommend continuing on to Emerald Lake via a portion of the Emerald Triangle. (See Hike 24 for more details.) Offering views of the Emerald Glacier, Michael Peak (2,696 m), Mount Burgess (2,599 m), Wapta Mountain (2,778 m), and other peaks, the Emerald Triangle highlights some of the most fantastic scenery in Yoho National Park. If you opt for either of these trails, your best bet is to have one car parked at Takakkaw Falls and another at Emerald Lake to avoid backtracking or hitchhiking.

19 Centennial Loop

Highlights:	This leisurely stroll leads you through the forest along the Yoho River.
Type of hike:	Short walk; loop.
Total distance:	2.5 kilometers.
Difficulty:	Easy.
Hiking time:	45 minutes–1 hour.
Elevation at trailhead:	1,305 meters.
Elevation gain/loss:	Minimal.
Topo maps:	Lake Louise & Yoho (GemTrek Publishing); Lake Louise, 82 N/8.

Finding the trailhead: Follow TransCanada Highway 1 approximately 5.9 kilometers east of the town of Field to the turnoff for Kicking Horse Campground. Take a left (north) off the highway and continue past the campground approximately 2.3 kilometers on Yoho Valley Road. The trailhead is located on the left (north) side of the road, immediately after the small bridge crossing the Yoho River. Although there's a small gravel parking lot, this trailhead is not marked, and there's no directional signage along the way.

Key points:
- 0.0   Trailhead.
- 1.1   Yoho Valley Road; turn left (north) over the bridge and left (northeast) onto the campground road.
- 1.9   Campground road; continue left (northeast).
- 2.5   End of trail.

The hike: This trail is perfect as a leisurely after-dinner stroll or a quick stretch break. Besides the Emerald Lake Circuit, it's also the only other short walk in Yoho National Park that's almost entirely flat.

The trail skirts the Yoho River, which flows from the Yoho Glacier in the Wapta Icefields. Exactly how high and fast the river flows depends on how quickly the glacial ice melts. Typically, glacially fed rivers run low in the morning, with water volume peaking in the early evening, after the water travels from the glacier to the valley floor.

Lined with juniper, Englemann spruce, and Douglas fir, this trail offers only limited mountain views. Just 200 meters into the trail you'll enjoy views of Mount Field (2635 m) on your right (northwest), Mount Burgess (2,599 m) straight ahead (southwest), and Cathedral Mountain (3,189 m) on your left (south). At night alpenglow on Cathedral Mountain creates a soft orange color. Also to your left (south) you'll see Mountain Stephen (3,199 m), on which you'll spot several cavelike openings—remnants of old mine shafts from the Monarch mines.

At 800 meters you'll cross a small stream, and at 1.1 kilometers you'll find yourself back on Yoho Valley Road, across from Cathedral Mountain Lodge & Chalets. Take a left (north) over the bridge and another left (northeast) onto the campground road.

Centennial Loop

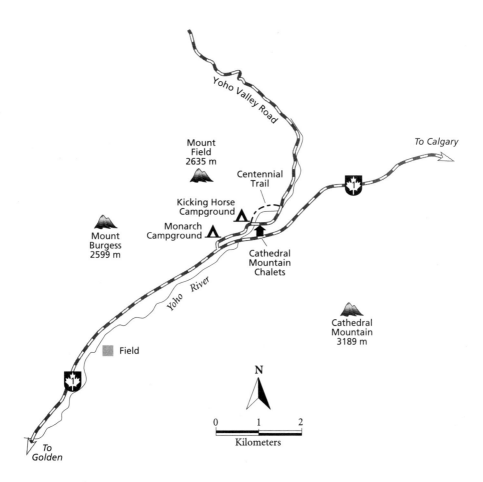

At 1.5 kilometers, just before the campground playground, you can either take a left (west) back into the trees and walk closer to the river or continue along the campground road. Either way, at 1.9 kilometers you'll wind back out onto the campground road; continue left (northeast). At the north end of the campground, follow the gravel service road to your left (north) back to your car. The bridge over the Yoho River at the end of the trail offers a natural spot for a photo.

20 A Walk in the Past

Highlights:	An interpretive historical walk from Kicking Horse Campground to the "Big Hill." You will come across an abandoned narrow-gauge work engine that was used during construction of the Spiral Tunnels.
Type of hike:	Short hike; out-and-back.
Total distance:	2.7 kilometers.
Difficulty:	Easy.
Hiking time:	1–2 hours.
Elevation at trailhead:	1,255 meters.
Elevation gain:	120 meters.
Topo maps:	Lake Louise & Yoho (GemTrek Publishing); Lake Louise, 82 N/8.

Finding the trailhead: Follow TransCanada Highway 1 approximately 5.9 kilometers east of the town of Field to the turnoff for Kicking Horse Campground. Take a left (north) off the highway onto the Yoho Valley Road and turn into Kicking Horse Campground. Stay right, heading north toward the picnic area, approximately 0.4 kilometer into the campground. The trailhead sign is just left of the washrooms.

Key Points:
0.0	Trailhead.
0.3	Trail Marker 1.
0.5	Trail Marker 2.
0.7	Trail Marker 3.
1.0	Trail Marker 4.
1.1	Trail Marker 5.
1.2	Trail Marker 6.

The hike: History or train buffs will love this trail, and even if you don't fall into one of these classifications, you'll find this walk interesting. It's perfect for a rainy day.

In 1884, 12,000 men from across the country came to work on the Canadian Pacific Railway—building the railroad through the steep Kicking Horse Pass. This trail takes you along the worker's old tote road from Kicking Horse Campground, once their work camp, to the pass, which was not so fondly referred to as "The Big Hill." At the end of this short hike you will encounter an abandoned narrow-gauge work engine that once hauled rock out of the Spiral Tunnels.

At the trailhead it's worth picking up an interpretive brochure for this self-guiding trail. The brochures are put together by the Friends of Yoho; you pay by dropping one dollar into the cash box, and at the end of the trail, you can return the brochure for reuse.

Take the trail to the left of the washrooms and head up the hill about 100 meters before crossing Yoho Valley Road. You will regain the trail on the other

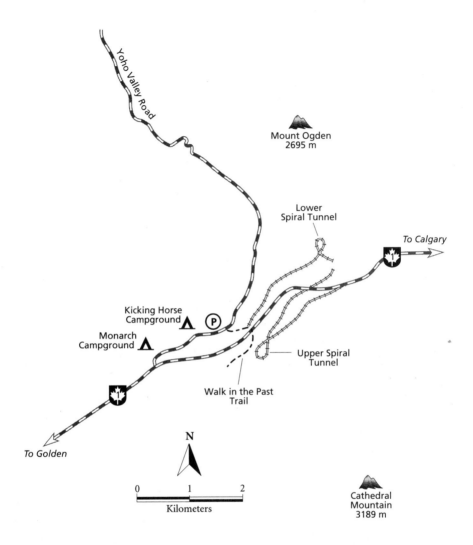

Mount Ogden
2695 m

Yoho Valley Road

Lower
Spiral Tunnel

To Calgary

Kicking Horse
Campground

Monarch
Campground

Upper Spiral
Tunnel

Walk in the Past
Trail

To Golden

N

0   1   2
Kilometers

Cathedral
Mountain
3189 m

side of the road, passing through a forest filled with coastal plants—red cedar and devil's club. You'll reach the first trail marker at 0.3 kilometer into the trail as you continue on a gradual incline through the lush wet montane forest. At 0.5 kilometer you will reach the second historical trail marker. You will follow a few switchbacks to reach Trail Marker 3 at 0.7 kilometer. Here and a few other places along the Big Hill track, "clinkers," deposits of cinders and soot lie inches deep—proof that fifteen steam locomotives passed along this track every day for the last fifty years of the track's use. In 1885 four engines were required to push fourteen freight cars to the top of the pass 400 meters above Field; it took nearly an hour to travel this 13-kilometer section.

Beyond Marker 3, you walk parallel with the highway; it's here that you gain a great view of Cathedral Mountain (3,189 m) straight ahead (southeast), which houses the upper Spiral Tunnel. Built in 1909, the new track doubled the length up Big Hill but reduced the grade by half. The upper loop is 3,255 feet long, with a curvature of 288 degrees. The difference in elevation between the upper and lower portal is 14.4 meters. As you continue along the trail, pass beneath the highway and carefully cross over the railway tracks. Those tracks lead to the renowned Spiral Tunnels. The tracks head east to Mount Ogden, then loop around the inside of the mountain, and come back across the valley to Cathedral Mountain. One kilometer into the hike you will reach Marker 4. Above you is the upper tunnel, where the track makes its second loop inside Cathedral Mountain and continues upward to the top of the pass. It's the highway that actually follows the route of the original Big Hill track. If you look closely as you drive into Yoho Park from the east, you can see the old tunnel pass alongside the highway.

At the 1.1-kilometer point you will reach Trail Marker 5. Above you is the portal of the upper tunnel; below you is where the lower track of the Spiral Tunnel runs into Field. Going downhill caused many problems for engineers of the day. Wheels and brakes had to be tested constantly and safety switches always had to be manned, ready to slow down a speeding train by turning them onto uphill runaway tracks. Occasionally the switches couldn't be operated in time and the runaway train would plunge into the river below.

From here continue walking along the forest service road on Big Hill until you see the trail marker to the south (your left). You'll see a footbridge surrounded by orange Indian paintbrush, which is followed by the last trail marker, number 6 (1.2 km into the trail). Here lies the rust-covered narrow-gauge work engine that was used to haul rock out of the Spiral Tunnels as workers built them almost a century ago.

21 Emerald Lake Circuit

Highlights:	This pancake-flat interpretive trail provides excellent views of Emerald Lake and area mountain peaks. The trail includes a 3.4-kilometer wheelchair-accessible section.
Type of hike:	Day hike; loop.
Total distance:	4.6 kilometers.
Difficulty:	Easy.
Hiking time:	1–2 hours.
Elevation at trailhead:	1,310 meters.
Elevation gain:	Minimal.
Topo maps:	Lake Louise & Yoho (GemTrek Publishing); Golden, 82 N/7.

The most popular lake in Yoho, Emerald Lake attracts more than 14,000 visitors a day.

Finding the trailhead: The turnoff for Emerald Lake is located on the north side of Highway 1, approximately 2.5 kilometers west of the town of Field and 26.5 kilometers east of Yoho National Park's west gate. Follow signs for the Natural Bridge and Emerald Lake. You'll travel 8.7 kilometers on a paved road, which ends at the parking lot for Emerald Lake. The trailhead is located on the west side of the lake, just behind the gift shop. Follow the trail clockwise around the lake.

Near the trailhead you'll find washrooms and a gift shop that rents canoes, rowboats, and hiking gear. Emerald Lake Lodge, located on the south side of the lake, offers accommodations, restaurants, and a lounge.

Key points:
0.0   Trailhead.
1.6   Emerald Basin Trail junction; continue straight ahead (east).
1.7   Yoho Pass Trail junction; continue straight ahead (east).
1.8   Stream crossing.
2.3   Stream crossing.
2.4   Stream crossing.
2.5   Burgess Pass Trail junction; continue straight ahead (south).
3.3   Emerald Lake Lodge Trail junction; turn right (northwest).
4.6   Parking lot.

The hike: Gorgeous, but incredibly busy. That's how we'd sum up our experience at Emerald Lake—a regular stop on the tour bus circuit. The good news is that relatively few tourists venture past the lodge and gift shop at the south end of the lake.

Follow the trail clockwise around the lake. The first part of the trail features information on the avalanche chute, two different types of forest, the

Emerald Lake Circuit

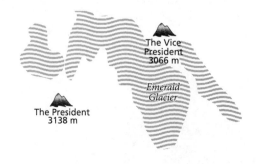

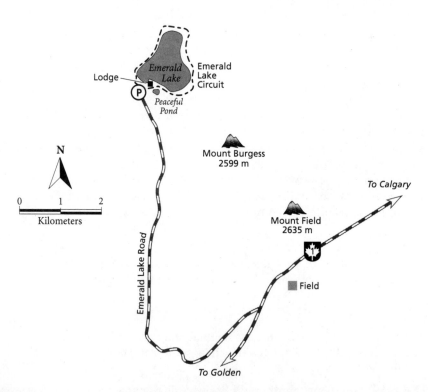

alluvial fan, and the glacial moraine you'll pass along the trail, as well as the nearby Burgess Shale fossils. Rain or shine, you'll notice Emerald Lake's brilliant aquamarine color, caused as light reflects on the fine glacial rock powder suspended in the water. Nearby glaciers create this powder over time by grinding up the underlying rock.

If you're hiking this trail in mid to late summer, an array of wildflowers, including yellow lady's slippers, columbine, Indian paintbrush, and fleabane, add a splash of color along the way. Strategically placed log benches also provide places to rest and enjoy the scenery.

At 1.6 kilometers you'll reach the alluvial fan on the south side of the lake and the junction for the Emerald Basin Trail. This is an ideal spot to rest, have lunch, and snap a few photos of Mount Burgess (2,599 m) and Mount Field (2,635 m) to your left (southeast) before continuing straight ahead (east) on the Shoreline Trail.

Just 100 meters later you'll reach the end of the wheelchair-accessible trail at the trail junction for Yoho Pass. To complete the circuit, continue straight ahead (east) on the Shoreline Trail. At 1.8 kilometers you'll cross an unnamed stream, which originates in the President Range. Look behind you (west) for fantastic views of the President Range and Emerald Glacier.

The second part of the trail consists of a moist, shady forest, which can be quite muddy year-round. You'll cross small unnamed streams at 2.3 and 2.4 kilometers respectively. Just 500 meters later you'll reach the Burgess Pass trailhead; continue straight ahead (south) on the Shoreline Trail.

You'll reach the final trail junction at 3.3 kilometers. From here you can either branch left (west) to reach the parking lot via a wooded trail and Peaceful Pond or right (northwest) to reach the parking lot via Emerald Lake Lodge.

22 Hamilton Falls and Hamilton Lake

Highlights: This short but incredibly steep climb passes Hamilton Falls and offers superb views of Mount Vaux and Mount Goodsir.
Type of hike: Day hike; out-and-back.
Total distance: 12.2 kilometers.
Difficulty: Strenuous.
Hiking time: 3½–5 hours.
Elevation gain/loss: 840 meters.
Topo maps: Lake Louise & Yoho (GemTrek Publishing); Golden, 82 N/7.

Finding the trailhead: The trail to Hamilton Falls and Hamilton Lake starts in the southwest corner of the Emerald Lake parking lot. The turnoff to Emerald Lake is located on the north side of TransCanada Highway 1, approximately 2.5 kilometers west of the town of Field and 26.5 kilometers east of Yoho National Park's west gate. Follow the sign for the Natural Bridge and Emerald Lake. You'll travel 8.7 kilometers on a paved road, which ends at the Emerald Lake parking lot.

Near the Emerald Lake trailhead, you'll find washrooms and a gift shop that rents canoes, rowboats, and hiking gear. Emerald Lake Lodge, located on the south side of the lake, offers accommodations, restaurants, and a lounge.

Key Points:

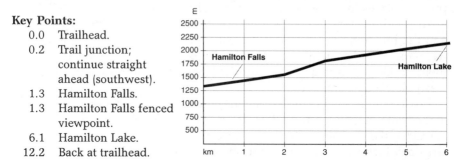

0.0   Trailhead.
0.2   Trail junction; continue straight ahead (southwest).
1.3   Hamilton Falls.
1.3   Hamilton Falls fenced viewpoint.
6.1   Hamilton Lake.
12.2   Back at trailhead.

The hike: You may feel a bit like a mountain goat on this seemingly never-ending climb—one of the most strenuous in Yoho National Park. But you'll be well rewarded for your efforts.

For your hiking enjoyment, don't venture onto this trail too early in the season. Wait until mid-July at the earliest, or you may find yourself plowing through thigh-deep snow like we did. We hiked this trail in mid-June—only to arrive at a frozen lake blanketed with more than a meter of heavy snow. Keep in mind that you'll be gaining some impressive elevation, so this trail will take considerably more time than most other 12-kilometer trails.

On your 700-meter stroll to Hamilton Falls (the easy part of the trail), you'll pass through a moist, mossy forest of western red cedar, hemlock, and Douglas fir on a narrow, single-file path. Just 200 meters into the trail you'll reach a trail junction; continue straight ahead (southwest). At 700 meters you'll arrive at Hamilton Falls, which flow over a limestone cliff in a series of steps, carving deep paths into the underlying bedrock in the process.

From here the steep ascent to the lake starts immediately with a seemingly never-ending series of switchbacks. At 1.1 kilometers follow the side trail 100 meters to your left (south) to enjoy a panoramic view of the Hamilton Spur and Hamilton Ridge to the southeast. You'll be able to hear, but not see, Hamilton Falls rushing below you (south). On your way back to the main trail, enjoy a lofty view of Emerald Lake straight ahead (northeast).

At 1.3 kilometers you'll take in the best view of Hamilton Falls to your left (south) at a fenced viewpoint. From here the ascent to Hamilton Lake becomes a bit tedious as you climb switchback after switchback through a forest of Englemann spruce, whitebark pine, hemlock, western red cedar, juniper, and lodgepole pine. Along the way you may notice both dark-green and black hairy-looking moss dangling from some of these trees; they're known as old man's beard and horsehair lichen, respectively, and do not harm the trees. Early in the season you're also likely to see bright-yellow glacier lilies lining the trail, a favorite treat for the grizzly bears that roam this area.

At 4.6 kilometers the trail begins to open up. Take a good look to your left (south) at the Ottertail Range, particularly Mount Hurd (2,993 m), Mount Vaux (3,307 m), and the two towers of Mount Goodsir (North Tower, 3,520 m;

Hamilton Falls and Hamilton Lake

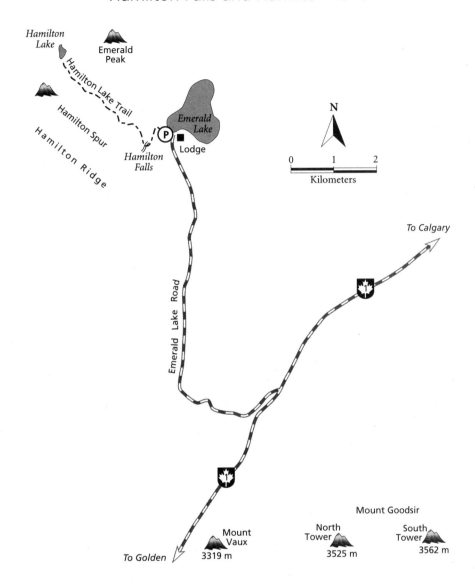

South Tower, 3,581 m)—the highest mountains in Yoho National Park. With only 500 meters to go, you'll pass through an open shale area from which you can see Mount Carnavon (2,545 m) and Emerald Peak (2,300 m) straight ahead (north and northeast).

Hamilton Lake is a gorgeous place to relax; just keep an eye out for bears. You may also spot hoary marmots and Columbian ground squirrels in this area. The lake was named for C. E. Roxy Hamilton, who ran a hotel in the town of Field and later worked for the park.

23 Emerald Basin

Highlights:	This steep, forested climb crosses several avalanche chutes, ending with views of hanging glaciers.
Type of hike:	Day hike; out-and-back.
Total distance:	9.4 kilometers.
Difficulty:	Easy.
Hiking time:	2½–4 hours.
Elevation at trailhead:	1,310 meters.
Elevation gain:	240 meters.
Topo maps:	Lake Louise & Yoho (GemTrek Publishing); Golden, 82 N/7.

Finding the trailhead: The Emerald Basin trailhead is located at Emerald Lake. You'll find Emerald Lake on the north side of Highway 1, approximately 2.5 kilometers west of the town of Field and 26.5 kilometers east of Yoho National Park's west gate. Follow signs for the Natural Bridge and Emerald Lake. You'll travel 8.7 kilometers on a paved road, which ends at the parking lot for Emerald Lake. To reach the Emerald Basin Trail junction, walk 1.6 kilometers left (northwest) around the lake.

Near the Emerald Lake trailhead, you'll find washrooms and a gift shop that rents canoes, rowboats, and hiking gear. Emerald Lake Lodge, located on the south side of the lake, offers accommodations, restaurants, and a lounge.

Key points:

0.0   Emerald Lake trailhead.
1.6   Emerald Basin Trail junction; turn left (north).
4.7   Emerald Basin.
9.4   Back at Emerald Lake trailhead.

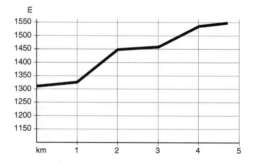

The hike: If you're out of shape like we were the first time we hiked this trail, you're bound to feel a bit of pain on your ascent to Emerald Basin. But the prime views from the natural ampitheater at the end of the hike make it all worthwhile.

Starting at the south end of Emerald Lake, follow the Emerald Lake Circuit left (northwest) 1.6 kilometers to the Emerald Basin trailhead. This is the easy part of the trail; enjoy it while it lasts. Turn left (north) at the trail junction. You'll catch occasional glimpses of the President Range straight ahead (north) through the trees on the first part of this trail—a short but steep climb through a forest of Douglas fir, spruce, and cedar. After the initial ascent, the trail levels out as it passes through a forest of yew and hemlock. You'll cross several avalanche chutes from the President Range to your left (west)—and likely will slip and slide across the remaining drifts of snow—before arriving at Emerald Basin.

Emerald Basin

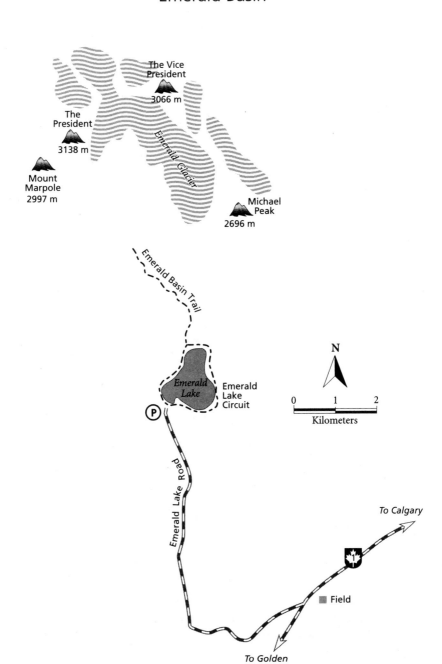

No the photo isn't crooked—the trees are. You'll hike through several avalanche chutes to reach Emerald Basin.

From Emerald Basin you'll soak up fabulous views of the President (3,138 m), the Vice President (3,066 m), and the Emerald Glacier straight ahead (north and northeast); Michael Peak (2,696 m) to your right (northeast); and Mount Marpole (2,997 m) as well as numerous avalanche chutes from the President Range to your left (northwest and west). If you're hiking this trail in early summer, wear gaiters and be prepared for snow and mud. It's also wise to check with the visitor center in nearby Field for potential avalanche danger on the trail.

24 Emerald Triangle

Highlights:	This all-day hike offers fantastic views of the President Range, the Emerald Glacier, Mount Burgess, and Wapta Mountain.
Type of hike:	Day hike; loop.
Total distance:	18.5 kilometers.
Difficulty:	Moderate.
Hiking time:	8–10 hours.
Elevation at trailhead:	1,310 meters.
Elevation gain:	890 meters.
Topo maps:	Lake Louise & Yoho (GemTrek Publishing); Golden, 82 N/7; Lake Louise, 82 N/8.

Finding the trailhead: You can tackle the Emerald Triangle from either the north end or the south end of Emerald Lake. The turnoff for Emerald Lake is located on the north side of Highway 1, approximately 2.5 kilometers west of the town of Field and 26.5 kilometers east of Yoho National Park's west gate. Follow signs for the Natural Bridge and Emerald Lake. You'll travel 8.7 kilometers on a paved road, which ends at the parking lot for Emerald Lake.

The trailhead is located on the east side of the parking lot; follow the Emerald Lake Circuit Trail counterclockwise around the lake, and begin the Triangle via either the Burgess Pass Trail or the Yoho Pass Trail. The Yoho Pass Trail provides the easiest climb to the Burgess Highline, but the Burgess Pass Trail offers the most scenic views (that's where we opted to start).

Near the Emerald Lake parking lot, you'll find washrooms and a gift shop that rents canoes, rowboats, and hiking gear. Emerald Lake Lodge, located on the south side of the lake, offers accommodations, restaurants, and a lounge.

Key Points:
- 0.0   Trailhead.
- 1.0   Burgess Pass Trail junction; turn right (east).
- 6.5   Burgess Highline Trail junction; continue straight ahead (east).
- 12.6 Yoho Pass Trail junction; turn left (southwest).
- 16.2 Trail junction; continue straight ahead (south).
- 16.9 Emerald Lake.
- 18.5 Emerald Lake parking lot.

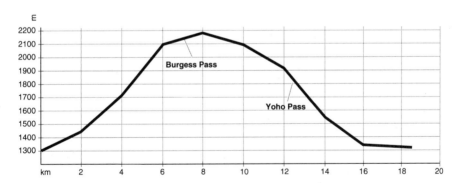

The hike: The first time we hiked this trail, in mid-July, deep snow and avalanches on the Burgess Highline forced us to turn around early. You're better off waiting until August or September to hike this trail; and it's well worth the wait.

You'll have to work for your views though—especially if you start with the Burgess Pass Trail, on which you'll gain 840 meters in just 5.5 kilometers. It doesn't sound so bad—until you realize that the raspy noise you keep hearing is your own labored breathing.

Follow the Emerald Lake Circuit 1.0 kilometer counterclockwise (northeast) around the lake to the Burgess Pass Trail junction; take a right (east) here. There's no resting on this damp, shady trail, which starts climbing

Emerald Triangle

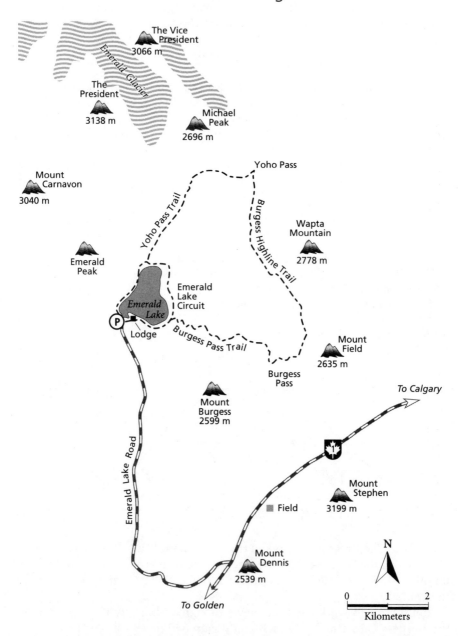

immediately through a forest of Douglas fir, hemlock, and western red cedar. Look for bright-yellow glacier lilies and globeflowers sprinkled along this part of the trail.

At 4.6 kilometers you'll enjoy a fantastic view of Emerald Lake, the President Range, and Mount Carnavon (3,040 m) to your left (west). As you continue up the switchbacks to 5.8 kilometers, look to your right (south) for an impressive view of Mount Burgess (2,599 m). We also spotted a few deer tracks in the patches of snow lingering amidst the trees.

At 6.5 kilometers you'll reach the trail junction; continue straight ahead (east) toward the Burgess Highline. Less than 100 meters past the junction, you'll notice a giant hill (a high spot on Burgess Pass) to your left (west). Before continuing on the trail, scramble up this hill to enjoy majestic views of the Kicking Horse River Valley, Mount Dennis (2,539 m), and Mount Stephen (3,199 m) to your right (southeast); Wapta Mountain (2,778 m) straight ahead (east); and the President Range behind you to your left (northwest). You'll then head down (northeast) through the trees toward the Burgess Highline.

After emerging from the forest, you'll pass several steep avalanche slopes on Mount Field (2,635 m) and Wapta Mountain (2,778 m) to your right (east). You'll also enjoy fantastic views of Emerald Lake far beneath you to your left (west) and the President Range straight ahead (northwest).

At 8.6 kilometers you may spot a congregation of tents off to your left on a small plateau. These tents belong to scientists researching the Burgess Shale fossils. At 9.1 kilometers you'll cross a small stream, which eventually drains into Emerald Lake. Just 500 meters later you'll walk through an orange-and-gray-colored rocky slide section as you continue past Wapta Mountain.

From here to Yoho Pass, the trail winds through sections of heavily wooded forest, rocky slides, and avalanche slopes overflowing with brightly colored arnica, valerian, Indian paintbrush, and yellow columbine. The fattest marmot we've ever seen waddled into the forest ahead of us here.

At 11.6 kilometers you'll soak up spectacular bird's-eye views of Emerald Lake and the alluvial fan along the north end of the lake, along with the President Range and the Emerald Glacier to your left (north and northwest). Follow the trail past the red-and-white sign on the Burgess Shale fossils through the woods to Yoho Pass at 12.6 kilometers.

From the Yoho Pass Trail junction, turn left (southwest) for an easy descent to Emerald Lake. At 13.4 kilometers you'll gain views of Emerald Lake to your left (south), along with Mount Burgess and Mount Dennis to the southeast.

At 13.8 kilometers the trail opens up with prime views of Michael Peak (2,696 m) to the northwest, as well as Mount Carnavon and Emerald Peak straight ahead (west). Depending on the time of year, you may also see pink mountain heather, yellow columbine, and purple orchids on this section of the trail.

At 14.7 kilometers you'll begin a series of gentle switchbacks down to Emerald Lake. Don't miss the great view of the President Range and the small waterfall to your right (east) here. You'll pass through a sparse forest of lodgepole pine and Douglas fir at approximately 15.7 kilometers on your way to the alluvial fan.

Just 100 meters later you'll cross a wooden bridge over a small stream, which originates in the President Range. You may spot wild strawberries, Columbia lilies, Indian paintbrushes, and lady's slippers on this section of

The green water of Emerald Lake is visible from the Wapta Highline.

trail. At 16.2 kilometers you'll reach a trail junction; continue straight ahead (south) toward Emerald Lake.

At 16.6 kilometers you'll cross another stream on a wooden bridge, followed by several subsequent bridges over this wet section of trail. You'll reach the Emerald Lake Trail junction at 16.9 kilometers. At this point, you may head either right (west) 1.6 kilometers around the lake or left (east) 3 kilometers around the lake to the Emerald Lake parking lot.

25 Emerald River

Highlights:	This pleasant walk along Emerald River crosses Hamilton Creek and Russell Creek.
Type of hike:	Day hike; shuttle.
Total distance:	7.1 kilometers.
Difficulty:	Easy.
Hiking time:	2–3 hours.
Elevation at trailhead:	1,310 meters.
Elevation loss:	135 meters.
Topo maps:	Lake Louise & Yoho (GemTrek Publishing); Golden, 82 N/7.

Finding the trailhead: The turnoff for Emerald Lake is located on the north side of TransCanada Highway 1, approximately 2.5 kilometers west of the

Emerald River

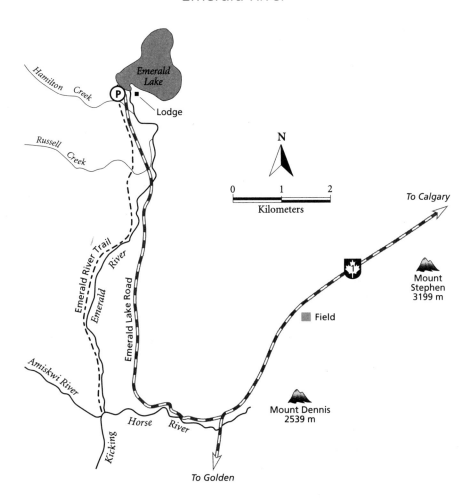

town of Field and 26.5 kilometers east of Yoho National Park's west gate. Follow signs for the Natural Bridge and Emerald Lake. You'll travel 8.7 kilometers on a paved road, which ends at the parking lot for Emerald Lake. Look for the Hamilton Falls/Hamilton Lake trailhead at the southwest end of the parking lot, and follow the trail straight ahead (west) 200 meters to arrive at the Emerald River Trail junction.

Near the Emerald Lake trailhead, you'll find washrooms and a gift shop that rents canoes, rowboats, and hiking gear. Emerald Lake Lodge, located on the south side of the lake, offers accommodations, restaurants, and a lounge.

Key points:
- 0.0   Trailhead.
- 0.2   Emerald River Trail junction; turn left (south).
- 0.6   Hamilton Creek crossing.
- 1.8   Russell Creek crossing.

3.6   Unmarked Trail junction; stay right (west).

5.3   Trail junction; continue straight ahead (south).

7.1   Kicking Horse River; end of trail.

The hike: If you're looking for a long but gentle walk in the woods, this is it. You're guaranteed to leave Emerald Lake's camera-waving tourists behind you on this less-traveled trail.

From the trailhead you'll walk 200 meters straight ahead (west), taking a left (south) at the Emerald River Trail junction. Just 400 meters later you'll cross Hamilton Creek. As you continue along this relatively flat, forested trail you'll cross several small streams, many of which are bridged only by fallen logs—great if you have good balance, not so great if you don't.

At approximately 1.8 kilometers you'll cross Russell Creek. At 3.2 kilometers you'll start walking alongside Emerald River to your left (east), which you'll follow closely for the remainder of the trail. Three Kootenay Indian campsites believed to date back to at least 1800 have been discovered at the mouth of this river.

At 3.6 kilometers you'll arrive at an unmarked trail junction; stay right (west). You'll reach another trail junction at 5.3 kilometers—continue straight ahead (south) to complete the trail. The trail gradually opens up, providing majestic views of Mount Stephen (3,199 m) and Mount Dennis (2,539 m). From 6.4 kilometers on, you can look down into a modest canyon to your right (east) and watch the tumbling falls of Emerald River head toward the greater Kicking Horse River. The trail ends at the junction of these two rivers.

Follow the secondary road left (east) to walk 2.3 kilometers to the Natural Bridge Parking area. From here you may be able to hitchhike back to Emerald Lake. Or leave a second vehicle in the parking area, approximately 500 meters from the end of the trail to your right (west).

26 Burgess Pass

Highlights:	To make the most of this trip, you may want to take a guided hike of the Burgess Shale fossil find with Parks Canada. Or you can hike to the top of the Burgess Pass just to gain the spectacular views.
Type of hike:	Day hike; out-and-back day.
Total distance:	16.4 kilometers.
Difficulty:	Strenuous.
Hiking time:	5–6 hours.
Elevation at trailhead:	1,090 meters.
Elevation gain:	1,085 meters.
Topo maps:	Lake Louise & Yoho (GemTrek Publishing); Lake Louise, 82 N/8.

Finding the trailhead: Follow TransCanada Highway 1 approximately 1.3 kilometers northeast from the Field Information Centre and turn left (north) into the unmarked secondary road. Immediately turn left (west) again and follow the gravel road about 500 meters to the trailhead.

Key points:

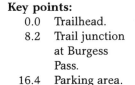

0.0 Trailhead.
8.2 Trail junction at Burgess Pass.
16.4 Parking area.

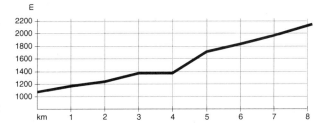

The hike: Forty-eight switchbacks. Need we say more? Yes, it's uphill—for every step of the 8.2 kilometers—but it's worth every one of them. Even if you're not interested in fossils, the variety of alpine flowers you'll see along the way could fill a book, and the views of Mount Stephen (3,199 m), Mount Dennis (2,359 m) and the Kicking Horse Valley are breathtaking on a clear day. There is one thing this trail could do without though, and that's the hum of traffic; you can still hear it at the top.

Ranked as one of the most important fossil localities in the world, the Burgess Shale was declared a World Heritage Site in 1980. In 1886 trilobite fossils were discovered on Mount Stephen by Otto Klotz, a railway engineer/surveyor. Upon learning of the discovery, Charles Walcott, a paleontologist with the Smithsonian Institution of Washington, D.C., came to the site in 1909 as part of a general study on Cambrian rock. Walcott discovered many creatures new to science high on the ridge that connects Mount Burgess to Wapta Peak—a discovery that changed many scientists' views about the earth's evolution. Fossil collecting by the public is not allowed. However, if you're interested in learning more about the fossils of the Burgess Shale, Yoho National Park, in partnership with the Yoho–Burgess Shale Foundation, offers Earth Science educational hikes. The cost is CDN $48.15 per adult; CDN $26.75 per child under twelve, and you can book by calling (800) 343-3006 or by e-mailing burgshal@rockies.net. You can also take a look at a few fossil samples at the Field Information Centre.

At the trailhead you'll notice that the sign says 7.3 kilometers; we found the trail to the pass to be 8.2 kilometers. Follow the single-file path south parallel to the highway. You'll immediately encounter some crimson-red and orange-colored Indian paintbrush—maybe even a little bear scat in early July. About 100 meters down the trail you'll turn right (west) into a lovely forest filled with poplar, aspen, mountain ash, Rocky Mountain maple, hemlock, and lodgepole pine. This lush trail is lined by moss and is initially root filled. At 0.4 kilometer you'll cross a small stream. Just beyond it, you're bound to see some dogwood, partridge foot, and maybe even some blue clematis; you'll also notice the constant sound of traffic. Approximately 1.0 kilometer into the trail you'll gain your first view of Mount Stephen through the trees (south); at 2 kilometers your view will be completely clear. Just to your right (southeast) you'll see Mount Dennis behind the town of Field.

You'll have trouble keeping your eye on the trail as the wildflowers provide constant distraction—yellow columbine, calypso orchid, western meadow

Burgess Pass

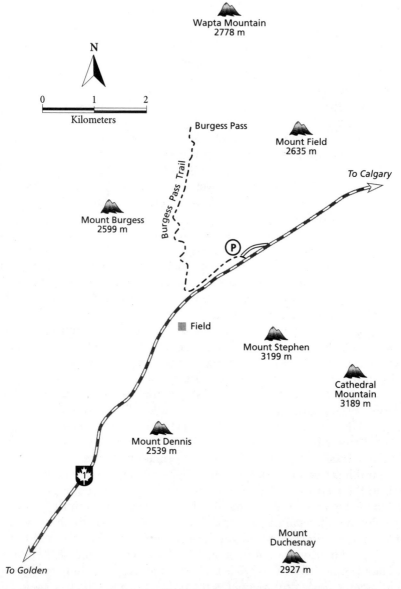

Wapta Mountain
2778 m

N

0 1 2
Kilometers

Burgess Pass

Mount Field
2635 m

To Calgary

Burgess Pass Trail

Mount Burgess
2599 m

P

Field

Mount Stephen
3199 m

Cathedral
Mountain
3189 m

Mount Dennis
2539 m

Mount
Duchesnay
2927 m

To Golden

rue, common blue violet, and Utah honeysuckle, as well as juniper, can be spotted all along the way. After a continuous climb, Mount Burgess (2,599 m) will come into view to your left (west). In early June we passed over a fresh avalanche chute at 2.7 kilometers.

Just beyond the 3-kilometer point, the trail really begins to open up as you enter into the first of several alpine meadows. You can see the Crags of Cathedral Mountain (3,073 m) and its peak (3,189 m) to the southeast, and behind Mount Dennis (southeast) you can now see Mount Duchesnay (2,927 m). At 4.2 kilometers you'll pass through an old rockfall and once again gain a great view of Mount Burgess looming over you. About 300 meters farther down the trail, you can look back for a panoramic view of Kicking Horse Valley. If you make this hike just as the snow is melting, you may even see glacier lilies and a little watermelon snow. Continue on the forested trail, and at 8.2 kilometers you'll stand on the top of Burgess Pass. The view to the south from here is awesome. If you continue on above the tree line (which we highly recommend), you'll see the Emerald Triangle Trail to the east as it skirts Wapta Mountain (2,778 m), as well as the tree-filled valley below with Micheal Peak (2,696 m) as its backdrop to the north.

27 Amiskwi Trail

Highlights: An unmaintained trail used primarily for mountain biking.
Type of hike: Out-and-back mountain-bike ride or a 4- to 6-day backpack. Hikers should note that there are no campgrounds on this trail; random camping is allowed, and there is a hut at 37.9 kilometers.
Total distance: 71 kilometers.
Difficulty: Moderate.
Hiking time: 4–6 days.
Elevation at trailhead: 1175 meters.
Elevation gain: 805 meters.
Topo maps: Lake Louise & Yoho (GemTrek Publishing); Golden, N/7; Blaeberry, 82 N/10.

Finding the trailhead: Take the turnoff for Emerald Lake, which is located on the north side of TransCanada Highway 1, approximately 2.5 kilometers west of the town of Field and 26.5 kilometers east of Yoho National Park's west gate. Follow the signs for the Natural Bridge and Emerald Lake. Travel 2.4 kilometers to the Natural Bridge turnoff, and follow the gravel road to the right (northwest) for 1.5 kilometers to reach the trailhead.

Key points:
- 0.0 Trailhead.
- 13.2 Cross Fire Creek.
- 15.8 Fork in the road; stay right (northeast).
- 17.5 Cross Otto Creek.
- 24.0 Cross the Amiskwi River (the bridge is out).
- 29.0 End of fire road.
- 31.0 Amiskwi Falls.
- 35.5 Amiskwi Pass.

The hike: Remote and long. This is how we would describe the trip to Amiskwi Pass. You'll follow an old fire road for approximately 30 kilometers before

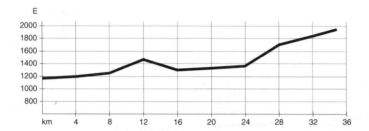

you see Amiskwi Falls and clamber up to the pass. We would recommend a pass on this trail, opting instead for the Ottertail Trail if you're looking for a good bike ride or the Emerald Triangle as a hike with jaw-dropping views. If you're in search of solitude, though, this may just be the trail for you.

Leaving the trailhead, you will begin a gradual ascent for the first 1.5 kilometers on a nice wide-open trail. You'll then head northwest, into the trees, where you'll stay for the next 7 kilometers. At approximately 7.6 kilometers you'll have to walk through a small creek; the time of year will determine just how much water you'll be walking through. At the end of June it was midcalf level. At 8.75 kilometers, approximately 50 meters of the trail is partially submerged by runoff. At this point the trail begins to open up a little, and you'll be able to see the Hamilton Ridge to your right (east). Continue on through several 0.6-meter creek crossings; there are too many to mention, but they're mainly just runoff and are pretty easy to get through.

When you've traveled approximately 10.6 kilometers you'll reach a really nice spot to stop for a break, as there's a pretty clear view of the Hamilton Ridge. Approximately 12.3 kilometers into the trail you'll notice that it gets quite wet again; there are a lot of trees and roots damming the flow of the runoff. At the 13-kilometer point you'll enter a large clearing in the Amiskwi Valley. You'll be able to see Burnt Hill and Sea Shoal Mountain off to your left (northwest). Travel another 200 meters and you'll cross Fire Creek— and this time there's a bridge. Just after the bridge, you may see a 1.8-meter-long sawblade on the side of the trail; this is a remnant of an old sawmill that was situated here during the 1950s. At 15.8 kilometers you'll reach an unmarked fork in the road; head right (northeast). At approximately 17.5 kilometers and 22.5 kilometers, respectively, you'll reach two creek crossings; again, depending on the time of year, the creeks can be pretty deep. From here you'll notice that the trail narrows, and soon you'll be level with the Amiskwi River. There are some really nice views of the ranges from the 24-kilometer point on; you may even spot a few eagles. However, the trail is covered in shrubs, so it can be a bit of a tough go from here.

To continue along this trail you'll have to cross the Amiskwi River. At the end of June, during heavy runoff, the river is approximately 10 meters wide; if you're planning on continuing to Amiskwi Pass, it may be best to try this trail later in the season. From here you can see Mount McArthur to the northeast, Amiskwi Peak to the northwest, and Horsey Peak to the east. Stay on this narrow trail for another 11 kilometers before reaching the Amiskwi hut.

Amiskwi Trail

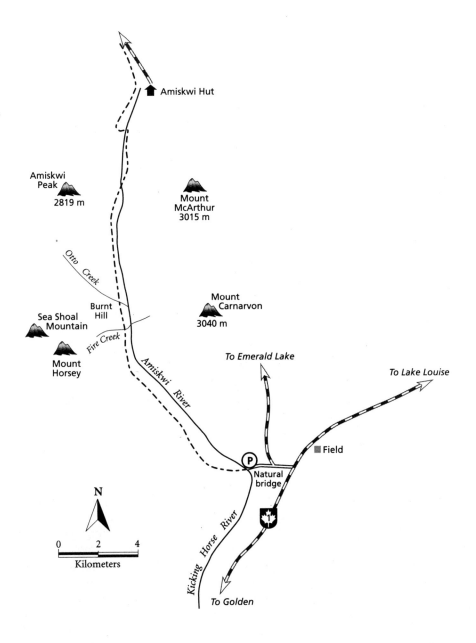

28 Kicking Horse Trail

Highlights:	An unmaintained trail that follows the Kicking Horse River to Chancellor Peak Campground.
Type of hike:	A shuttle mountain-bike ride or day hike. On your bike this trail could be completed in 1½–3 hours. If you're hiking, plan to spend at 4–5 hours.
Total distance:	15.4 kilometers.
Difficulty:	Easy.
Hiking time:	4–5 hours.
Elevation at trailhead:	1,175 meters.
Elevation gain:	Minimal.
Topo maps:	Lake Louise & Yoho (GemTrek Publishing); Golden, N/7.

Finding the trailhead: Take the turnoff for Emerald Lake, which is located on the north side of TransCanada Highway 1, approximately 2.5 kilometers west of the town of Field and 26.5 kilometers east of Yoho National Park's west gate. Follow the signs for the Natural Bridge and Emerald Lake. Travel 2.4 kilometers to the Natural Bridge turnoff, and follow the gravel road to the right for approximately 1.5 kilometers to reach the trailhead. The Kicking Horse Trail is not listed on the trailhead marker; it is the unnamed trail to the left.

Key points:
```
 0.0   Trailhead; follow the Kicking Horse Trail to the left (south).
 4.1   Trail junction; continue straight ahead (south).
 4.9   Bridge crossing the Otterhead River (trail not maintained past this point).
 6.7   Creek crossing.
 8.1   Creek crossing.
15.4   Chancellor Peak Campground.
```

The hike: This trail is more often cycled than hiked. While flat, it is extremely challenging and is not maintained past 4.9 kilometers (many adventurers end up abandoning the trail out of frustration and return to the trailhead). From this point on the trail is overgrown with shrubs; even on the warmest day, you should wear pants to protect your legs from a needless lashing. Sunglasses are also a must, as much of the overgrowth is eye-level. (I attempted to ride with my eyes closed, and I certainly would not recommend this to others.) Once you're prepared for some heavy bushwhacking—climbing over fallen trees and through the dense shrubbery—you can attempt this trail.

From the parking area, follow the unnamed trail to your left (south). This is the Kicking Horse Trail, an old fire road surrounded by trees and wildflowers that is wide open and well maintained. At 4.1 kilometers you'll reach the junction for the Otterhead Trail; continue straight ahead (south). At about 4.9 kilometers you'll cross the Kicking Horse River over a small footbridge; from this point on the trail is not maintained and becomes much more challenging because of the downed trees and dense undergrowth.

Kicking Horse Trail

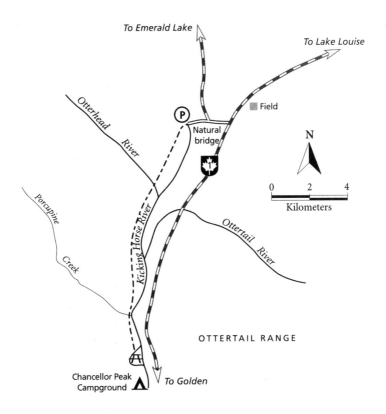

Off the trail, near the junction of the Otterhead and Kicking Horse Rivers, lie the historical remnants of Camp Otter, an internment camp from World War I. This camp, which closed in June 1916, housed men from eastern and central Europe. These men, who had emigrated to North America to work on the railways and development projects, had drifted into the cities in search of employment during the recession in 1912. Because of the war, these workers were considered "enemy aliens." To calm fears these men were removed from urban centers by the government, which had established detention camps across the country. While in the camps these men provided coveted labor to the expanding parks. Incidentally, the first of the four camps to be established was in Banff; the camp in Yoho was built only after a camp in the Mount Revelstoke area had to be relocated due to bad weather. Camp Otter, which was named after William Otter, director of Canadian Internment Camp Operations, was shut down after six months because the area it had been built on was too wet and was prone to flooding. If you're looking for more information on the internment camps, Bill Waiser has written an excellent book on this subject, called *Park Prisoners*.

The old camp, which is surrounded by bits of barbwire, has now become a wolf den. Parks Canada does not recommend travel to this area, as it considered environmentally sensitive. The camp is also incredibly difficult to find unless you're with someone who knows how to get there.

Follow the trail as it narrows, and reach a creek crossing at 6.7 kilometers. You'll meet yet another creek at 8.1 kilometers, and, depending on the time of year, crossing this second creek could be impossible (even in July, we could not cross this creek). From here continue south along this trail, climbing deadfall and gaining the occasional view of the Ottertail Range through the trees to the southeast. You'll spot a lot of Indian paintbrush and mauve fleabane along the way before you're forced to cross the raging Kicking Horse River if you wish to enter the north end of Chancellor Peak Campground at 15.4 kilometers.

29 Otterhead Trail
(marked TOCHER RIDGE on the park signage)

Highlights:	An unmaintained trail that follows the Otterhead River before heading northeast to the Tocher Ridge Lookout. Views from the lookout are fantastic.
Type of hike:	An out-and-back mountain bike ride or day hike.
Total distance:	33 kilometers.
Difficulty:	Moderate.
Hiking time:	10–12 hours.
Elevation at trailhead:	1,175 meters.
Elevation gain:	960 meters.
Recreational Topo maps:	Lake Louise & Yoho (GemTrek Publishing); Golden, N/7.

Finding the trailhead: Take the turnoff for Emerald Lake, which is located on the north side of Trans Canada Highway 1, approximately 2.5 kilometers west of the town of Field and 26.5 kilometers east of Yoho National Park's west gate. Follow the signs for the Natural Bridge and Emerald Lake. Travel 2.4 kilometers to the Natural Bridge turnoff, and follow the gravel road to the right for approximately 1.5 kilometers to reach the trailhead. Follow the unnamed trail to the left (south).

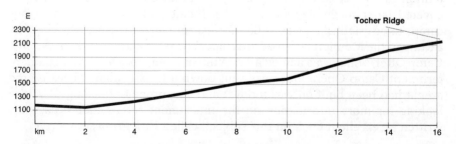

Otterhead Trail

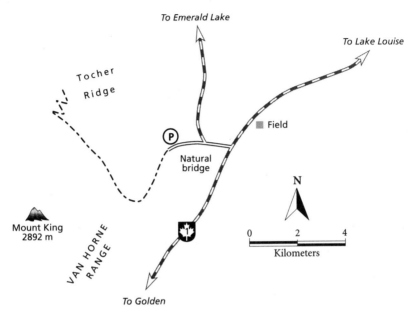

Key points:
- 0.0   Trailhead; follow the Kicking Horse Trail to the left (south).
- 4.1   Trail junction; turn right (northwest) for the Otterhead Trail, marked as Tocher Ridge.
- 11.0 Trail junction; turn right (north) to Tocher Ridge lookout.
- 16.5 Tocher Ridge Lookout.
- 22.0 Tocher Ridge junction.
- 33.0 Trail junction back to parking area.

The hike: While you can hike or bike this trail, it is most often traveled by cyclists who ride to the Tocher Ridge Lookout junction, where they hang their bikes from trees (hungry porcupines like to chew through the rubber tires), then ascend the final 5.5 kilometers to the lookout on foot.

From the parking area follow the unnamed trail to your left (south). This is the Kicking Horse Trail—an old fire road that is well maintained and wide open. At 4.1 kilometers you'll reach the junction for the Otterhead Trail (the sign says 6.4 KILOMETERS TO THE TOCHER RIDGE TRAIL, 11.8 KILOMETERS TO THE TOCHER RIDGE LOOKOUT). Follow this trail right (northwest) as you climb toward the ridge with the Otterhead River to your left (west). At 6.3 kilometers you'll notice that the trail is ascending more steeply.

At 11 kilometers you'll reach the junction for the lookout. Head right (north), following the steady switchbacks and crossing an unnamed creek several times on the 500-meter ascent. Continue on, and at approximately 16.5 kilometers you'll reach the old fire lookout. The view from here is spectacular. You'll see just about every mountain range in Yoho Park; the awesome Van Horne Range sits off to the southwest with the President Range to the northwest, and down the valley you just passed through sits the Ottertail Range.

30 Ottertail Trail

Highlights:	This easy backpacking trip skirts the Ottertail River, ending with prime views of Mount Goodsir, the Goodsir Glacier, and Sentry Peak.
Type of hike:	Backpack trip; out-and-back.
Total distance:	37.8 kilometers.
Difficulty:	Easy.
Hiking time:	2–3 days.
Elevation at trailhead:	1,200 meters.
Elevation gain:	275 meters.
Topo maps:	Lake Louise & Yoho (GemTrek Publishing); Lake Louise, 82 N/8.

Finding the trailhead: The Ottertail trailhead is located on the south side of TransCanada Highway 1, approximately 20 kilometers east of Yoho National Park's west gate and 9 kilometers west of the town of Field. Park in the small lot on the side of the highway.

Key points:
- 0.0 Trailhead.
- 0.5 Haygarth Creek crossing.
- 2.8 View of hoodoos.
- 4.0 Giddie Creek crossing.
- 6.2 Float Creek Campground.
- 7.8 Silverslope Creek crossing.

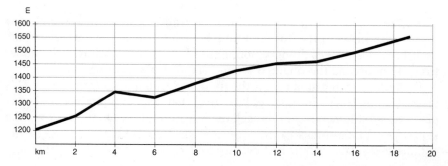

Ottertail Trail

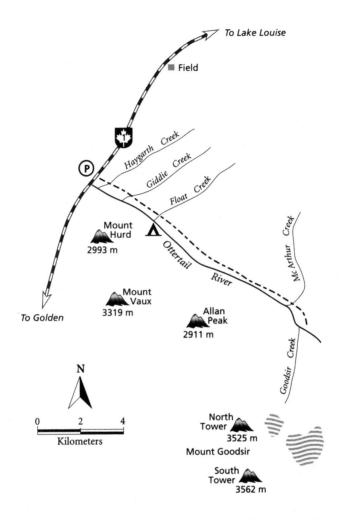

14.9   McArthur Creek Trail junction; continue straight ahead (south).
15.1   McArthur Creek crossing and campground.
15.9   Ottertail River crossing.
16.1   Trail junction; head left (northeast) to Ottertail Falls or right (southeast) to the Goodsir Pass Trail and the Rockwall.
18.9   Ottertail Falls.

The hike: If you want to get to the good views faster, consider mountain biking the Ottertail Trail. This fire road's gentle incline offers an easy, pleasant trip—whether you're riding or hoofing it. The trail skirts the Ottertrail River on your right (south) and crosses a number of small creeks as it winds gradually upward through a forest of lodgepole pine, trembling aspen, and spruce. Early in the season, the trail may be quite muddy; we noticed several mud slides midtrail when we hiked here in June. But because it's south facing, it's also one of the first longer trails in Yoho to become snow free.

Just 500 meters into the trail you'll cross Haygarth Creek. Although the trail initially offers only limited views, it opens up at 2.8 kilometers with views of hoodoo formations below to your right (south). You'll also enjoy brief but excellent views of Mount Hurd (2,993 m), Mount Vaux (3,319 m), and the Hanbury Glacier to your left (south).

At approximately 4 kilometers you'll cross Giddie Creek; 1.5 kilometers later you'll enjoy a gradual 0.7- kilometer descent to Float Creek Campground. Just 100 meters beyond the campground you'll find a quiet spot to stop for a snack alongside the Ottertail River.

From there the trail starts to climb again as it winds away from the river through a forest of Engelmann spruce and Douglas fir. At 7.8 kilometers you'll cross Silver Slope Creek, and at 14.9 kilometers, you'll reach the McArthur Creek Trail junction. Continue straight ahead (south) here. Just 200 meters later you'll reach McArthur Creek Campground, followed by a small clearing overlooking McArthur Creek, where the warden's cabin is located. From here you'll enjoy fantastic views straight ahead (southeast) of Mount Goodsir's North Tower (3,525 m) and South Tower (3,562 m), the Goodsir Glacier, and Sentry Peak (3,267 m).

At 15.9 kilometers you'll cross the Ottertail River, which marks the end of the portion of the trail open to mountain bikes. Just 200 meters later you'll reach a trail junction; head left (northeast) 2.8 kilometers (about thirty minutes) to reach Ottertail Falls—an excellent viewpoint en route to Goodsir Pass. From here you can either return the way you came or continue east on the Goodsir Pass/Rockwall Trail. (See Hike 40 for more details.)

31 Hoodoo Creek

Highlights:	This steep, uphill climb ends with fantastic views of hoodoo formations.
Type of hike:	Day hike; out-and-back.
Total distance:	5.2 kilometers.
Difficulty:	Moderate.
Hiking time:	1½–2½ hours.
Elevation at trailhead:	1,210 meters.
Elevation gain:	340 meters.
Topo maps:	McMurdo, 82 N/2.

Finding the trailhead: The Hoodoo Creek Trail is located in Hoodoo Creek Campground, on the south side of TransCanada Highway 1, approximately 6.5 kilometers east of Yoho National Park's west gate and 22.5 kilometers west of the town of Field. Turn southeast off the highway onto the paved campground road, and park in the gravel lot on your left (north) just before the campground kiosk.

Hoodoo Creek

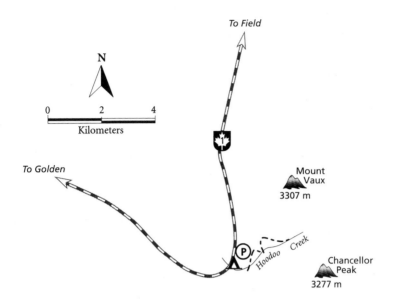

To reach the trailhead follow the paved campground road behind the campground kiosk 800 meters to your left (southwest) toward campsites D through F. Take a left (north) at the brown-and-yellow directional signage and walk 100 meters to the trailhead alongside Hoodoo Creek. A picnic area and outhouse are located closer to the highway on the north side of the campground road.

Key points:

- 0.0 Trailhead.
- 0.8 Trail junction; turn left (north).
- 0.9 Hoodoo Creek crossing.
- 2.3 Trail junction; head left (north) to upper viewpoint or right (south) to lower viewpoint.
- 2.6 Upper viewpoint.
- 2.9 Lower viewpoint.
- 5.2 Back at trailhead.

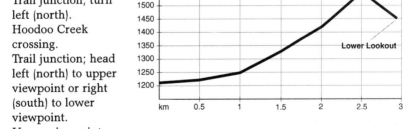

The hike: Pay attention to those warning signs at the trailhead. The Hoodoo Creek Trail involves one heck of a steep climb. After the 900-meter stroll through the campground, you'll cross Hoodoo Creek and start climbing immediately.

It's a steep climb to reach these nicely formed hoodoos, giant pillars of glacial debris.

As you're clambering up the steep switchbacks, keep an eye out for Hoodoo the bear, a black bear who's lived near the campground for the last nine years. You'll travel through a cool forest lined with Douglas fir, juniper, and lodgepole pine and occasionally catch glimpses of Chancellor Peak (3,280 meters) to your right (south) through openings in the trees.

At 2.3 kilometers you'll reach the junction for the upper and lower lookouts. Stay left (north) here toward the upper lookout for the best view. You'll catch your first glimpse of the hoodoos just 100 meters later. Hoodoos are simply giant pillars of sand, gravel, and other glacial debris. Because they're protected by large boulder "caps," which shelter them from rain and snow, they don't erode like the sand and gravel around them—over time molding these giant pillars.

The trail ends at 2.6 kilometers. If you're looking for a place to have lunch, head for the lower viewpoint alongside Hoodoo Creek. There are plenty of large logs and boulders here where you can relax.

32 Ice River Trail

Highlights: A relatively flat fire road that follows the east side of the Beaverfoot River before reaching the Lower Ice River warden cabin and then the Upper Ice River warden cabin. Mountain views are limited.

Type of hike: Backpack.
Total distance: 47.8 kilometers.
Difficulty: Easy.
Hiking time: Allow 3–4 days.
Elevation at trailhead: 1,210 meters.
Elevation gain: 360 meters.
Topo maps: McMurdo, 82 N/2; Mount Goodsir 82 N/1.

Finding the trailhead: The Ice River Trail is located in Hoodoo Creek Campground, on the south side of TransCanada Highway 1, approximately 6.5 kilometers east of Yoho National Park's west gate and 22.5 kilometers west of the town of Field. Turn southeast off the highway onto the paved campground road, and turn right just before the entrance (the sign says DEER LODGE). Follow the gravel road about 500 meters to the Hoodoos Trail parking area. The Ice River Fire Road begins at the locked access gate on the southwest corner of the parking lot. There is an outhouse beside the parking area.

Key points:
0.0 Trailhead.
0.9 Trail junction, left (east) to Ice River.
10.0 Tallon Creek and warden cabin.
17.5 Lower Ice River warden cabin; end of fire road.
17.6 Bridge crossing over Ice River.
17.7 Trail junction; stay left (north) for Ice River.
19.9 Clawson Creek.
23.9 Upper Ice River warden cabin.

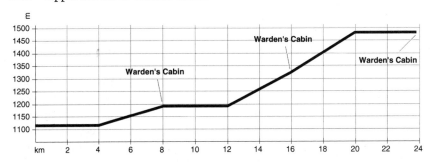

The hike: This low-elevation valley trail certainly does not attract the number of backcountry hikers found on any other trail in Yoho; in fact, you'd be lucky if you pass another human being the entire time you're on the trail. You may, however, encounter some other forms of wildlife. As I was sprinting down the trail with the bush crashing behind me, I did not stop to

Ice River Trail

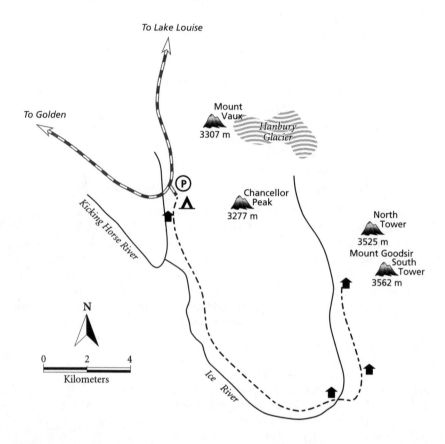

identify the stalking creature; I just scrambled on with the hope of never finding out what it was.

The trail climbs out of Hoodoo Campground on a gradual grade along a wide open, flat, well-graded fire road spotted with oxeye daisy. You'll meet up with the Beaverfoot River nearly 1.0 kilometer into the trail, where you'll also come across three abandoned buildings that once served as a warden station. From this point on the trail travels through a forest of Douglas fir and western red cedar; you'll gain the occasional view of the Beaverfoot Range to the south high above the trees. This trail, although completely wooded, is quite pleasant apart from the amount of scattered deadfall you'll have to climb over to continue on your merry way. It's much easier on foot than on a mountain bike, though; on a bike you'll have to dismount every few hundred meters.

Continue through the woods; you'll cross Tallon Creek at approximately 10 kilometers as you reach the first of three warden cabins on this trail. At 17.5 kilometers the fire road ends as you come across the Lower Ice River warden cabin. Some hikers reach this point after only a 2-kilometer journey; they drive down the Beaverfoot Road until they come across an old logging route, where they park their vehicles and take the shortcut in. You have to know where you're going to find this route, though; otherwise you could end up hiking over Wolverine Pass on the Rockwall in Kootenay National Park (which by all accounts wouldn't be that bad either).

At 17.6 kilometers you'll reach a trail junction where the Kootenay River Trail intersects the main trail from the right. Stay left to continue toward the Upper Ice River warden cabin, not before crossing Clawson Creek. From the top of the valley you'll spot Mount Goodsir's North (3,520 m) and South (3,581 m) Towers to the northeast as well as Mount Ennis, Hanbury Peak, and the Hanbury Glacier to the northwest. If you were to continue along the rough trail from here, you'd eventually reach Sodalite Creek (Sodalite is a gem mineral known to occur only at this site), the heart of the Ice River intrusion, which is famous among geologists because of the rare rock types found here. In fact, the ranges south and east of Goodsir—Zinc Mountain and Manganese Mountain—are made up of pluton, a mass of once-molten rock that crystalized deep underground. This is the only source of true pluton to be found in the Canadian Rockies.

33 Wapta Falls

Highlights:	A quick and easy hike offering views of spectacular Wapta Falls.
Type of hike:	Short hike; out-and-back.
Total distance:	4.2 kilometers; 7.4 kilometers if the road is closed.
Difficulty:	Easy.
Hiking time:	1 hour–2 hours.
Elevation at trailhead:	1,000 meters.
Elevation gain:	Minimal.
Topo maps:	Lake Louise & Yoho (GemTrek Publishing); Golden, 84/N7; Parson, 82 N/2.

Finding the trailhead: Wapta Falls is located on the south side of TransCanada Highway 1, approximately 4.5 kilometers from Yoho National Park's west gate. The trail is not marked if you're traveling west, and there is no left-turn lane. Your best bet when traveling west is to continue to the park's west gate and backtrack. There are picnic tables at the trailhead.

Key points:
    0.0   Trailhead.
    1.7   Upper viewpoint.
    1.77 Lower viewpoint.
    2.1   Base of Wapta Falls.

The hike: Wapta Falls is the largest waterfall in terms of volume of water in Yoho National Park. Even better than that, it's a quick and easy hike that

Wapta Falls

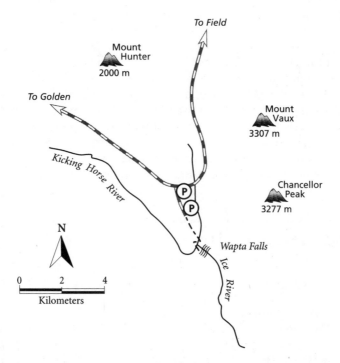

ends with the thundering falls, which you can view either from the upper lookout or, early in the season, from their base.

In May or June, before the road is open, the trailhead starts with a 1.6-kilometer hike on a gravel road alongside the Leanchoil Marsh. On a quiet day, with a bit of luck you may spot some whitetail deer bounding across the road. At the true trailhead, the road turns into a single-file path through the woods, which is lined with lodgepole pine, white spruce, and poplar. Straight ahead of you is Coral Mountain of the Beaverfoot Range. Occasionally you'll catch glimpses of Chancellor Peak (3,277 m) to the east, and don't forget to look behind you (north) for fantastic views of Mount Hunter. Initially, the trail is lined with wild strawberries and common blue violets.

Approximately 150 meters into the trail, you'll reach the trees as you enter the dense forest, where the nice flat trail becomes root filled. One kilometer into the hike you'll begin a gradual climb toward the falls; here you may see a few spring sunflowers.

At 1.7 kilometers you'll reach the upper viewpoint, with your first glimpse of the falls below. The falls were formed through the powerful action of the Kicking Horse River, which, over time, has carved a new channel through

It's a short hike to the upper viewpoint at the spectacular Wapta Falls.

the rock. You'll also notice a few resistant bands of rock, which formerly marked the edge of the falls but now are only downstream islands. Shortly after this viewpoint (1.77 kilometers) you'll reach the fork in the trail. Take a left and you'll reach the lower viewpoint and the best place to take photos. The right-hand trail leads to the same level as the river and offers a closer glimpse of the falls as well as the common Indian paintbrush.

In late May and even early June, you can catch an even closer view of the falls. Venture out onto the rocky area that marks the former path of the Kicking Horse and you'll actually feel their spray. But be careful; the rocks are wet and very slippery. Once the spring melt begins and the river swells to full capacity, this additional trek is not possible.

34 Mt. Hunter Lookout

Highlights:	A steep trail to Mt. Hunter's two fire lookouts.
Type of hike:	Day hike; out-and-back.
Total distance:	13.4 kilometers.
Difficulty:	Moderate.
Hiking time:	3½–5 hours.
Elevation at trailhead:	1,025 meters.
Elevation gain:	930 meters.
Topo maps:	Lake Louise & Yoho (GemTrek Publishing); McMurdo, 82 N/2; Golden, 82 N/7.

Finding the trailhead: Follow TransCanada Highway 1 approximately 24 kilometers west of Field to the Wapta Falls turnoff, and turn south. There is no sign for westbound travelers; it's best to keep driving for 4.5 kilometers to the park's west gate, where it is safe to turn around. Follow the highway east and turn south into Wapta Falls. Park in the small parking area adjacent to the highway. You'll have to carefully cross to the north side of the highway to reach the trailhead for Mt. Hunter.

Key points:
- 0.0 Trailhead.
- 3.8 Trail junction to lower lookout; turn left (west).
- 4.0 Lower lookout.
- 4.2 Trail junction to upper lookout; turn left (west).
- 6.7 Upper lookout.

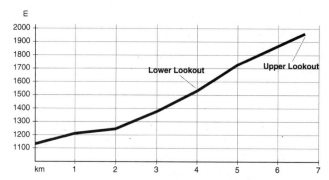

The hike: Mt. Hunter is one of the first high-elevation trails of the season to open in Yoho. While the lower lookout is often open toward the end of May, the upper lookout is usually not clear of snow until mid-June. Although this hike is quite steep in places, the effort spent is well worth it for the breathtaking 240-degree views the upper lookout affords. However, we would be remiss if we didn't advise you to be sure the sky is clear; otherwise, you may be disappointed by limited visibility.

From the highway, the trail heads east into a forest filled with white spruce and lodgepole pine. Even as early as June, you may spot rare yellow lady's slippers and shooting stars on the trail. At 0.25 kilometer you must carefully cross the Canadian Pacific Railway tracks. To regain the trail look to your left to spot the trail sign, about 7 meters to the west. From here you will ascend a root-filled trail into a thick forest of aspen and white birch. At about 1.6 kilometers the trail parallels the cliff edge, with natural lookouts along the way. From these you can gain spectacular views of the pale-brown-weathering dolomite and limestone of the Beaverfoot Range and the deep green Kicking Horse Valley below (southwest). The Beaverfoot Range forms the east wall of the Rocky Mountain Trench, which spans 50 kilometers west all the way to Golden.

At 2.4 kilometers you will also glimpse a view of the natural blowdown area (just off to the west). This is the result of an Arctic cold front colliding with a Pacific system that brought 110 kph winds to the flanks of Mt.

Mt. Hunter Lookout

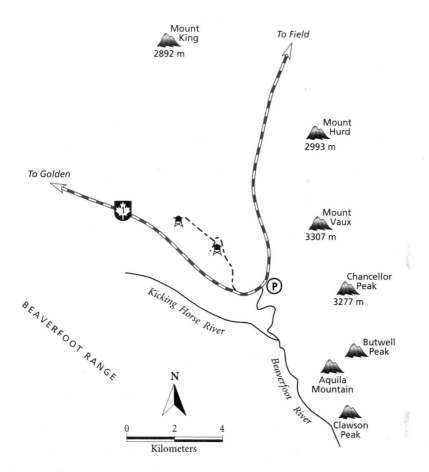

Hunter, flattening a 200-hectare area on both sides of the TransCanada Highway. From this natural viewpoint, the trail winds in and out of the forest and parallels the cliff edge. As you ascend out of the trees on the east side of the trail, you will gain views of both Mt. Vaux (3,307 m) and Chancellor Peak (3,277 m) (south).

At 3.8 kilometers you will reach the trail junction to the lower lookout to your left (west). If you decide to take the walk, you'll gain views of the Kicking Horse Valley and the Beaverfoot Range to the southwest. You will also come across a lookout tower that is unsafe to climb. There's also a day-use shelter here if you wish to take a break for lunch. The huge white-and-black panels just south of the lookout are part of a communications system for the park.

Back at the junction to the upper lookout, you will notice that the trail begins a more aggressive ascent. Heading up through the forest of Douglas

The upper lookout, which was removed in 1992, affords jaw-dropping views of the Beaverfoot Range and the Kicking Horse River below.

fir and lodgepole pine, we also came across bear digs more frequently; we stopped counting at thirty and continued onward, making enough noise to scare any of the grizzlies away. The unfortunate thing about making that much noise is that it also makes it pretty unlikely that you'll spot any of the other wildlife, such as deer or owls, known to frequent this trail. Onward and upward in and out of the trees, you hike in anticipation of the upper lookout. The views all along the way are so fantastic that it's hard to believe they can get better. At about 5.8 kilometers you will reach a series of switchbacks that lead to the lookout. You know you're there when you reach the second tower jack's cabin (1,955 m). In 1992 the tower at the upper lookout was removed.

From the upper lookout you have a great view of the Kicking Horse Valley and River below (southeast). At an altitude of 1,955 meters, you feel as though you're above the Beaverfoot Range. With at least a 240-degree view, you can see ranges outside Yoho's boundaries on the southeast end. Mt. Hurd, Mt. Vaux, and Chancellor Peak as well as the rest of the Ottertail Range, Buttwell Peak, Aquila Mountain, and Clawson Peak stand off to the south.

Kootenay National Park

Kootenay National Park is full of surprises. It's the only Canadian national park where you'll find glaciers and cactus in the same region. However, it's the hot springs just north of Radium that attract the most visitors—not the park's 200 kilometers of hiking trails.

Established in 1920, the park protects 1,406 kilometers of Rocky Mountain wilderness in the southeastern corner of British Columbia. Along with Yoho, Banff, and Jasper National Parks, as well as Mt. Robson, Mt. Assiniboine, and Hamber Provincial Parks, Kootenay forms one of the largest protected wilderness areas as part of UNESCO's Rocky Mountain Parks World Heritage Site.

Kootenay is centered around the headwaters of the Kootenay River. It is suspected that the Blackfoot Indians may have adopted the name "Kootenay," which means the "people of the water" in the Kootenay language. The "ay" spelling of Kootenay was fixed in 1864 by Frederick Seymour, first governor of British Columbia, to differentiate it from Kootenai, the form used in the United States.

The park lies 170 kilometers west of Calgary and 888 kilometers east of Vancouver. You can reach it from the north by traveling south on Highway 93 from Castle Junction (TransCanada Highway 1 and Highway 93). From the south you can reach the park by traveling north on Highway 93 from Highway 95 near Radium.

Traveling south on Highway 93 takes you through the park along the Vermilion and Kootenay Rivers and through the narrow gorge of Sinclair Canyon. Given a choice of entries into the park, this is by far the most spectacular. Many of the park's scenic attractions can be experienced along this route, including the Continental Divide and Fireweed Trail, which takes you through the site of a 1968 forest fire, the paint pots, Marble Canyon, and the Kootenay Valley Viewpoint.

Kootenay offers more of an off-the-beaten-track experience. Less-traveled than its neighbors, the park has a variety of landscapes from glacier-clad peaks in the north to dry, cactus-bearing slopes in the south. The important thing to remember about Kootenay is that, with the exception of the Stanley Glacier and Hawk Creek Trails, you'll have to hike nearly 10 kilometers to see the great mountain views. That's because the valley here is much wider than in the other parks.

Wildlife in the area includes elk, whitetailed deer, mule deer, mountain goats (at Mount Wardle), and bighorn sheep in the Radium Hot Springs area. Black bear, moose, coyotes, and wolves are less common visitors in Kootenay.

SEASONS AND WEATHER

North-south prevailing winds give this natural area a moderate climate and grasslands unlike most other high-mountain regions. Current weather reports

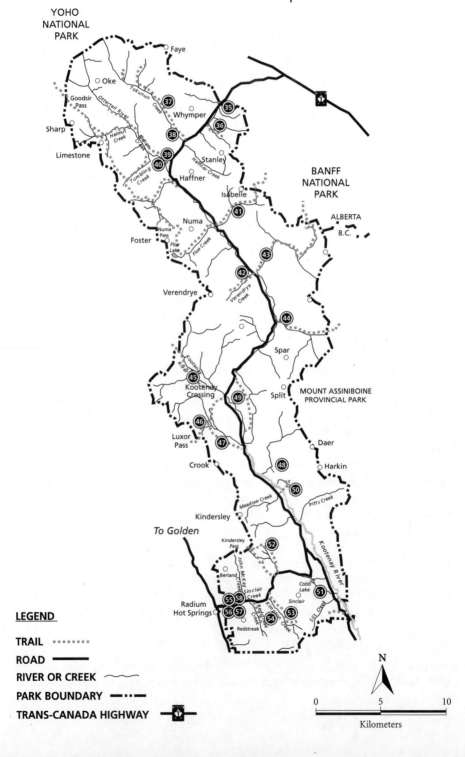

Kootenay National Park
Trail Locator Map

YOHO
NATIONAL
PARK

○ Faye

○ Oke

Goodsir
Pass

○ Sharp

Limestone

Helmut Creek

Ottertail River

Tokunun Creek

(37)

Whymper ○

(38)

(39)

(40)

Tumbling Creek

Stanley ○

Haffner Creek

Haffner ○

Isabelle ○

(35)

(36)

BANFF
NATIONAL
PARK

ALBERTA
B.C.

Numa ○

Foster ○

Numa
Pass

Floe
Lake

Floe Creek

(41)

(42)

(43)

Verendrye ○

Verendrye Creek

(44)

Spar ○

Kootenay River

(45)

Kootenay
Crossing

(49)

Split ○

MOUNT ASSINIBOINE
PROVINCIAL PARK

(46)

Luxor
Pass

(47)

Daer ○

Crook ○

(48)

Harkin ○

(50)

Meadow Creek

Pitts Creek

Kootenay River

Sill Creek

Kindersley ○

To Golden

Kindersley
Pass

(52)

Berland ○

John McKay Creek

Sinclair
Creek

(55) (58)

(56) (57)

Radium
Hot Springs ○

Redstreak ○

(54)

Redstreak Creek

Cobb
Lake

(51)

Sinclair ○

Kimpton Creek

(53)

LEGEND

TRAIL ·······

ROAD ━━━

RIVER OR CREEK ∿

PARK BOUNDARY ━·━·

TRANS-CANADA HIGHWAY

N

0   5   10
Kilometers

are available at the information center in Radium and on-line (see Appendix A). You may also want to pick up a copy of Falcon's *Reading Weather* at your local bookstore.

BASIC SERVICES

Limited services are available in Radium Hot Springs, just outside the park's west gate. Banff, 33 kilometers northeast of the park's east entrance, and Invermere, approximately 11 kilometers south of the park's west gate, offer full services, including large grocery stores, camping/hiking equipment, and a variety of restaurants and accommodations.

Kootenay is open year-round, but the two information centers are seasonal. The Kootenay National Park Information Centres are located on Highway 95 in Radium (open May 29 to September 19) and at the Vermilion Crossing Visitor Centre (open April 2 to September 26), which is in the north end of the park on Highway 93, 63 kilometers north of the Radium Hot Springs townsite, or 31.2 kilometers south of the Banff/Kootenay boundary.

FRONTCOUNTRY CAMPGROUNDS

There are four highway-accessible campgrounds in Kootenay National Park—Redstreak, McLeod Meadows, Marble Canyon, and Crook's Meadow Campground. All sites, with the exception of Crook's, operate on a first-come, first-served basis. Fees range from CDN $13 to $22 per night.

- **Redstreak,** located 2.5 kilometers from the village of Radium Hot Springs, is a fully serviced site with showers, electricity, water, and sewer hookups. It has 242 sites; 50 fully serviced and 38 with electricity only.

- **McLeod,** located 27 kilometers from the west gate entrance, is an unserviced campsite with 98 sites. It does have kitchen shelters, piped water, firewood, and interpretive activities.

- **Marble Canyon,** located 86 kilometers north of the west gate entrance or 7.0 kilometers southwest of the Banff–Kootenay boundary, is also an unserviced campground with 61 sites. It does have kitchen shelters, piped water, and interpretive activities.

- **Crook's Meadow Group Campground,** which is set aside for nonprofit groups, is located 34 kilometers north of the west gate entrance. For reservations call (250) 347–9615 or e-mail: kootenay_reception@pch.gc.ca.

BACKCOUNTRY CAMPGROUNDS

Many of Kootenay's trails offer overnight backcountry opportunities.

- Kaufmann Lake (6 sites)

- Tokumm Creek (6 sites)

- Helmet/Ochre Junction (6 sites)

- Hemet Falls (18 sites)

- Tumbling/Ochre Junction (6 sites)

- Tumbling Creek (18 sites)

- Numa Creek (18 sites)

- Floe Lake (18 sites)

- Verdant Creek (6 sites)

A Wilderness Pass is required for all backcountry campsites. To limit the environmental impacts of these experiences, there is a quota on the number of sites available per campground. Seventy-five percent of the campsites can be reserved up to three months in advance. Passes for the remaining 25 percent are issued at information centers within twenty-four hours of your trip. You can buy a pass for CDN $6.00 per person per night (or an annual pass for CDN $42.00) at the Kootenay National Park Information Centre in Radium Village from June to September. Call the Lake Louise Visitor Centre at (403) 522–3833 when the Kootenay Information Centre is closed.

35 Fireweed Trail

Highlights:	On this short interpretive hike, you can learn about the natural evolution that takes place after a forest fire.
Type of hike:	Short loop.
Total distance:	0.8 kilometers.
Difficulty:	Easy.
Hiking time:	20–30 minutes.
Elevation at trailhead:	1,650 meters.
Elevation gain:	Minimal.
Topo maps:	Kootenay National Park (GemTrek Publishing); Mount Goodsir, 82 N/1.

Finding the trailhead: The turnoff for the Fireweed Trail is located on the east side of Highway 93, approximately 700 meters north of Kootenay National Park's east gate. There are washrooms in the parking area.

Key points:
- 0.0   Trailhead.
- 0.8   End of trail.

The hike: This short, easy, interpretive hike is perfect for stretching those driving legs; it's good for all fitness levels. Beware, though, staying so close to the highway has its drawbacks; traffic noise is apparent regardless of where you are on this trail.

Lodgepole pine charred in the 1968 Vermilion burn still stand today.

Fireweed Trail

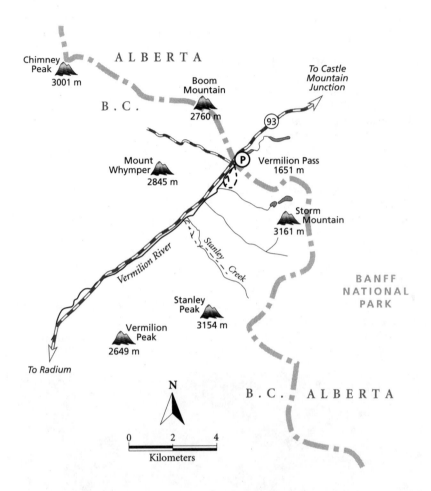

The trail consists of two loops: an upper walk through the charred lodgepole pine forest and a lower interpretive trail. Both can be completed in under thirty minutes, but it's best to begin with the lower loop at the southeast end of the parking area.

This trail is set on the Continental Divide; water flows to the Atlantic Ocean to the east and the Pacific Ocean to the west. The divider between Banff National Park and Kootenay National Park was drawn here in 1913.

As you begin the lower loop, you will immediately meet several interpretive signs that explain the ecological impacts of the eight-day Vermilion Pass burn in July 1968. Directly ahead of you (southwest) lie the headwaters of the Vermilion River. The small glacier that feeds it once fed the entire valley. In the 10,000 years since the glacier's retreat, these forests have evolved through recurring fires. At one time the national parks fought forest fires, creating a lot of deadfall and limiting new growth. Today one of the national parks' goals is to preserve natural forests; for that reason, a fire in the park is left to burn unless it is threatening people or buildings.

Let a forest fire burn its natural course? It seems sort of strange until you come to accept that a forest fire, like forest maturity, has its place in the age-old ecological cycle, enabling the growth of new plant species and improving the habitat for small mammals like pine martens and weasels. On this trail you see the forest succession up close—the mass of fireweed, the Englemann spruce, and the aspen, which will one day stand as tall as the charred lodgepole pine.

From the lower loop you will see Boom Mountain (2,760 m), Mount Whymper (2,845 m), and Chimney Peak (3,001 m) across the highway to the northwest.

The trail on the upper loop is more narrow and rocky; there are two benches approximately 200 meters apart if you care to stop and enjoy the scenery. If it's a clear day you'll have an impressive view of Castle Mountain to the north as it guards Banff National Park.

36 Stanley Glacier

Highlights:	A moderate climb to the hanging valley of Stanley Glacier.
Type of hike:	Day hike; out-and-back.
Total distance:	9.6 kilometers.
Difficulty:	Easy.
Hiking time:	3–4 hours.
Elevation at trailhead:	1585 meters.
Elevation gain:	365 meters.
Topo maps:	Kootenay National Park (GemTrek Publishing); Mount Goodsir 82 N/1.

Finding the trailhead: Follow Highway 93 approximately 86.8 kilometers northeast from the Kootenay National Park's west gate and approximately 3 kilometers southwest of the park's east boundary. Turn east into the Stanley Glacier parking area. The trail is well marked and begins just to the left of the outhouse.

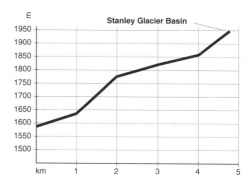

Stanley Glacier Basin

Stanley Glacier

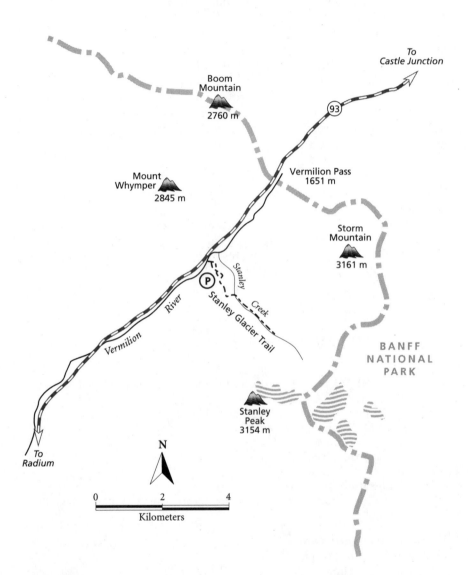

Key points:
- 0.0   Trailhead.
- 2.2   Enter the hanging valley.
- 2.4   Cross over Stanley Creek on a small wooden footbridge.
- 4.8   Stanley Glacier Basin.

The hike: This trail differs in two ways from many of the other short hikes open in June in Kootenay National Park. Unlike other low-elevation trails, Stanley Glacier provides breathtaking views of Stanley Peak (3,154 m) to the

These caves are just a short scramble away from the basin of Stanley Glacier.

south, its glacier, Storm Mountain (3,161 m) to the northeast, Mount Whymper (2,845 m), and Boom Mountain (2,760 m) to the northwest. Most important, it is heavily hiked. If you're looking for the sanctity afforded by many of the other trails in Kootenay, begin your hike at 9:00 A.M., if not before. By noon this trail is packed with eager visitors—and for good reason.

This particular valley was shaped by fire—the 1968 Vermilion Pass burn, which charred 2,500 hectares of forest—and ice, the Stanley Glacier. As you begin this trek you will cross the Vermilion River into a forest of predominantly lodgepole pine, a lot of which, as you'll notice, remains charred. The many young fir and spruce trees here, will eventually grow to the heights of the blackened pines. Follow the switchbacks; at 0.5 kilometer you will gain a nice view of Stanley Creek as it rolls down the eastern flank of Stanley Peak. From here you will also see Banff's Castle Mountain off to your left (north), with Mount Whymper and Boom Mountain directly behind you (northwest). At 0.9 kilometer you gain a great view of Storm Mountain off to your left (east).

Continue upward; at 2.2 kilometers the trail will flatten out as you enter the hanging valley. Once there the trail remains fairly level across Stanley Creek, where it parallels the sheer 450-meter Cambrian limestone walls of Stanley Peak to the right (south). In spring, when we hiked this trail, waterfalls were cascading over the edge of the face; you'll notice this if you visit the caves just past the boulder field, as you'll likely be soaked by their spray. The avalanche path on the east side of the valley provides good habitat for moose, and in the summer months, you can spot black bears eating berries. At 2.4 kilometers you will cross Stanley Creek on a small wooden footbridge; you may spot northern anemones alongside the trail as well as several types of moss, including Thuidium, which is bright green and branched like small feathers, and golden-brown Drepanocladus. At 2.7 kilometers you gain a nice view of the bowl through the sparse, charred lodgepole pine. Continue; at the 3.7- kilometer point you will begin to climb some rocky steps as you leave the trees to climb the open-valley slopes of this spectacular amphitheater filled with avalanche chutes.

When the trail reaches a field of large boulders, the path splits and you can head out on either side of the valley. This is a perfect spot to enjoy lunch, as you will often see golden-mantled ground squirrels, marmots, and pikas; if you don't see them, you will at least hear their chirping. If you take the path to your right (southeast), you can scramble approximately 200 meters to reach two caves that were hollowed out when the glacier once filled the basin; they are home to brown bats. You can then follow the scree slope around to the plateau, where you can view the toe of the Stanley Glacier. Taking the left trail (northeast) through the valley, you can also climb the last 900 meters to this plateau. If you're really eager, you can scramble the remaining 300 meters to the glacier.

37 Kaufmann Lake

Highlights:	This easy backpacking trail leads you through Prospector's Valley, offering excellent views of area mountain peaks, before ending at Kaufmann Lake.
Type of hike:	Backpack; out-and-back.
Total distance:	32 kilometers.
Difficulty:	Easy (except short, strenuous climbs to Fay Hut and Kaufmann Lake).
Hiking time:	2 days.
Elevation at trailhead:	1,480 meters.
Elevation gain:	580 meters.
Topo maps:	Kootenay National Park (GemTrek Publishing); Lake Louise, 82 N/8.

Finding the trailhead: The turnoff for Kaufmann Lake is located on the west side of Highway 93, approximately 84 kilometers north of Kootenay National Park's west gate and 17 kilometers south of Castle Junction (High-

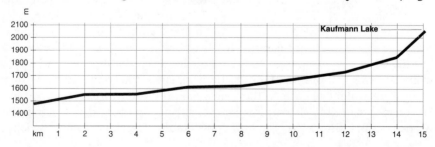

Kaufmann Lake

way 93 and TransCanada Highway 1). Follow the signs for Marble Canyon, and park in the Marble Canyon parking lot. The trailhead is located near the northwest corner of the parking lot. Just north of the trailhead you'll find washrooms and a small picnic area.

Key points:
- 0.0   Trailhead; head right (northwest).
- 0.7   Trail junction; continue straight ahead (northwest).
- 3.3   Stream crossing and scenic viewpoint.
- 10.4   Fay Hut Trail junction; turn right (north) to Fay Hut or continue straight ahead (northwest) toward Kaufmann Lake.
- 11.3   Tokumm Creek Campground.
- 12.8   Fay Hut.
- 13.6   Kaufmann Lake Trail junction; turn right (northeast).
- 15.1   Kaufmann Lake.

The hike: The first time we hiked this trail, we turned around after just 5 kilometers because of an aggressive grizzly bear. An early-July snowstorm surprised us on our second trip. Even so, we still recommend this easy backpacking hike, which leads you through Prospector's Valley, offering excellent views of nearby mountain peaks on the way to Kaufmann Lake.

Head right (northwest) at the trailhead in the northwest corner of the parking lot. If you'd prefer, take a 700-meter detour through the highly traveled but interesting Marble Canyon interpretive trail to your left (southwest).

The early part of the trail, an old fire road, parallels the Marble Canyon interpretive trail and leads you through a forest of Englemann spruce, lodgepole pine, and Douglas fir. Calypso orchids, wild strawberries, early blue violets, alpine forget-me-nots, and pink mountain heather also add a splash of color to the trail.

Just 700 meters into the hike you'll reach a trail junction; continue straight ahead (northwest). At 800 meters the trail opens up for excellent views of Mount Oke (2920 m) to your left (west) and Mount Whymper (2,845 m) to your right (east). You'll also hear Tokumm Creek rushing through Marble Canyon (to your east).

From 1.7 to nearly 3 kilometers you'll cross eleven small streams as the trail narrows to a single-file, mossy path. Toward the end of this section you'll leave the forest and enter Prospector's Valley, with Tokumm Creek bubbling beneath you to your left (west).

At 3.3 kilometers take a good look around as you're crossing another small creek. You'll enjoy views of Mount Oke to your left (northwest), Chimney Peak (3001 m) to your right (northeast), and Vermilion Peak (2,649 m) and Stanley Peak (3,154 m) behind you (southeast). Just 100 meters later the trail skirts Tokkum Creek to your left (west).

At 4.3 kilometers you'll reach a natural viewpoint to your left (west) offering prime views of Mount Oke to your left (west), Tokumm Creek to your left (west), and Mount Allen (3,310 m) straight ahead (northeast). Early in the season, sunny globeflowers, harebells, red clover, western meadow rue, and yellow glacier lilies line this section of trail.

From 5 to 6.9 kilometers you'll cross eight streams—all of which eventually feed Tokumm Creek. Take your time crossing the last bridge, where you'll enjoy a great view of the mountains on all sides of the valley, including Vermilion Peak and Stanley Peak behind you (southeast), Chimney Peak to your right (northeast), and Mount Oke to your left (northwest). You'll cross two more small streams at 8.4 and 9.8 kilometers, respectively.

You'll reach a trail junction at 10.4 kilometers, and the direction you head from here will depend primarily on where you're spending the night. If you're headed to Fay Hut, take a right (north) at the junction for a challenging 2.4-kilometer climb to the hut, including a precipitous 25-meter section with built-in ropes on your final ascent. If you're camping, continue straight ahead (northwest) toward Kaufmann Lake. You'll pass Tokumm Creek Campground at 11.3 kilometers and reach the Kaufmann Lake Trail junction at 13.6 kilometers. Turn right (northeast) at the trail junction for a steep 1.5-kilometer climb to the lake and Kaufmann Lake Campground.

The Fourth of July at Fay Hut brings a snowstorm.

Framed by several of the Wenkchemna peaks—the same peaks you see from Moraine Lake—including Mount Allen (3,310 m), Mount Tuzo (3,245 m), and Deltaform Mountain (3,424 m). Kaufmann Lake offers a quiet, picturesque backcountry experience.

38 Marble Canyon

Highlights:	This self-guided, easy walk explains the geology of Marble Canyon and Prospectors Valley.
Type of hike:	Short walk; out-and-back.
Total distance:	1.4 kilometers.
Difficulty:	Easy.
Hiking time:	30 minutes–1 hour.
Elevation at trailhead:	1,450 meters.
Elevation gain:	Minimal.
Topo maps:	Kootenay National Park (GemTrek Publishing); Mount Goodsir, 82 N/1.

Finding the trailhead: Marble Canyon is located on the west side of Highway 93, approximately 84 kilometers north of Kootenay National Park's west gate and 17 kilometers south of Castle Junction (Highway 93 and Trans-Canada Highway 1). The trailhead is located near the northwest corner of the Marble Canyon parking lot. Just north of the trailhead you'll find a small picnic area and washrooms.

Marble Canyon

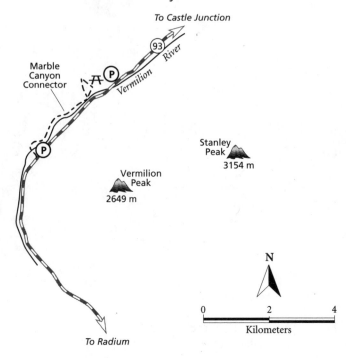

Key points:
   0.0 Trailhead.
   0.2 Tokumm Creek crossing.
   0.3 Natural arch.
   0.7 Tokumm Creek Falls.

The hike: Ideal for families and seniors, this easy stroll tells the geological story of Marble Canyon and Prospectors Valley. A series of interpretive signs highlights topics including how glaciers carved Marble Canyon, how mountains are formed, and the process of erosion. Strategically placed benches provide spots to rest and enjoy the view. At 200 meters you'll cross Tokumm Creek for the first time; several other bridges follow as you continue through the canyon. Don't miss the natural arch to your right (east) at 300 meters and the falls Tokumm Creek creates as it forces its way through the canyon at 700 meters.

Options:

Marble Canyon/Paint Pots Connector (3 kilometer shuttle; one-way).
This short downhill walk along the Vermilion River offers more solitude than the Marble Canyon and Paint Pots Trails, which can often be overflowing with tourists. However, you'll hardly find yourself "out in the wilderness." The Banff–Windermere Highway can be heard throughout your short journey through the woods.

Follow the Marble Canyon trail; after crossing the first bridge, head right (south) down the connector trail.

The Vermilion Range sits—which is quite impressive—sits off to the south and the glass-blue Vermilion River rushes past you for most of the trail. If you're interested in alpine flowers there are a few nice ones to be spotted; Indian paintbrush, calypso orchids, and common blue violets in particular are prevalent. At 2.1 kilometers you'll reach a trail junction, follow the path straight ahead to reach the Paint Pots Trail. At 2.7 kilometers you'll reach another trail junction; immediately cross the suspension bridge over the Vermilion River. Stay left and head 300 meters west toward the parking lot. Hike the remaining 500 meters to the Paint Pots (see Hike 39 for a full description), or head back along the connector to the Marble Canyon parking lot.

39 Paint Pots

Highlights: This self-guided walk explores the history behind the area's ochre mineral beds.
Type of hike: Shorttwalk; out-and-back.
Total distance: 2 kilometers.
Difficulty: Easy.
Hiking time: 30 minutes–1 hour.
Elevation at trailhead: 1,325 meters.
Elevation gain: Minimal.
Topo maps: Kootenay National Park (GemTrek Publishing); Mount Goodsir, 82 N/1.

Finding the trailhead: The Paint Pots Trail is located on the west side of Highway 93, approximately 19 kilometers south of Castle Junction (Highway 93 and TransCanada Highway 1) and 82 kilometers north of Kootenay National Park's west gate. You'll find the trailhead on the north side of the large parking lot. Picnic tables and an outhouse are located nearby.

Key points:
0.0 Trailhead.
0.2 Trail junction; continue straight ahead (west).
0.3 Vermilion River crossing.
0.6 Trail junction; turn left (west).
1.0 Trail ends at Paint Pots.

Paint Pots

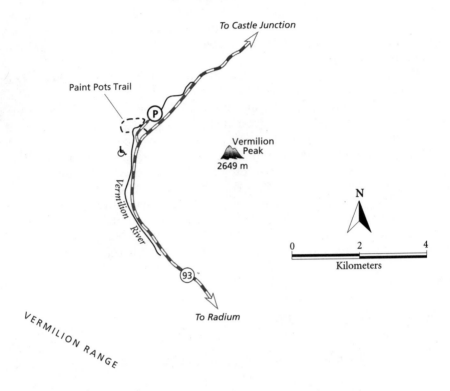

The hike: If you're interested in the history of ochre in the area, this hike's for you. This popular interpretive trail explores how Indians and early settlers mined and used the burnt-orange-colored substance that one hiker described as "big orange mud puddles."

From the trailhead you'll enter a forest of Douglas fir and lodgepole pine, along with arrowhead balsam root and dogwood. At 200 meters you'll reach a trail junction; branch left (south) for the wheelchair-accessible trail or continue straight ahead (west). Just 100 meters later you'll cross a bridge over the Vermilion River. Look to your left (west) from the bridge for great views of the Vermilion Range. At 600 meters you'll reach another trail junction; turn left (west) to continue along the trail past the ochre beds to the three paint pots at the end of the trail.

40 The Rockwall

Highlights:	This premier hike passes one of the highest waterfalls in the country before you reach a 30-kilometer trail that traverses beneath the Rockwall's extraordinary 53-kilometer-long limestone cliffs and hanging glaciers. You'll climb three alpine passes and through wildflower meadows to reach the breathtaking Floe Lake before you complete this 4- to 5-day journey.
Type of hike:	Backpack hike; shuttle.
Total distance:	53.8 kilometers.
Difficulty:	Moderate.
Hiking time:	Allow 4–6 days.
Elevation at trailhead:	1,450 meters.
Elevation gain:	See elevation chart.
Topo maps:	Kootenay National Park (GemTrek Publishing); Mount Goodsir, 82 N/1.

Finding the trailhead: Most hikers start the Rockwall Trail at either the Paint Pots or the Floe Lake trailhead. The Paint Pots trailhead (where we started) is located on the west side of Highway 93 approximately 82 kilometers north of Kootenay National Park's west gate and 19 kilometers south of Castle Junction (Highway 93 and TransCanada Highway 1). The Floe Lake trailhead, also located on the west side of Highway 93, is approximately 70 kilometers north of the park's west gate and 32 kilometers south of Castle Junction.

Either way you'll need to arrange for transportation back to the trailhead where you parked your car to avoid a 12-kilometer trudge along the highway at the end of your hike (that's if you decide to complete the entire Rockwall—as opposed to just hiking into Helmet or Tumbling Creek Campgrounds).

To start at the Paint Pots trailhead, park in the large lot on the west side of Highway 93, and follow signs for the Ochre Creek Trail. An outhouse and picnic tables are available in the parking lot. To begin at the Floe Lake trailhead, park in the lot on the west side of Highway 93, and follow the signs for Floe Lake. There's an outhouse in the parking area.

Key points:
- 0.0   Trailhead.
- 1.3   Trail junction; stay right (northwest).
- 3.4   Trail junction; stay right (northwest).
- 4.1   Stream crossing.
- 6.1   Helmet Ochre Campground/trail junction.
- 14.2   Helmet Falls Campground.
- 14.6   Trail junction; turn left (south).
- 17.8   Summit.
- 19.2   Unnamed lake.
- 22.7   Trail junction; continue straight ahead (northeast).
- 26.5   Tumbling Creek Campground/trail junction; turn right (south).

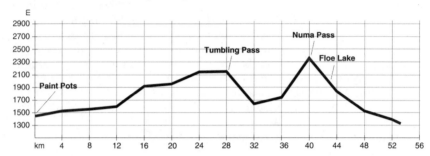

The hike: Get ready for the most stunning scenery in Kootenay National Park. You'll hike through the trees a bit to reach the alpine meadows, crystal-clear glacial lakes, and towering limestone cliffs that everyone raves about, but you won't be disappointed. Be prepared for crowds though; this is one of the most popular backcountry hikes in the area—especially during late July and August.

While many hikers spend their first night at Floe Lake (715-meter elevation gain), we recommend starting at the Paint Pots, because you'll follow a relatively flat trail to reach your first night's destination at Helmet Falls (310-meter elevation gain). Although it's farther than Floe Lake, it's a much easier hike, and it's best to save the finest swimming hole in the Canadian Rockies for your final night on this coveted trail. Plus it's only a 10.7-kilometer hike out from there, so you can spend the morning enjoying Floe Lake before you leave. (We'd be remiss if we didn't mention that the water can be just a little chilly.)

The trail begins with the 1.0-kilometer Paint Pots interpretive hike (see Hike 39). Near the ochre pools at the end of the hike, you'll notice a small wooden sign pointing to the Ochre Creek Trail to your left (northwest). Follow that trail into a forest lined with Douglas fir, Englemann spruce, and dwarf dogwood. If you're lucky you also may spot a few pine martens along this section of trail.

At 1.3 kilometers you'll reach a trail junction; stay to your right (northwest) and continue along the Ochre Creek and Helmet Creek Trails. Just past this point, to your left (southwest) you'll catch a glimpse of the Vermilion Range. You're in for a real treat as you continue along the trail through some absolutely enormous lodgepole pine and meadows virtually overflowing with brightly colored wildflowers. We spotted fringed Grass of Parnassus, Indian paintbrush, wild white roses, cow parsnip, wild strawberries, and broad-leaved willowherb.

At 1.7 and 2.1 kilometers, you'll cross two small streams. You'll then pass through several meadows, which the powerful forces of avalanches have com-

The Rockwall

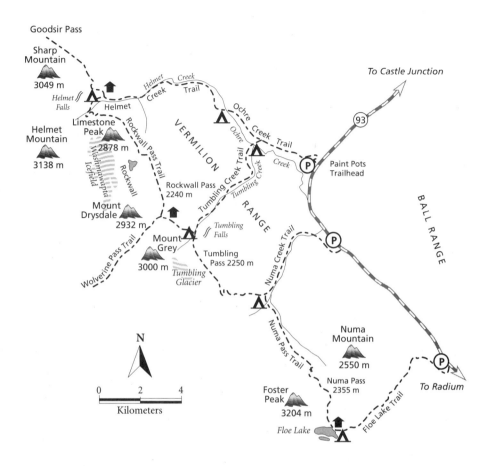

pletely cleared of trees, before arriving at the trail junction at 3.4 kilometers. Stay right (northwest) here to continue along the Ochre Creek/Helmet Creek Trail. At 4.1 kilometers, you'll cross another small stream.

At approximately 6 kilometers you'll arrive at the Ochre Creek and Helmet Creek junction, which you'll cross over a wooden bridge. Located on the other side of the bridge is Helmet Ochre Campground—an ideal spot to stop for lunch or a snack. Continue northwest 100 meters through the campground to arrive at the trail junction. Stay left (northwest) here, and follow signs for the Helmet Creek Trail.

From the trail junction to Helmet Falls Campground, you'll start to gain elevation. At 7 kilometers you'll cross Helmet Creek before heading back into the trees. Don't miss the small falls created as water flows into the creek to your left (west). Just before 14 kilometers you'll reach the Helmet Creek warden's cabin to your right (north). Look right (north) from here for a fantastic view of the thundering Helmet Falls. Less than 100 meters later you'll cross Helmet Creek to arrive at Helmet Falls Campground, which is nestled below Limestone Peak (2,878 m).

Continue straight (southeast) through the campground. At 14.6 kilometers you'll reach a trail junction; head left (south) toward Tumbling Creek. Just a few meters later you'll cross Tumbling Creek twice. You'll enjoy a fabulous view straight ahead (southeast) of Limestone Peak from here before heading back into the woods to begin your ascent over a pass leading to your first view of the Rockwall—a seldom-broken 53-kilometer cliff of Ottertail limestone.

At 15.7 kilometers, with Helmet Falls still thundering in the background, you'll start approaching the Rockwall to your right (west) and head parallel to it (southeast) into the forest. At 16.9 kilometers you'll cross a small stream. One kilometer later you'll enter a forest of graceful kelly-green larch.

You'll emerge from the forest for a fantastic view of the Rockwall to your right (south) along with the West Washmawapta Glacier at 18.2 kilometers. From here you'll weave in and out of trees and meadows sprinkled with heather, globeflowers, arnica, Indian paintbrush, and yellow columbine.

At 18.8 kilometers you'll start climbing through a rocky moraine. Just 400 meters later you'll reach a small unnamed lake to your right (west)—an ideal spot to stop for lunch. From here you'll walk through alpine tundra to the left (east) of the Rockwall. You'll feel just how exposed you really are in this area as the wind keeps trying to pry your hat off your head. The mammoth Rockwall towering above you to your right (west), along with Mount Drysdale (2,932 m), Wolverine Pass (2,210 m), and Mount Gray (3,000 m) almost seem too good to be true.

At 20.6 kilometers you'll cross a small creek. A spruce grouse and its chicks waddled along just ahead of us on this section of trail. At 22.7 kilometers you'll reach a trail junction; continue straight ahead (southeast) toward Tumbling Creek, or, for a quick diversion, drop your pack and head right (southwest) to Wolverine Pass (2,210 m) where you'll enjoy a fantastic view of a sea of mountain peaks.

Starting at 23.2 kilometers you'll enjoy a great view of the Tumbling Glacier ahead on your right (southwest). Just 3 kilometers later, before starting your descent toward Tumbling Creek Campground, you'll cross three streams and skirt both Tumbling Creek and Tumbling Falls to your right (southeast) before reaching the trail junction at 26.5 kilometers—and Tumbling Creek Campground.

From the campground you'll have to climb 270 meters to reach Tumbling Pass—and it's worth every step. Through the trees to your right (southwest), the view of Tumbling Glacier hanging on the side of Mount Gray (3,000 m) is awesome. If you time it right, you can easily sit on the pass for an hour or so to enjoy the view before heading down through a beautiful green grassy meadow with the odd trailer-size boulder tossed throughout. You'll also meet the Vermilion Range to your right (west) and the snow-capped peaks of the Ball Range, which sit off in the distance to your left (east). If it's a clear day, you may even see as far as Storm Mountain (3,161 m) to the northeast.

The trail from here to the Numa Creek Campground is quite steep, so if

Climbing over Numa Pass, you'll be rewarded by this view of Floe Lake and the enormous Rockwall.

you have poles, you may want to pull them out to descend the rocky switchback trail that leads you down through a lush valley. As you reach the avalanche chutes, you'll walk along a rocky trail lined by the willows and alders that are common in these old chutes; that's when you know you're close to the campground. You'll then enter a mossy forest filled with one-leafed foamflower, dwarf dogwood, and pearly everlasting as you drop the final 2 kilometers with the soothing sound of Numa Creek following you toward the junction that will lead you right (south) to the campground.

As we crossed the creek leaving the campground, hikers who'd come from Floe Lake said "you're pretty brave" as we passed by; others spoke muffled "good lucks" and warnings that we'd need to find some sticks if we were going to make the climb to Numa Pass. We ambled along through the heavily forested, fern-filled path in fear of the 800-meter ascent, but it wasn't as bad as we'd been told.

Admittedly, it looks a little daunting as you pass by a set of beautiful waterfalls in the second of two alder-filled alpine meadows (where we also spotted a large bull moose who was not at all pleased that we'd interrupted his lunch) before you begin the tough ascent at 36.5 kilometers. But if you take it at your own pace, it doesn't seem that bad—until you hike past the last larches above tree line and see the sand-colored pass ahead of you in the distance. Take a deep breath and forge on.

Numa Mountain (2,550 m) sits to the left (southeast), and you can see all the snow-covered peaks of the Ball Range across the highway (east). Take a minute to look north up the huge valley you've spent days climbing through;

it's at this point you realize how far, and just how high, you've traveled. As you climb over the pass, Foster Peak (3,204 m) ahead of you (southwest) eggs you on, and as you take those final steps, you'll be immediately overcome by a sense of accomplishment as you gain a fantastic view of Floe Lake beneath you. The Rockwall's sheer gray 600-meter cliff of Ottertail limestone looms as the awesome backdrop for the glistening midnight-blue lake. It's phenomenal.

You'll traverse along the green moraine above tree line before you meet the larch-filled forest that will help you complete your 2.7-kilometer descent to Floe Lake Campground. A garden of wildflowers—arnica, mauve alpine daisy, red and pink Indian paintbrush, hairy western anemones, and valerian—will lead you to the campground, which is on the lakeshore. Arrive as early as 11:00 A.M. to secure a tent spot with a view; otherwise you may be tucked behind a few trees. Most important, bring your bug spray—you'll need it here.

From here it's just a 10.7-kilometer hike back to Highway 93, so be sure to grab a dip in the lake before heading out refreshed and ready for a really hot shower. The trail climbs to your left (northeast) out of the campground before it drops steeply through a switchback section for about 2.5 kilometers. At this point the grade begins to soften. You'll have nice views down the lush green valley with unnamed peaks off to the southeast covered in deep green meadow as you pass in and out of forest and through overgrown avalanche chutes. On a hot day, this is a nice shady trail.

At 50.2 kilometers you'll see the highway ahead of you; unfortunately, you'll hear it as well. Continue through the forest, crossing Floe Creek at 51.5 kilometers, which you've followed most of the way down this trail. At 53.3 kilometers you'll cross the creek one more time as it passes through a nicely carved canyon. Once you reach the other side, you'll pass the final trail sign, which indicates it's just 500 meters to the parking area.

Options:
Goodsir Pass (8.0 to 27.2 kilometers; 450-meter elevation gain). You'll miss some fantastic scenery if you skip this excellent day hike from Helmet Falls Campground to Goodsir Pass. You can also leave the Rockwall Trail via Goodsir Pass and the Ottertail Trail, which runs northwest into Yoho National Park (27.2 km). The trailhead is located just east of the campground.

For the first 4 kilometers the trail climbs 450 meters via a series of forested switchbacks to Goodsir Pass (2,210 m). You can hear the pikas chirping amidst the rocky moraine to your right (west) just beyond the pass. From there the trail continues an additional 4 kilometers to the Kootenay National Park boundary. You'll enjoy fantastic views of Sharp Mountain (3,049 m), Mount Goodsir's North Tower (3,525 m) and South Tower (3,562 m), along with the Goodsir Glacier, and Hanbury Peak (2,911 m) to your left (west and northwest); and Mount Oke (2,920 m) and Misko Mountain (2,902 m) to your right (east and northeast).

This is a great spot from which to watch the sunrise, as we did.

Note: Slather on the mosquito spray before embarking on this trail, and travel in groups. Although we didn't spot any bears, we saw too many grizzly bear digs to count.

Return to Paint Pots via Tumbling Creek Trail (10.9 kilometers one way). If you'd like to see what everyone's raving about but you prefer to shave a few days or kilometers off the full 53.8-kilometer trail, consider a shorter version of the Rockwall. Head in from the Paint Pots trailhead as described above, and return to the Paint Pots via the Tumbling Creek Trail. From Tumbling Creek Campground, the Tumbling Creek Trail heads northeast through the woods, crossing a series of small streams and avalanche slopes along the way. The trail skirts Tumbling Creek to your right (southeast).

At approximately 4.1 kilometers you'll reach an unmarked fork in the trail; stay to your left (northeast) and cross Tumbling Creek over a steel bridge. At 6.4 kilometers you'll reach Helmet/Ochre Campground, where Ochre Creek and Helmet Creek intersect. Cross the bridge and continue heading northeast on the trail. Just 400 meters later you'll hit a trail junction. Take a right (southeast), and return 4.1 kilometers through the trees, passing the Paint Pots interpretive trail on your way back to the parking lot.

Return to Numa Falls Parking area via the Numa Creek Trail (6.7 kilometers one-way). If you just don't have the time or desire to complete the entire trip, leaving the Rockwall via the Numa Creek Trail is a nice option. If you just want to do a two-night trip, consider hiking to Floe Lake, over Numa Pass, and out via the Numa Creek Trail.

From the trail junction at 33.2 kilometers, follow the left (north) fork toward Highway 93. As you hike through a forest filled with Englemann spruce, Numa Creek will lead you back to the parking area. You'll pass in and out of the forest and through several old avalanche chutes with the occasional view of the softly sculpted Vermilion Range off to the left (north). At 3.6 kilometers you'll cross Numa Creek over a steel footbridge. Along the way you'll see thousands of wildflowers, including hairbells, Indian paintbrush, arnica, mauve-colored subalpine daisy, fireweed, wild clover, one-leafed foamflower, pearly everlasting, dwarf dogwood, cow parsnip as well as fringed Grass of Parnassus—a little white flower that's shaped like a star. At 4.7 kilometers you'll cross a small wooden footbridge over a dried out creek; at 6.6 kilometers you'll cross over the Vermilion River and beautifully carved Numa Falls just before reaching the parking area.

41 Hawk Creek to Ball Pass

Highlights: Up to one-third of the park's nineteen orchid species line this trail, which ends with fantastic views of the glaciers atop Mount Ball.
Type of hike: Day hike; out-and-back.
Total distance: 19.4 kilometers.
Difficulty: Moderate.
Hiking time: 5–7 hours.
Elevation at trailhead: 1,325 meters.
Elevation gain: 885 meters.
Topo maps: Kootenay National Park (GemTrek Publishing); Mount Goodsir, 82 N/1; Banff, 82 O/4.

Finding the trailhead: The Hawk Creek trailhead is located on the east side of Highway 93, approximately 69 kilometers north of Kootenay National Park's west gate and 32 kilometers south of Castle Junction (Highway 93 and TransCanada Highway 1). Park in the small lot on the west side of Highway 93 directly across the road from the trailhead. You'll find an outhouse in the southwest corner of the parking lot.

Key points:
- 0.0   Trailhead.
- 4.4   Creek crossing.
- 6.1   Creek crossing.
- 7.0   Hawk Creek waterfall.
- 8.3   Stream crossing.
- 8.9   Stream crossing.
- 9.7   Ball Pass.

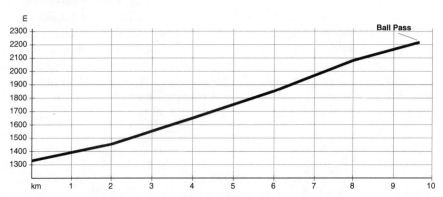

The hike: You'll travel uphill through the trees for two hours before spotting any impressive scenery along this trail. But the bird's-eye view at the end more than compensates for your efforts. The trail starts 100 meters from the parking lot on the east side of Highway 93. For the first 600 meters, you'll skirt the highway, passing Hawk Creek on your right (east) before heading into a forest of Douglas fir and lodgepole pine to your right (northeast).

Hawk Creek to Ball Pass

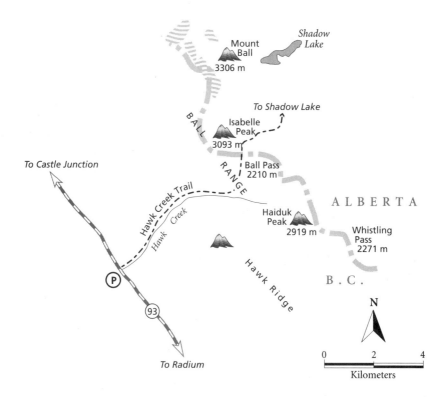

Enjoy the first kilometer—the only part of this hike that's relatively flat. Orange-flowered hawkweed, wild strawberries, red clover, potentilla, white buttercup, and dogwood provide bursts of color along the way.

At 1.2 kilometers you'll start your ascent with the sound of Hawk Creek rushing in the background (south). If you're lucky, you can find up to one-third of Kootenay National Park's nineteen known orchid species on this trail. We didn't spot them all, but we did recognize a medley of wildflowers en route to Ball Pass (2,210 m), including calypso orchids, yellow columbine, blue clematis, early blue violets, and Columbia lilies. We also noticed fresh moose tracks.

At 3.5 kilometers you'll enjoy a great view of Hawk Ridge to your right (south). The trail opens up 500 meters later as you enter an alpine meadow. Here's where we spotted a wood frog, a rare amphibian that freezes solid in the winter only to thaw and hop away in the spring.

At 4.4 kilometers you'll cross Hawk Creek. For the next 2 kilometers you'll traverse rocky avalanche slopes with great views of the rock wall to your left (northwest), Hawk Ridge to your right (southeast), and the Ball Range straight ahead (northeast).

You'll see many glaciers hanging atop Mount Ball.

At approximately 6.1 kilometers, as you cross a small creek you'll spot a series of waterfalls on the rock wall to your left (north)—the result of meltwater from the Ball Range. Hawk Creek creates an unexpected waterfall of its own, to your right (southeast) at 6.5 kilometers. Just 500 meters later you'll encounter the final series of switchbacks up to the pass. Yellow glacier lilies and globeflowers brighten this part of the trail.

At 8.3 and 8.9 kilometers you'll cross two small streams as you enter an open valley filled with stands of larch and colorful wildflowers before finally reaching Ball Pass (2,210 m) at 9.7 kilometers. Pack a lunch, and enjoy the spectacular views of mountains and glaciers from the pass. On a clear day you'll see Isabelle Peak (3,093 m) and the many hanging glaciers atop of Mount Ball (3,306 m) to your left (west and northwest), Shadow Lake in Banff straight ahead (north), and Haiduk Peak (2,919 m) and Whistling Pass (2,271m) in Banff to your right (southeast and east).

42 Verendrye Creek

Highlights: An easy walk along Verendrye Creek with limited views of Mount Verendrye.
Type of hike: Day hike; out-and-back.
Total distance: 7 kilometers.
Difficulty: Easy.
Hiking time: 2–3 hours.
Elevation at trailhead: 1,265 meters.
Elevation gain: 335 meters.
Topo maps: Kootenay National Park (GemTrek Publishing); Banff, 82 O/4; Mount Goodsir, 82 N/1.

Special considerations: We've heard that this trail is no longer maintained by Parks Canada. The last time we checked it was in poor condition.

Finding the trailhead: Follow Highway 93 approximately 61.6 kilometers southeast from the Kootenay National Park's west boundary and approximately 40 kilometers northeast of the park's eastern boundary. Turn west into the picnic area directly across the highway from the Vermilion Crossing Information Centre. There is no Verendrye Creek Trail sign on the highway; however, the trail is well marked. It begins at the north end of the covered picnic area beside the outhouses.

Key points:
  0.0   Trailhead.
  2.3   Ford Verendrye Creek (there is no bridge here).
  3.5   End of trail.

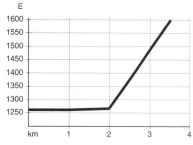

The hike: The simple fact is, some mountain views are just better from the highway; this is the case for the Verendrye Creek trail. However, if you're just looking for a walk in the woods, this one is quite easy—apart from the number of mud slides you'll have to traverse prior to reaching the creek at the 2.3-kilometer point. You may also catch a glimpse of Mount Verendrye (3,08 6m) straight ahead (west), yet the views are always limited by trees. And that's only if you've been eager enough to ford Verendrye Creek—crossing to the north side of the valley; the bridge was washed out many years ago. At this point many hikers turn around and head back down the trail.

You will begin this hike by walking parallel to the highway along the Vermilion River. About 100 meters into the trail you pass into a thick forest of white spruce and lodgepole pine. The trail is quite narrow and is lined by *Drepanocladus* moss. Heading west through the forest you will hear, but not see, Verendrye Creek. At 0.3 kilometer you will gain a nice view of Mount Verendrye straight ahead (west)—the best one you will have on this trail.

Verendrye Creek

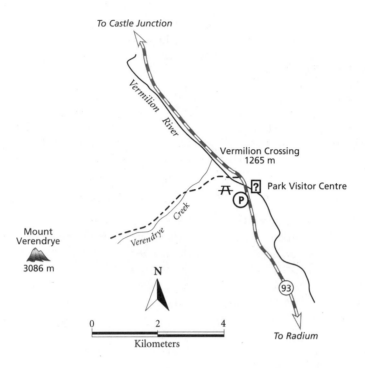

To Castle Junction

Vermilion River

Vermilion Crossing
1265 m

Park Visitor Centre

Mount
Verendrye

3086 m

Verendrye Creek

N

93

To Radium

0   2   4
Kilometers

Approximately 0.7 kilometer into the trail, you will follow a route of switch-backs as you gain a little elevation. At this point you will still hear the hum of vehicles traveling along Highway 93. At 1.4 kilometers you will gain your first clear view of Verendrye Creek (north) as you encounter a small natural lookout. From this point on you will gain the occasional glimpse of creek as you walk along this forested path. Approximately 2.3 kilometers into this trail the trees open up, as you are almost level with the creek; at this point you should cross to the north side of the valley and regain the trail. Early in the season, and even in the summer months, this will be a difficult task as the creek is wide and fast. After you have crossed the creek, the unmaintained trail is rough. At 3.5 kilometers the trail ends at the gravel by the side of the creek near the top of the valley filled with avalanche chutes. Even here, the view of Mount Verendrye is less than spectacular.

43 Honeymoon Pass

Highlights:	An uphill hike to Honeymoon Pass with views of Hawk Ridge and the Ball Range before you descend through the valley to the Verdant Creek backcountry campground.
Type of hike:	Backpack; out-and-back.
Total distance:	14.2 kilometers.
Difficulty:	Moderate.
Hiking time:	2 days.
Elevation at trailhead:	1,265 meters.
Elevation gain:	730 meters.
Topo maps:	Kootenay National Park (GemTrek Publishing); Banff, 82/04 (trail not shown on map).

Finding the trailhead: Follow Highway 93 to a small parking area approximately 61.6 kilometers south of the park's western boundary, or 40 kilometers north of the east gate. The trailhead is on the east side of Highway 93, just north of Vermilion Crossing and the Park Visitor Centre.

Key points:

- 0.0 Trailhead.
- 0.1 Creek crossing over a wooden footbridge.
- 2.6 Creek crossing over a wooden footbridge.
- 3.4 Creek crossing over a wooden footbridge.
- 4.3 Creek crossing over a wooden footbridge.
- 5.6 Honeymoon Pass.
- 6.0 Creek crossing over a wooden footbridge.
- 6.5 Cross Verdant Creek; no bridge.
- 7.1 Verdant Creek Campground.

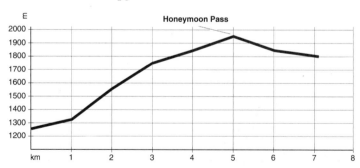

The hike: If you're looking for solitude, you'll find it on this trail. It's a steep, 730-meter climb up to Honeymoon Pass, then a quick, 200-meter descent into the valley bottom—only to ford the creek that will lead you to the lonesome Verdant Creek Campground. Strong, intrepid hikers can trek the remaining 12 kilometers to reach Redearth Pass and another 2.4 kilometers to

Honeymoon Pass

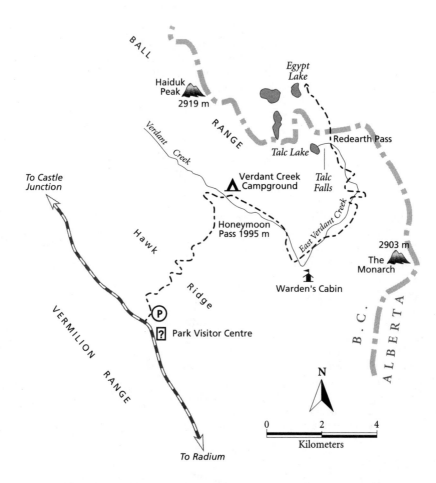

reach Egypt Lake in Banff National Park. However, the Verdant Creek Trail is seldom traveled, and excellent route-finding skills are a necessity.

From the trailhead this narrow wooded path lined by lodgepole pine and Douglas fir is rarely trodden and is overgrown by ferns, shrubs, and alpine wildflowers. Depending on the time of year, you'll spot mauve fleabane, wild rose, wild strawberry, pink Indian paintbrush, alpine buttercup, dwarf dogwood, yellow columbine, arnica, valerian, western anemone, and white mountain heather.

Alongside the softly ascending trail, you'll hear a quiet creek. Once you reach the 1.5- kilometer point, you'll have fantastic views of the Vermilion Range across the highway off to your right (west), including Mount Verendrye (3,086 m) and Mount Wardle (2,810 m) to the southwest; you'll also notice that the climb becomes much steeper from this point. Continue along this rising trail of switchbacks; at about 3.4 kilometers you'll come out of the trees into an alpine meadow. The scree slopes of Hawk Ridge are visible on either side of you.

After the 4-kilometer point, the trail is a little less trampled down; in fact, in places it can barely be spotted, so look for the red-and-white wooden trail markers (they are about 3 feet high) ahead of you. Walk along the scree slope to your left (north) and gain a nice view of the Ball Range in the distance (northeast).

Stay on the left-hand (north) side of the meadow to regain the trail once you've picked your way through the boggy flat; it's quite easy to spot the trail markers. From here descend through the valley, passing in and out of a forest of Douglas fir before reaching Verdant Creek. We were lucky enough to see a lot of fresh grizzly prints and bear scat as we got closer to the creek; thankfully, we did not spot the accompanying bear.

Walk parallel to the creek for about 700 meters before you come to what was once a bridge at about 6.5 kilometers. We had to ford the creek; however, it was far too dangerous to cross where the trail leads out on the other side. We walked about 50 meters upstream and crossed in thigh-deep, ice-cold water—and we can't emphasize the ice-cold enough. Once we reached the other side of the creek, we ran into the remains of a moose as we bushwhacked back along the other side of the creek to find the trail. Look for orange flagging in the trees, as the trail is difficult to follow from this point on.

At 7.1 kilometers you'll walk through a meadow filled with 1-meter-high shrubs and into Verdant Creek Campground. When we visited this spot in late July, it was obvious that nobody had stayed at the site for some time. The bear poles were knocked down, the outhouse walls were filled with holes, the area was very overgrown, and there was no firewood supplied, although there was a small firebox. The spot, though, is really quite peaceful; the slopes of the Hawk Ridge and Ball Range surround you, and the rumble of Verdant Creek is everlasting. We opted to camp about 500 meters from the firebox beneath the trees in a nearby clearing.

If you're intent on hiking to Redearth Pass from here, follow the trail leading east out of the campground; the creek will be to your right (south). After hiking 1.0 kilometer, you'll meet Verdant Creek again. This time there is an old log you can walk across, but it is very wet and slippery (two members of our hiking party ended up in chest-deep icewater here; OK, I was one of them). Continue for approximately 3 kilometers to reach the warden cabin, then cross the creek again as you meet up with East Verdant Creek. This creek will take you the remaining 8 kilometers to the Kootenay Park boundary and Redearth Pass. From here you can continue another 2.4 kilometers (north) to reach Egypt Lake in Banff National Park.

44 Simpson River

Highlights: A pleasant hike along the Simpson River.
Type of hike: Day hike; out-and-back.
Total distance: 20 kilometers.
Difficulty: Easy.
Hiking time: 6–8 hours.
Elevation at trailhead: 1,250 meters.
Elevation gain: 150 meters.
Topo maps: Kootenay National Park (GemTrek Publishing); Mount Assiniboine, 82J/13.

Finding the trailhead: Follow Highway 93 approximately 56 kilometers northeast from the Kootenay National Park west gate, or 45.8 kilometers south of Castle Junction (Highway 93 and TransCanada Highway 1). Turn east into the Simpson River parking area. The well-marked trail begins at the north end of the parking area, just before the footbridge that crosses the Vermilion River.

Key points:
0.0   Trailhead.
0.2   Trail junction to Simpson River; head right (east).
8.8   Kootenay National Park boundary.
10.0   Surprise Creek shelter.

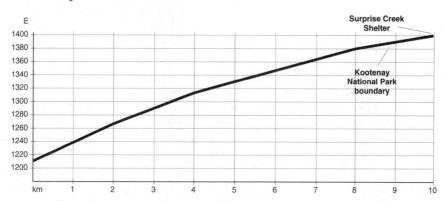

The hike: Although this hike is generally completed as an out-and-back day hike, we would also recommend it as an introductory backcountry trip. Hike 10.2 kilometers to the Surprise Creek shelter, about 2 kilometers past the Kootenay Park boundary, stay overnight, then hike back out. The shelter is well maintained and will sleep four comfortably; be sure to book it in advance through one of the park's information centers (Vermilion Crossing is closest). If you intend to complete this trip in a day, as we did, you may be disappointed if you hike only to the official park boundary, which is hidden away in the trees. The only uninterrupted mountain view to be had on this

Simpson River

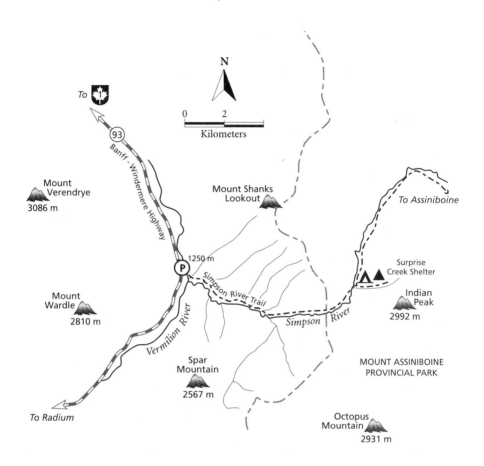

trail is about 100 meters before the shelter, where you'll pass over the Simpson River, gaining a nice view of Indian Peak (2,992 m).

From the trailhead cross the footbridge that will take you over the Vermilion River. Initially the trail is quite wide and is lined by juniper. At approximately 0.24 kilometer you will reach the trail junction that will point you right (southeast) toward Simpson River. The sign says the trail is 8.6 kilometers—keep in mind this only marks the Kootenay National Park official boundary—and we tracked this to be at 8.8 kilometers. The view to the north here is of Mount Shanks (2,800 m).

At 0.3 kilometer you may encounter a boggy area that will require careful navigation; if wet, it is deeper than it looks (yes, we soaked our hiking boots here). At 1.2 kilometers you will see blue clematis before you cross a small unnamed creek. Looking right (south) you will gain views of the Simpson River and Spar Mountain (2,567 m) as you follow a slight incline into

A hiker enjoys the view of Indian Peak from the suspension bridge on the Simpson River Trail.

the woods away from the river. You will come back out by the river at approximately 1.5 kilometers before heading back into the trees until approximately 2.5 kilometers, when the trail opens up again.

At 4 kilometers you will reach another stream crossing before heading up a gradual incline. At 1,365 meters you've gained a slow 100 meters since leaving the trailhead. At 4.5 kilometers you will cross logs that span another unnamed creek; you'll notice a lot of golden-brown peat moss along the trail. This particular type, *Drepanocladus,* is the most common species found in the Canadian Rockies.

At 5.2 kilometers you will pass over another stream, and just after it you may see some Kinnikinnick. At 5.7 kilometers you will join the Simpson River on your right (south), but you will see it only through the trees. You will also see Octopus Mountain (2,931 m) and Indian Peak (2,992 m) to your right (southeast) through the trees for the next few kilometers. At 6.8 kilometers you will pass by the river over a rocky portion on the trail. At 7.5 kilometers you will cross yet another stream before heading up a gradual incline to the national park boundary at 8.8 kilometers.

From here, we would recommend that you hike the remaining 1.2 kilometers into Mount Assiniboine Provincial Park and the Surprise Creek shelter. You'll know you're almost there when you cross a small suspension bridge over the Simpson River. You can see the shelter just beyond the bridge. If you're out on a day hike, this is a great place to stop for lunch (there's an outhouse here), with a great view of Indian Peak and Surprise Creek. From here it's 20.7 kilometers to Magog Lake at the base of Mount Assiniboine.

45 West Kootenay Trail

Highlights:	Follow this well-maintained fire road to the Kootenay National Park boundary. If you're looking for a quiet place to fish, you can continue about 1.0 kilometer to an old bridge over the Kootenay River.
Type of hike:	Day hike; out-and-back.
Total distance:	20.6 kilometers.
Difficulty:	Easy.
Hiking time:	4–6 hours on foot; 1 hour, 30 minutes by bike.
Elevation at trailhead:	1,250 meters.
Elevation gain:	Minimal.
Topo maps:	Kootenay National Park (GemTrek Publishing); Spillimacheen, 82/K16.

Finding the trailhead: The West Kootenay Fire Road begins at the Kootenay Crossing warden station, on the west side of Highway 93, approximately 42 kilometers north of Kootenay National Park's east gate, or 60 kilometers south of Castle Junction (Highway 93 and TransCanada Highway 1). Turn left (west) off Highway 93 at the warden's station and follow the signs for West Kootenay Trail. Follow the dirt road in the southwest corner of the warden's station approximately 0.8 kilometer until you reach the end of the road. You can park here, just before the rocks that mark the trailhead.

Key points:
  0.0   Trailhead.
  1.1   Trail junction; turn right (west).
  6.4   Creek crossing over a wooden footbridge.
 10.2   Fork in the trail; continue straight ahead 100 meters to reach the park boundary, or head right (north) to meet the Kootenay River.
 10.3   Kootenay National Park boundary.

The hike: There are no mountain views whatsoever on this trail, but if you're looking for an easy hike along a nice wide-open fire road, or an excellent fly-fishing spot, this is a good pick.

You'll begin the trail by immediately climbing up the Dolly Varden Fire Road, which also serves as a mountain bike trail. This relatively flat, well-maintained road is lined with spruce, aspen, lodgepole pine, and Douglas fir. In August you'll spot a lot of oxeye daisy and bright-red Indian paintbrush, as well as the occasional glimpse of pearly everlasting and valerian.

At 1.1 kilometers you'll reach a trail junction; turn right (west) to travel the West Kootenay Trail. The old fire road is windy and wide open and is really quite fun if you're on a bike. If you're walking it can get a bit tiresome, as there's nothing to see but trees and a few wildflowers. At about 5.7 kilometers the trail is slightly overgrown with grass. At this point you'll catch a glimpse of a peak in the Vermilion Ridge (east); you'll see it above the trees for only a few hundred meters though. Continue on; at 10.2 kilometers, about 100 meters before the park boundary, you'll reach a fork in

West Kootenay Trail

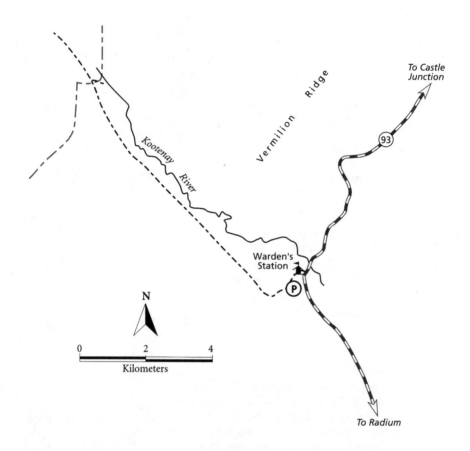

the trail. If you want to do some fine fly-fishing, head right (north) to take the 1.0-kilometer branch road up a short hill to descend to an old bridge on the Kootenay River.

From here you have three options: (1) Follow the trail 100 meters to the boundary, just to say you made it, then turn around and head back to the trailhead; (2) head back 9.4 kilometers to the first trail junction and follow the Dolly Varden Trail (see Hike 47 for a description) to Crooks Meadow Campground; or (3) go fishing!

46 Luxor Pass

Highlights:	This long, forested hike offers views of Luxor Pass, Mount Crook, and the Mitchell Range.
Type of hike:	Day hike; out-and-back.
Total distance:	17.8 kilometers.
Hiking time:	4½–6½ hours.
Difficulty:	Moderate.
Elevation at trailhead:	1,250 meters.
Elevation gain/loss:	655 meters.
Topo maps:	Kootenay National Park (GemTrek Publishing); Spillmacheen, 82/K16.

Finding the trailhead: The Luxor Pass Trail starts at the Kootenay Crossing warden station, on the west side of Highway 93, approximately 42 kilometers north of Kootenay National Park's west gate. Turn left (west) off Highway 93 at the warden's station and follow the signs for West Kootenay Trail. Follow the dirt road in the southwest corner of the warden's station approximately 800 meters until the road ends; this is the parking area. You'll find directional signage here.

Key points:
- 0.0 Trailhead.
- 1.1 Trail junction; continue straight ahead (southwest).
- 3.6 Dolly Varden Creek crossing.
- 3.9 Luxor Pass Junction; turn right (southwest).
- 8.9 Luxor Pass/Kootenay National Park border.

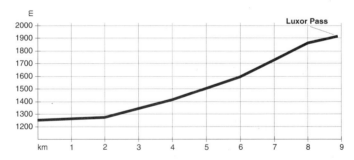

The hike: You'll get better views from the parking lot than you will on this prolonged walk in the woods. On the way to Luxor Pass, you'll scramble up some extremely strenuous sections, which offer limited views compared with other trails in the area. Unless you're simply interested in some fantastic exercise, we'd suggest skipping this trail.

The trail starts on the Dolly Varden Fire Road, which doubles as a mountain bike trail. Spruce, aspen, lodgepole pine, and Douglas fir line this well-maintained trail, with blue clematis and tiny northern anemones providing a splash of color.

At 1.1 kilometers you'll reach a trail junction; continue straight ahead

Luxor Pass

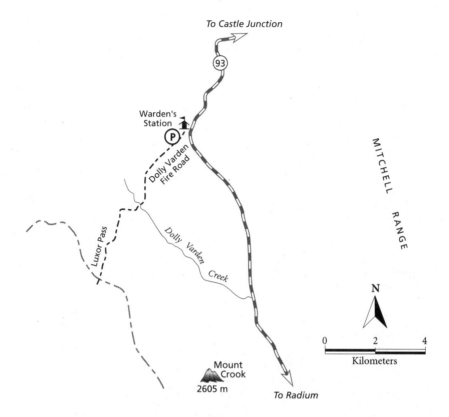

(southwest) along the Dolly Varden Fire Road. Just 1.0 kilometer later you'll catch a glimpse of Luxor Pass directly ahead of you (southwest) and Mount Crook (2,605 m) slightly to your left (south). At 3.6 kilometers you'll cross Dolly Varden Creek. We spotted two spruce grouse—the highlight of our hike—on this section of trail.

Just 300 meters later you'll reach the Luxor Pass trailhead. Here's where the tough stuff starts. Turning right (southwest) you'll start your ascent on a single-file path through dense forest carpeted with varied mosses. A kaleidoscope of brightly colored northern anemones, Indian paintbrush, glacier lilies, and calypso orchids line this section of trail.

At 5.7 kilometers look directly behind you (east) for a view of the Mitchell Range across the valley. This view and a similar view to your east at 6 kilometers are about the best you'll get on this trail. At 8.1 kilometers you'll be directly even with Mount Crook to your left (south). From here the trail continues 700 meters through the trees to a sign marking the Kootenay National Park border.

Although you've gained considerable elevation, you won't enjoy the spectacular views offered by some of the park's other trails. The good news is that the trip down is far easier than the hike up.

47 Dolly Varden Trail
(Also referred to as the West Kootenay Fire Road)

Highlights: This forested hike or mountain bike ride offers limited views of Luxor Pass, Mount Crook, and the Mitchell Range.

Type of hike: Day hike; out-and-back or shuttle.

Total distance: 22 kilometers (out-and-back) or 11 kilometers (shuttle).

Difficulty: Easy.

Hiking time: 4½–6½ hours on foot; 30 minutes–1½ hours by bike.

Elevation at trailhead: 1,250 meters.

Elevation gain/loss: Minimal.

Topo maps: Kootenay National Park (GemTrek Publishing); Spillmacheen, 82/K16.

Finding the trailhead: The West Kootenay Fire Road begins at the Kootenay Crossing warden station, on the west side of Highway 93, approximately 42 kilometers north of Kootenay National Park's west gate. Turn left (west) off Highway 93 at the warden's station, and follow the signs for West Kootenay Trail. Follow the dirt road in the southwest corner of the warden's station approximately 800 meters until you reach the end of the road. This is the parking area. You'll see directional signage for the trail next to the parking area. You can also begin this trail at Crooks Meadow Group Campground, also on the west side of Highway 93, approximately 34.4 kilometers north of Kootenay National Park's west gate.

Key points:
- 0.0   Directional trail sign.
- 1.1   Trail junction.
- 2.1   View of Luxor Pass and Mount Crook.
- 3.6   Bridge over Dolly Varden Creek.
- 4.1   Junction; head south.
- 11.0   Crooks Meadow Campground.

The hike: Unfortunately, the mountain view from the highway is better than the one you'll have on this trail. It's a long walk in the woods, yet it makes for a nice leisurely mountain bike ride.

The trail begins on the Dolly Varden fire road, which also serves as a mountain bike trail. The well-maintained road is lined with spruce, aspen, lodgepole pine, and Douglas fir. You may also spot blue clematis, tiny white northern anemones, purple common fleabane, wild strawberries, and Indian paintbrush.

At 0.9 kilometer you'll reach a trail junction; continue straight ahead (southwest) along the Dolly Varden fire road. To your right is West Kootenay Trail, another popular mountain biking route. At 2.1 kilometers you'll catch a glimpse

Wildflowers add a splash of color to this nicely-graded, wide-open fire road on the inviting Dolly Varden Trail.

Dolly Varden Trail

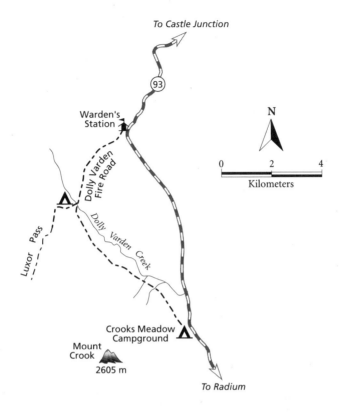

of Luxor Pass directly ahead of you (southwest) and Mount Crook (2,606 m) slightly to your left (south). At 3.6 kilometers you'll cross Dolly Varden Creek over a wooden footbridge.

You'll reach the Luxor Pass trailhead at 4.1 kilometers. Continue heading south along the fire road. You'll gain an occasional glimpse of Mount Crook (south) through the trees before you ride or hike into the meadow that will lead you to Crooks Meadow Campground.

48 East Kootenay Fire Road

Highlights:	This pancake-flat, overgrown trail offers limited views of the Kootenay Range.
Type of hike:	Day hike; out-and-back.
Total distance:	14.4 kilometers.
Difficulty:	Easy.
Hiking time:	5–6 hours on foot; 1–2 hours on by mountain bike.
Elevation at trailhead:	1,100 meters.
Elevation gain:	Minimal.
Topo maps:	Kootenay National Park (GemTrek Publishing); Mount Assiniboine, 82 J/13.

Finding the trailhead: Follow Highway 93 approximately 25 kilometers north of Kootenay National Park's west gate, or 76 kilometers south of Castle Junction (Highway 93 and TransCanada Highway 1) to the turnoff for McLeod Meadows Campground and Picnic Site. Turn east off Highway 93, and park near the back (east end) of the picnic site. The trailhead is located to the left (west) of the picnic shelter.

Key points:
- 0.0 Trail head; proceed straight ahead (east).
- 0.5 Bridge crossing over the Kootenay River.
- 0.8 Trail junction; head left (north).
- 3.0 Trail junction; continue left (north).
- 7.2 End of trail.

The hike: This overgrown, almost pancake-flat fire road makes for a peaceful, if slightly dull, hike, since there are only limited mountain views. You can also mountain-bike this trail—but watch for the nasty undergrowth, which will scratch and scrape against you as you ride by.

The first part of the trail parallels the highway as it passes through McLeod Meadows picnic site. This is the least-enjoyable section of the hike because of the constant buzz of traffic on Highway 93. At 400 meters you'll cross a service road and see another trail marker directing you northeast. Just 140 meters later you'll cross two consecutive wooden bridges over the glacier-fed Kootenay River. If it's fall, look for spawning Kokanee salmon in the river beneath you here.

Just 800 meters into the trail you'll reach a trail junction; head left (north) here toward Split Creek Junction. Although the trail sign indicates that you can travel 13.4 kilometers left (north) from here, the bridge that formerly connected the East Kootenay Trail and Hector Gorge (also known as East Kootenay Fire Road) to the north is out, so you can actually travel only approximately 7.2 kilometers farther.

You'll catch occasional glimpses of the Kootenay River and the Kootenay Range, including Mount Crook (2,605 m) and Mount Kindersley (2,696 m) to your left (west) through the trees. You may also spot Indian paintbrush

East Kootenay Fire Road

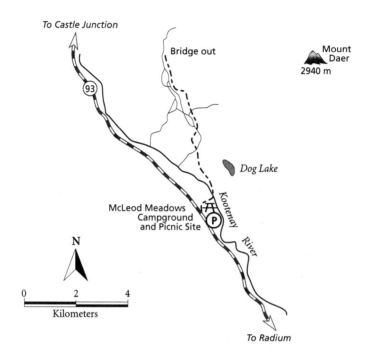

To Castle Junction

Bridge out

Mount Daer
2940 m

93

Dog Lake

McLeod Meadows
Campground
and Picnic Site

P

Kootenay River

N

0   2   4
Kilometers

To Radium

and oxeye daisies along this heavily forested trail, where views grow more limited the farther north you hike. At 7.2 kilometers you'll reach the end of the maintained trail, where the missing bridge prevents you from traveling any further. All in all, we'd recommend skipping this hike in favor of a hike like Hawk Creek to Ball Pass (see Hike 41), which ends with fantastic mountain views.

49 Hector Gorge/East Kootenay Fire Road

Highlights: This walk along an overgrown fire road is seldom traveled. You'll gain limited views of the Mitchell Range.

Type of hike: Day hike; shuttle.

Total distance: 9.5 kilometers.

Difficulty: Easy.

Hiking time: 2–3 hours.

Elevation at trailhead: 1,150 meters.

Elevation gain: Minimal.

Topo maps: Kootenay National Park (GemTrek Publishing); Spillimacheen, 82 K/16.

Finding the trailhead: Follow Highway 93 approximately 49 kilometers north of Kootenay National Park's west gate to an unmarked gravel road. Turn east off Highway 93 and park near the unmarked trailhead. The trail leaves the small parking area to the east. If you're looking to complete this hike as a shuttle, it's best to leave your second vehicle at the Hector Gorge Viewpoint; you'll still have to walk approximately 1.0 kilometer north along the highway once you've completed the trail. There is no parking area at the north end of this trail.

Key points:

0.0   Trailhead; continue straight ahead (east).
0.2   Bridge crossing the Kootenay River.
1.3   Trail junction; head left (north).
9.5   End of trail.

The hike: This hike travels along an old, overgrown fire road that traverses Hector Gorge (which you won't see). You'll gain the occasional view of Mount Selkirk (2,940 m) and Split Peak (2,928 m) of the Mitchell Range to your right (east), but your views will often be through the trees. If you're intent on hiking a fire road, you may want to consider Dolly Varden (Hike 47) or the West Kootenay Trail (Hike 45). The trails on these hikes are well maintained.

Follow the wide-open fire road east out of the parking area; this is the only section of trail that is well trodden. After hiking 200 meters you'll cross the Kootenay River over a small bridge. At 1.3 kilometers, right before you reach the Vermilion River, you'll come across a trail junction where you should head left (north). The trail to the right (south) used to link up with the East Kootenay Fire Road; however, the bridge at Daer Creek is out, and Parks Canada no longer maintains this section of the trail. Continue along the path and you'll likely spot bright-red Indian paintbrush, oxeye daisies, and mauve fleabane, as your legs take a lashing from the unruly undergrowth. From here the quality of the trail decreases; at times you'll be able to see only 1.5 meters in front of you because of overgrowth.

Hector Gorge/East Kootenay Fire Road

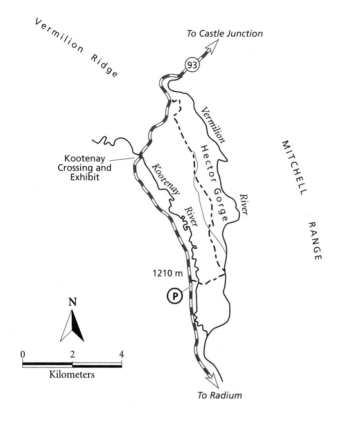

At approximately 5.8 kilometers you'll enter an alpine meadow filled with willows. Here you'll gain your best view of the Mitchell Range to your right (east). Continue along, climbing over a lot of deadfall as you navigate your way along the thick green trail until you reach its end. From here head left (west) and walk the remaining 50 meters to Highway 93, then up the road (north) to the Hector Gorge Viewpoint, where you've hopefully left another vehicle; otherwise, turn around and trek back to where you began this hike.

50 Dog Lake Trail

Highlights:	This gentle walk ends at Dog Lake with a view of Mount Harkin.
Type of hike:	Day hike; out-and-back.
Total distance:	5.4 kilometers.
Difficulty:	Easy.
Hiking time:	1½–2 hours.
Elevation at trailhead:	1,250 meters.
Elevation gain/loss:	Minimal.
Topo maps:	Kootenay National Park (GemTrek Publishing); Mount Assiniboine, 82 J/13.

Finding the trailhead: Follow Highway 93 approximately 25 kilometers north of Kootenay National Park's west gate, or 76 kilometers south of Castle Junction (Highway 93 and TransCanada Highway 1) to the turnoff for McLeod Meadows Campground and picnic site. Turn east off Highway 93, and park near the back (east end) of the picnic site. The trailhead is located to the left (west) of the picnic shelter.

Key points:
- 0.0   Trailhead.
- 0.9   Trail junction; continue straight ahead (northeast).
- 2.7   Dog Lake.

The hike: The lake is definitely a "dog" compared with others in Kootenay National Park, but this gentle walk in the woods is great for working off a big picnic dinner. The trail's first 900 meters parallels the highway as it passes through the McLeod Meadows picnic site. This is the least enjoyable section of the hike because of the constant buzz of traffic on Highway 93.

At 400 meters you'll cross a service road and see another trail marker directing you northeast. Just 140 meters later you'll cross two consecutive wooden bridges over the glacier-fed Kootenay River. If it's fall, look for spawning Kokanee salmon in the river beneath you here.

Head left (north) after the bridge another 360 meters, and cross the East Kootenay fire road to arrive at the trail junction. Continue straight ahead (northeast) here. From the junction it's another 1.7 kilometers through the woods to Dog Lake. In early summer you may find orange western wood lilies and calypso orchids lining the drier sections of trail.

The first question we asked at the lake is "where's the water?" The many reeds along the shore of this swampy lake have begun to take over. To find water, follow the trail to the right (southeast) across a wooden footbridge, which leads to an unmaintained trail on the east side of the lake. Mount Harkin (2,981 m), directly west of the lake, is named after the first commissioner of Canada's national parks, James Harkin.

Note: Slather up with bug spray before embarking on this hike to avoid the ravenous throng of mosquitoes here.

Dog Lake Trail

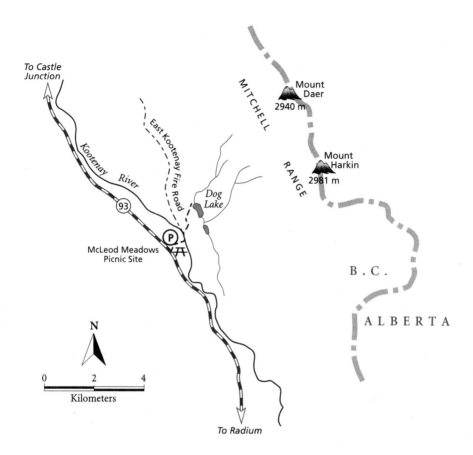

Options:

After enjoying the lake, you can either return the way you came or head right (north) to connect to the East Kootenay Fire Road. The fire road and its connecting trail create a 3.4-kilometer loop that eventually joins the Dog Lake Trail just east of McLeod Meadows Campground.

51 Cobb Lake Trail

Highlights:	A pleasant forested walk to Cobb Lake.
Type of hike:	Day hike; out-and-back.
Total distance:	5.6 kilometers.
Difficulty:	Easy.
Hiking time:	1–2 hours.
Elevation at trailhead:	1,410 meters.
Elevation gain:	Minimal.
Topo maps:	Kootenay National Park (GemTrek Publishing); Tangle Peak, 82 J/12.

Finding the trailhead: Follow Highway 93 to a small parking area approximately 14.5 kilometers from the park's west gate. The trailhead is on the south side of the highway.

Key points:
- 0.0 Trailhead.
- 1.7 Swede Creek.
- 2.8 Cobb Lake.

The hike: Leaving the parking area, this hike winds 1.7 kilometers downhill through a thick forest filled with lodgepole pine and white spruce, as well as some fire-scarred Douglas fir trees, whose thick bark has enabled

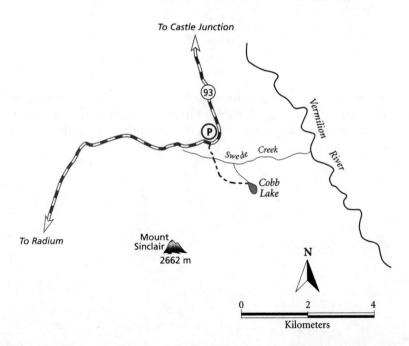

Cobb Lake Trail

them to withstand the heat of past forest fires. You may also see some blue clematis alongside this pleasant trail.

After crossing Swede Creek, the trail works uphill at a slight grade until it reaches a small boggy lake. The lake is filled with rarely caught brook and cutthroat (native) trout. Stocking lakes with non-native sport fish is no longer practiced in the mountain parks, as it diminishes the quality of our aquatic ecosystems. Although Mount Sinclair (2,662 m) sits to your right (southwest) of the lake, you may only glimpse a corner of its peak through the dense forest.

52 Kindersley Pass/ Sinclair Creek Loop

Highlights:	This hike features fabulous views of area mountains, including Devil's Tooth, Mount Sinclair, and Mount Kindersley.
Type of hike:	Day hike; shuttle.
Total distance:	16.2 kilometers.
Difficulty:	Moderate.
Hiking time:	4–5 hours.
Elevation at trailhead:	1,340 meters.
Elevation gain:	1,055 meters.
Topo maps:	Kootenay National Park (GemTrek Publishing); Tangle Peak, 82 J/12.

Finding the trailhead: You can start the Kindersley Pass/Sinclair Creek shuttle from one of two trailheads. The Kindersley Pass trailhead is located on the west side of Highway 93, approximately 10.8 kilometers north of Kootenay National Park's West Gate. The Sinclair Creek trailhead, also on the west side of Highway 93, is located 12 kilometers north of the park's west gate.

Starting at the Kindersley Pass trailhead makes for a gentle but longer ascent than the Sinclair Creek trail. However, you'll gain elevation more quickly from the Sinclair Creek trailhead, which offers better views. No matter which option you choose, leave a vehicle at both trailheads to avoid the 1.2-kilometer trudge back to your car at the end of the hike.

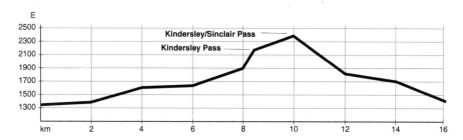

Kindersley Pass/Sinclair Creek Loop

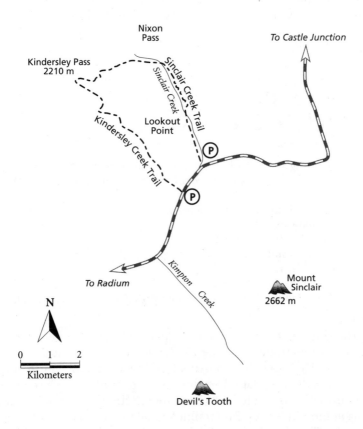

We started at the Kindersley Pass trailhead. You'll find the Kindersley Pass parking lot on the east side of Highway 93, directly across from the trailhead.

Key points:

0.0	Kindersley Pass trailhead.
7.3	Creek crossing.
7.9	Creek crossing.
8.4	Kindersley Pass; continue right (east).
8.6	Trail junction; continue right (east).
9.8	Kindersley/Sinclair Pass and trail junction; continue right (east).
10.3	Creek crossing.
14.2	Creek crossing.
16.2	Creek trailhead.

The hike: You may not develop buns of steel on the climb to Kindersley–Sinclair Pass (2,395 m), but this hike is no easy walk in the woods. While the initial part of the trail is heavily wooded, primarily by Douglas fir, it's also a flower-lover's paradise, especially after 2.2 kilometers where an avalanche chute opens up the trail.

Even if you're not interested in flowers, you can't help but enjoy the kaleidoscope of brightly colored fleabane, wild roses, Indian paintbrush, yellow columbine, cow parsnip, fireweed, and blue clematis. If you're really lucky or unlucky, depending on how you look at it, you may also spot an occasional grizzly bear scrounging for food along nearby avalanche chutes. Apparently there's a female grizzly with cubs who lives near this trail, but she's avoided encounters with hikers.

At 6.2 kilometers you'll skirt a large avalanche chute to your left (southwest). As you're crossing a creek at 7.3 kilometers, look to your right (east) for views of Lookout Point and Kindersley-Sinclair Pass. You'll then duck back into the woods for 500 meters before emerging to enjoy a crystal-clear view of Kindersley Pass (2,210 m) straight ahead of you (northwest).

At 7.9 kilometers you'll cross the creek again, and 500 meters later you'll arrive at Kindersley Pass, which is marked by a sign for the park boundary. You may not feel like you've reached the pass since the climb is fairly moderate and there isn't much to see besides the Kindersley Creek Valley straight ahead (north), but keep going—the best is yet to come.

From here you'll continue to your right (east) and ascend the flank of Kindersley Peak to Kindersley–Sinclair Pass—the steepest part of the trail. You'll reach another trail junction at 8.6 kilometers; continue right (east) here toward Kindersley–Sinclair Pass. After a brief shady section, you'll enter an exposed area above the tree line. From here to the pass you'll soak up fantastic views. Look to your right (south) for views of Devil's Tooth, Mount Sinclair (2,662 m), and the Kimpton Creek Valley; to your left (north and northeast) for views of Mount Kindersley (2,696 m) and Nixon Pass; and straight ahead for a view of Kindersley–Sinclair Pass. If you're lucky you may also spot Rocky Mountain bighorn sheep on nearby rocky ridges.

You'll reach the Kindersley Pass/Sinclair Creek Trail junction at 9.8 kilometers; head right (east). The good news is that it's all downhill (in terms of elevation only) from here. Be prepared to cross a number of snowy avalanche chutes on your way down—even in late July or early August. Wear gaiters, and enjoy a bit of "boot skiing" to speed your descent.

At 10.3 kilometers you'll cross a small stream and enter an alpine meadow. Just 300 meters later you'll enjoy a great view of Mount Sinclair (2,662 m) straight ahead (south). Don't forget to look behind you (northwest) as well for one of the last glimpses of Kindersley–Sinclair Pass.

Immediately after the meadow you'll face a series of steep downhill switchbacks. Yellow glacier lilies, alpine buttercups, western anemones, red clover, alpine forget-me-nots, and northern anemones line this part of the path. At 14.2 kilometers you'll cross a creek and enter a brief meadow area, which has been cleared by the many avalanche chutes to your right (west), before heading back into the trees.

Hikers climb past masses of yellow glacier lily on their way to Kindersley Pass.

There's not much to see on the rest of the trail, which descends through a dense, mossy forest lined with Douglas fir. The last 2.2 kilometers follows a creek, which you'll hear tumbling alongside you—even when you can't see it—almost all the way to the trailhead.

If you don't have a car at both trailheads, head (right) southwest along Highway 93 to the Kindersley Pass parking lot—an extra 1.2 kilometers.

53 Kimpton Creek Trail

Highlights: A short hike along Kimpton Creek with views of the Devils Tooth range.
Type of hike: Day hike; out-and-back.
Total distance: 9.6 kilometers.
Difficulty: Easy.
Hiking time: 2½–3½ hours.
Elevation at trailhead: 1,200 meters.
Elevation gain: 300 meters.
Topo maps: Kootenay National Park (GemTrek Publishing); Tangle Peak, 82/J12.

Finding the trailhead: Follow Highway 93 to a small parking area approximately 7.5 kilometers from the park's west gate. The trailhead is on the south side of the highway. Walk back down the highway 100 meters from the parking lot and cross the footbridge over Sinclair Creek to begin the hike.

Key points:
  0.0   Trailhead.
  4.8   End of trail sign.

Kimpton Creek Trail

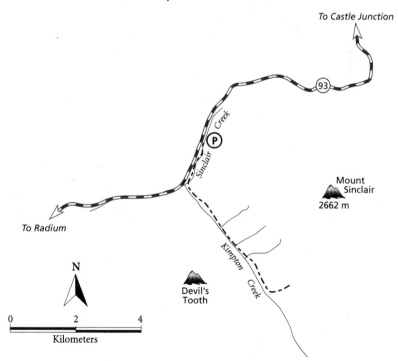

The hike: Avoid your instinct to follow the beaten path that heads north out of the parking area; that trail will lead you along Sinclair Creek, but that's about it. Leave the parking lot and head downstream along the highway approximately 100 meters until you reach the footbridge that will take you across

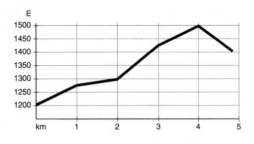

Sinclair Creek and onto Kimpton Creek Trail. Turn left (east) here. The trail is relatively flat for the first 1.5 kilometers before climbing gently to a high point of 1,470 meters. At this point the trail heads northeast and you drop back down into the densely forested valley before running into an end-of-trail sign that stops you quite suddenly.

Similar to the Redstreak Creek Trail, this hike runs through a forested valley along a creek. However, you do gain views of the Devils Tooth Range and its many avalanche chutes to your right (south) as you hike through the shaded banks of Kimpton Creek. We spotted our first black bear of the season on this trail and watched him momentarily as he dug for berries in one of the four avalanche chutes we passed by; he was at least 200 meters away from us.

54 Redstreak Creek Trail

Highlights:	A short walk through the trees.
Type of hike:	Day hike; out-and-back.
Total distance:	5.2 kilometers.
Difficulty:	Easy.
Hiking time:	1–1½ hours.
Elevation at trailhead:	995 meters.
Elevation gain:	160 meters.
Topo maps:	Kootenay National Park (GemTrek Publishing); Tangle Peak, 82J/12.

Finding the trailhead: Follow Highway 93 to a small parking area approximately 4.3 kilometers from the park's west gate. The trailhead is on the south side of the highway.

Key points:
- 0.0 Trailhead.
- 2.6 End-of-trail sign.

The hike: This is the perfect hike if you've been driving for some time and just want to get out of the car to stretch your legs on a short walk. The trail, which begins by crossing Sinclair Creek on a wooden foot bridge, starts out with a moderate climb through a series of switchbacks. You will hear Red-

Redstreak Creek Trail

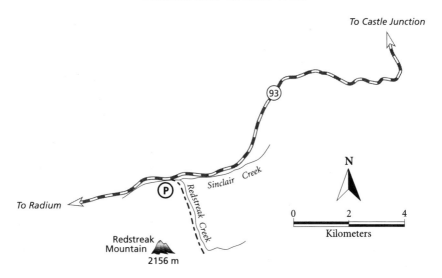

To Castle Junction

To Radium

Sinclair Creek

Redstreak Creek

Redstreak
Mountain
2156 m

N

0   2   4
Kilometers

streak Creek beneath you to your left (north) as you pass through a forest filled with lodgepole pine, white spruce, Douglas fir, and aspen. Approximately 1.0 kilometer into the trail you can catch a glimpse of Redstreak Mountain (2,156 m) through the trees to your right (south); otherwise, views are very limited. The trail ends abruptly alongside trickling Redstreak Creek in this heavily forested valley.

55 Juniper Trail

Highlights:	This short trail leads you through cool forest to Sinclair Falls and one of the driest sections of Kootenay National Park, which offers views of the Columbia Valley.
Type of hike:	Short walk; shuttle.
Total distance:	3.6 kilometers.
Difficulty:	Moderate.
Hiking time:	1½–2 hours.
Elevation at trailhead:	800 meters.
Elevation gain:	Minimal.
Topo maps:	Kootenay National Park (GemTrek Publishing); Radium Hot Springs, 82 K/9.

Finding the trailhead: You can start the Juniper Trail in one of two places: the west side of Highway 93 just past the Kootenay National Park west gate or the Radium Hot Springs parking lot on the west side of Highway 93. Washrooms are available just past the west gate on the east side of the road.

Juniper Trail

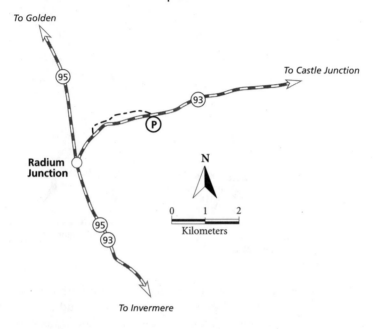

To Golden

To Castle Junction

(95)

(93)

P

**Radium
Junction**

N

(95)
(93)

0   1   2
Kilometers

To Invermere

This is a shuttle hike, so if you're traveling with a group, consider leaving one car at each end of the trail. That way you can avoid backtracking to your car after your hike.

Key points:
- 0.0   Trailhead.
- 0.4   Trail junction.
- 0.5   Sinclair Falls.
- 0.6   Creek crossing.
- 1.6   Fenced viewpoint.
- 2.3   View of Columbia Valley.
- 3.6   End of trail.

The hike: For an interpretive trail, this hike is surprisingly steep in places. But if you plan your route carefully, you can reward yourself afterward with a refreshing dip in Radium Hot Springs. That's why we started the trail just past the Kootenay National Park west gate instead of the more popular starting point, the Radium Hot Springs parking lot.

The trailhead is located on the west side of Highway 93 just past the Kootenay National Park west Gate. The first part of the trail descends 40 meters through a forest of lodgepole pine and western red cedar. This is the cool part of the trail, so enjoy it while it lasts. At 0.4 kilometer you'll reach a trail junction. Turn right here and head toward Sinclair Falls and Radium Hot Springs. Just 40 meters later you'll reach a directional sign for Sinclair Falls. Follow the trail 200 meters to your right for a great view of the falls, which have been carving a path through the underlying limestone for the last 10,000 years.

At 0.6 kilometer, you'll cross Sinclair Creek. Immediately after the bridge you'll start gaining elevation through a series of switchbacks. This dry, sunny section of the trail—the driest area of the park—is home to snakes, grasshoppers, Rocky Mountain bighorn sheep, and mountain lions (which are seldom seen). Black-eyed susans, harebells, arrowhead balsam root, dogwood, three varieties of juniper, and Douglas fir are among the flowers and trees you're likely to see on this part of the trail.

At 1.6 kilometers you'll reach a fenced viewpoint on the north rim of Sinclair Canyon. Look behind you (southwest) for a fabulous view of the Columbia Valley. You'll reach another great spot to view the Columbia Valley, as well as a bench where you can rest, at 2.3 kilometers. From here it's primarily downhill to the Radium Hot Springs parking lot. The fastest way back to your car (if it's parked at the other end of the trail) is the sidewalk along the highway.

56 Redstreak Campground/ Sinclair Canyon Trail

Highlights:	This well-traveled trail leads you through a shady forest to Sinclair Canyon.
Type of hike:	Short walk; shuttle.
Total distance:	3.2 kilometers.
Difficulty:	Easy.
Hiking time:	1–1½ hours.
Elevation at trailhead:	965 meters.
Elevation gain:	Minimal.
Topo maps:	Kootenay National Park (GemTrek Publishing); Radium Hot Springs, 82 K/9.

Finding the trailhead: You can start the Redstreak Campground/Sinclair Canyon Trail in one of three places—just after Kootenay National Park's west gate on the south side of Highway 93, at the Radium Hot Springs Pools, or from Redstreak Campground. We started at the Hot Springs, which are located on the south side of Highway 93, approximately 3 kilometers east of Radium Hot Springs Village. Parking is available on both the north and south sides of Highway 93 just before the springs. You'll find the trailhead just after the pool entrance to your right (south). Washrooms, refreshments, and souvenirs are available near the trailhead.

Key points:
- 0.0 Trailhead.
- 2.2 Redstreak Campground Trail junction; continue straight ahead (west).
- 2.4 Sinclair Canyon Viewpoint.
- 3.2 Highway 93.

Redstreak Campground/Sinclair Canyon Trail

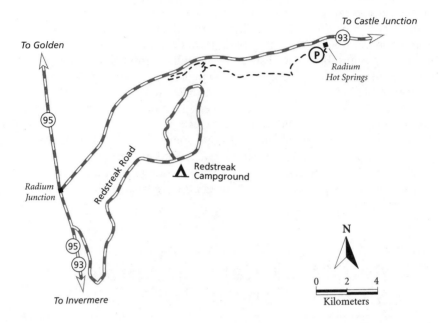

The hike: Used primarily by campers heading for the hot springs, this cool, shady trail offers a welcome break from the heat, along with views of Sinclair Canyon. After a surprisingly steep climb, the trail travels through a forest of western red cedar and Douglas fir and past the Place of Silence Peace Park—basically just a quiet place to relax. Several strategically placed benches provide spots to rest along the way.

At 2.2 kilometers you'll reach a trail junction; continue straight ahead (west) to complete the Sinclair Canyon Trail, or take a right (south) for Redstreak Campground. Approximately 200 meters later you reach a fenced viewpoint for Sinclair Canyon to your right (north). The view isn't much different here from what you see from the road. From here you'll descend 800 meters to a spot just north of the park's west gate on Highway 93.

57 Redstreak Campground Loop

Highlights:	Ideal for an after-dinner stroll, this trail offers views of the Columbia Valley.
Type of hike:	Short walk; loop.
Total distance:	2.2 kilometers.
Difficulty:	Easy.
Hiking time:	1 hour.
Elevation at trailhead:	970 meters.
Elevation gain:	Minimal.
Topo maps:	Kootenay National Park (GemTrek Publishing); Radium Hot Springs, 82 K/9.

Finding the trailhead: As the name implies, the Redstreak Campground Loop is located at Kootenay's Redstreak Campground. To get to the campground, take a left (east) off Highway 95 at the Kootenay National Park Information Centre and follow Redstreak Road to the campground. If you're not camping, look for a parking spot in the parking area just past the campground entrance on your right (south). To find the trailhead, head left (north) toward camping area A, and follow the dirt trail to your right (west) 400 meters through the campground.

Redstreak Campground Loop

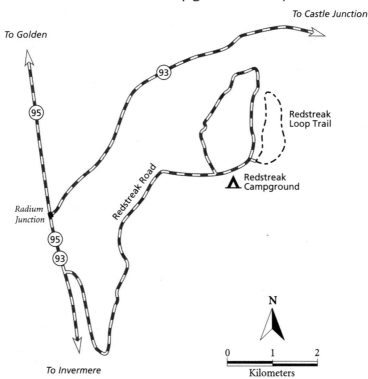

Key points:
- 0.0　Trailhead.
- 0.9　Scenic viewpoint.
- 2.2　Loop ends at campground.

The hike: Believe it or not, it's easy to lose your way on the unmarked dirt trails leading to the Redstreak Campground Loop trailhead; if you get lost, follow signs for the campground amphitheater.

Perfect for an after-dinner stroll, the Redstreak Campground Loop climbs steadily through a dry forest dominated by Douglas fir to a viewpoint overlooking the Columbia Valley at 900 meters. Mountain goldenrod, red clover, and fleabane provide a burst of color along the way. On your way to the viewpoint, bear right at all forks in the trail. The rest of the loop descends 1.3 kilometers through a cool, shady forest to the campground.

58　Valley View Trail

Highlights:	This quick, easy trail offers views of the Columbia Valley.
Type of hike:	Short walk; shuttle.
Total distance:	1.4 kilometers.
Difficulty:	Easy.
Hiking time:	1–1½ hours.
Elevation at trailhead:	975 meters.
Elevation loss:	Minimal.
Topo maps:	Kootenay National Park (GemTrek Publishing); Radium Hot Springs, 82 K/9.

Finding the trailhead: The Valley View Trail is located at Redstreak Campground. To get to the campground, take a left (east) off Highway 93 at the Kootenay National Park Information Centre, and follow Redstreak Road to the campground. If you're not camping, look for a parking spot in the parking area just past the campground entrance on your right (south). To find the trailhead, head left (north) toward camping area A and follow the dirt trail to your left (west) 100 meters through the campground.

Key Points
- 0.0　Trailhead.
- 0.8　Radium Hot Springs Trail junction; continue straight ahead (west).
- 0.9　Picnic area and scenic viewpoint.
- 1.4　Park Information Centre.

The hike: If you have limited time, the Valley View Trail is definitely not the way to go. Although it's quite easy compared with the park's other short hikes, there's not much to see and the constant traffic noise can be quite distracting.

Valley View Trail

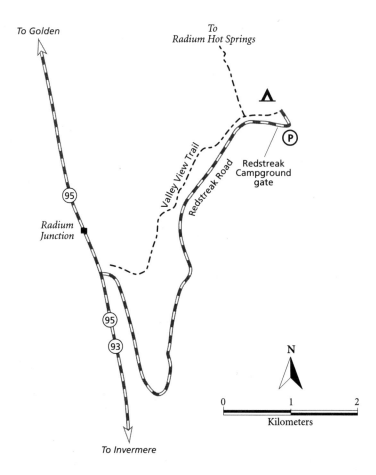

The self-guided Valley View Trail meanders through a dry Douglas fir forest, offering views of the Columbia Valley and the Village of Radium Hot Springs. You'll find a series of interpretive signs on your gradual descent to Radium Hot Springs.

At 800 meters you'll reach a trail junction; continue straight ahead (west) along the trail to reach Radium Hot Springs Village via the Valley View Trail. You can also turn right (northwest) at this point to head directly to Radium Hot Springs Village. Just 100 meters later you'll reach a small picnic area, which provides views of the Columbia River Valley and Radium Hot Springs Village. From here it's 500 meters downhill to Radium Hot Springs Village.

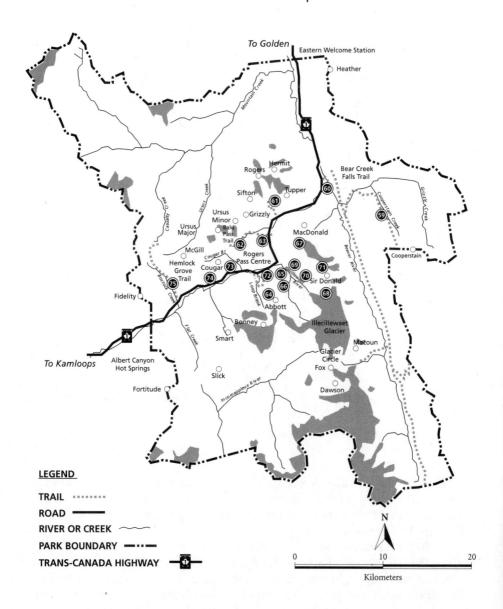

Glacier National Park
Trail Locator Map

To Golden

Eastern Welcome Station

Heather

Mountain Creek

Bear Creek
Falls Trail

Rogers

Hermit

Sifton

Tupper

60

59

Cooperstown Creek

Grizzly Creek

Grizzly

Ursus
Minor

Balu
Pass
Trail

Ursus
Major

62

63

MacDonald

67

Cooperstain

McGill

Cougar Bt.

Rogers
Pass Centre

Beaver River

Hemlock
Grove
Trail

Cougar

73

69

71

75

74

72

65

70

Sir Donald

Fidelity

66

68

64

Abbott

Bonney

Illecillewaet
Glacier

Smart

Macoun

To Kamloops

Albert Canyon
Hot Springs

Glacier
Circle

Fox

Slick

Fortitude

Incomaplewx River

Dawson

Illecillewaet River

Loop Brook

Flat Creek

Bartock Creek

Casualty Creek

Ursus Creek

LEGEND

TRAIL · · · · · · · ·

ROAD ——————

RIVER OR CREEK ～～～

PARK BOUNDARY —·—·—

TRANS-CANADA HIGHWAY

N

0   10   20

Kilometers

Glacier National Park

Glacier National Park is aptly named because of the 400 glaciers that cover a tenth of its overall area. This park also marks the history of the development of the Canadian Pacific Railway's transcontinental line, which attracts train enthusiasts from across the country.

The park was established in 1886 along with its easterly neighbor, Yoho National Park. These parks were revered by pioneers who were working on the Canadian Pacific Railway and who had chartered this territory to complete the country's transcontinental line.

Over one hundred years ago railway entrepreneurs determined that the scenery along the rail line suggested the potential for tourism. Lodges and hotels were built in what had been completely uncharted wilderness just a few years earlier. The Glacier House hotel and recreation complex was the first lodge built in the area, and it attracted visitors from all over North America. Following its closure in 1925, facility development in the park was limited to trail construction until the early '60s, when TransCanada Highway 1 was built. At this time facilities were built for the "automobile oriented" visitor, including viewpoints, campgrounds, and picnic areas.

Glacier is located 410 kilometers west of Calgary and 575 kilometers east of Vancouver. It's a two-and-a-half-hour drive from Banff and is located in the Selkirk and Purcell Mountains, which are part of the Columbia Mountain Range.

The park's 1,349 kilometers remain relatively unspoiled, despite the fact that the TransCanada Highway runs right through the middle of its famous valley—Rogers Pass. The pass was named after Major A. B. Rogers, who was said to have discovered the valley while working for the Canadian Pacific Railway.

Although it attracts millions of visitors a year, most visitors stop only for gas and snacks at the Rogers Pass Centre, taking little time to explore any of the park's fantastic history—like the Loop Brook pillars and Glacier House ruins. The Rogers Pass Centre, which serves both Glacier and Mount Revelstoke National Parks, features an eighty-seat theater and displays on railway history, park ecology, and recreation. Parks Canada staff are also available at the center to answer questions or assist with permit or park pass purchases.

Along with an almost guaranteed glimpse of wildlife, you'll find abandoned rights-of-way, stone bridges, equipment, and snow sheds as well as many other structures associated with construction of the railway. This area is well known for its spectacular mountain views, cedar and hemlock trees (similar to those found in coastal rain forests), valley-bottom strolls, and steep, tough hikes. It features a little something for every outdoor adventurer.

SEASONS AND WEATHER

Located in the Columbia Mountain region of British Columbia's interior wet belt, Glacier's climate is characterized by high precipitation, heavy snow- fall, and moderate winter temperatures. Generally, summer (July through August) and winter (December through February) are the best times to enjoy park trails—for hiking, cross-country skiing, or snowshoeing. Snow season is mid-October through mid-June, but snow can fall anytime at higher ele- vations, so it's a good idea to carry a good weatherproof jacket and to dress in layers—regardless of the weather at the trailhead.

Regular weather reports, including fire danger and lightning forecasts, are available at the Rogers Pass Centre or on-line (see Appendix A). You may also want to pick up a copy of Falcon's *Reading Weather* at your local bookstore.

BASIC SERVICES

The Rogers Pass Centre, located at the summit of Rogers Pass on Tran- sCanada Highway 1, offers services including gas, a restaurant, and limited convenience shopping. The nearest communities are Golden, 80 kilometers east of Rogers Pass Centre, and Revelstoke, 72 kilometers to the west. Full services, including emergency medical treatment, are available at either lo- cation. The only commercial accommodation available in Glacier is the Glacier Park Lodge at Rogers Pass. The nearest commercial airports are at Kamloops and Kelowna, British Columbia, and Calgary, Alberta.

FRONTCOUNTRY CAMPGROUNDS

There are two highway-accessible campgrounds in Glacier, which operate on a first-come, first-served basis. Illecillewaet Campground, the gateway to seven spectacular day hikes, has sixty sites and is located 3 kilometers west of Rogers Pass summit. Check in at the campground's staffed welcome cen- ter. Loop Brook Campground, with its interpretive trail, has twenty sites and is located 5 kilometers west of Rogers Pass summit. Both campgrounds are open June through October and feature flush toilets, log kitchen shelters, food lockers, firewood, and drinking water. There are also overflow camp- sites at the Sir Donald Picnic Area during July and August; these sites are assigned by staff at the Rogers Pass Centre and at the Illecillewaet Welcome Station. All campsites cost CDN $13.00 per night.

BACKCOUNTRY CAMPGROUNDS

Glacier has three designated backcountry campsites on the Bald Hills, above the Copperstain Trail: Copperstain Pass, Caribou Pass, and 20-Mile. Each site has tent pads and food storage poles, but no open fires are permitted. Ran- dom camping is also permitted 5 kilometers from the pavement throughout the park.

A Wilderness Pass is required for all backcountry camping in Glacier Na- tional Park. Available from the Rogers Pass Centre, passes cost CDN $6.00 per person per night or CDN $42.00 for an annual pass.

59 Copperstain Trail

Highlights:	An uphill hike through the trees to reach Copperstain Creek Valley and the Copperstain Pass Campsite. Once you've reached this backcountry destination, you can explore the alpine meadows of Bald Mountain.
Type of hike:	Backpack hike; out-and-back.
Total distance:	32 kilometers.
Difficulty:	Moderate.
Hiking time:	2 days.
Elevation at trailhead:	920 meters.
Elevation gain:	1,128 meters.
Topo maps:	Rogers Pass (Glacier National Park, The Adventure Map); Blaeberry, 82 N/6.

Finding the trailhead: Follow TransCanada Highway 1 approximately 12 kilometers west of Glacier National Park's east boundary or 33 kilometers south of the west boundary, and turn south at the Beaver Valley turnoff. Follow the short secondary road to the southwest end of the parking area, where you'll reach the trailhead for the Beaver River Trail. This trail joins the Copperstain Trail in 4.8 kilometers. There is an outhouse in the parking area.

Key points:

0.0	Trailhead.
4.8	Trail junction; head left (east).
6.3	Suspension bridge over Grizzly Creek.
7.7	Stream crossing.
9.2	Bridge, but no stream.
10.2	Stream crossing on a wooden footbridge.
10.9	Stream crossing.
11.2	Stream crossing.
12.9	Stream crossing.
13.4	Enter an old burn with a view of Copperstain Mountain.
16.0	Copperstain Pass Campsite.

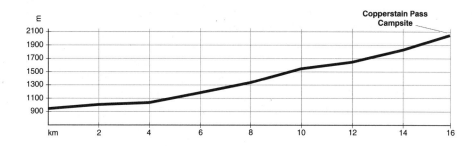

Copperstain Trail

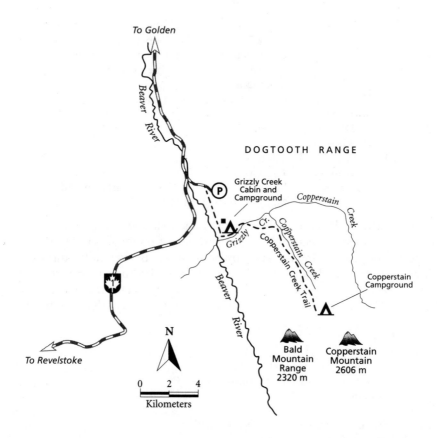

The hike: It's a long uphill hike to reach Copperstain Pass Campsite, and unlike many of the phenomenal day hikes in Glacier National Park, the views on this trail are limited. In fact, you won't see anything but trees for the first 13 kilometers on this trail. However, once you do reach the campsite, you will find solitude—and likely the largest alpine meadow you've ever seen.

Head southeast on the Beaver River Trail. You'll immediately gain a nice view of the Dogtooth Range to the left (east), but this will be the only view you have until you've hiked to the Copperstain Creek Valley, 13.4 kilometers farther down the trail. The trail turns right (southeast) onto a nice wide-open fire road in a forest filled with Douglas fir, lodgepole pine, beautiful western red cedar, and hemlock. Here you may see some fireweed, arnica, and Indian paintbrush, as well as the occasional mauve fleabane, but don't expect to see many more wildflowers along the way.

For the first hour you'll hear a lot of highway noise on this trail. At 4.6 kilometers you'll see Grizzly Creek to your right (north) before meeting the Copperstain Trail junction; head left (east) here along the north side of the

Badly charred lodgepole pine, the result of an old burn, remain standing along the Copperstain Trail.

creek. At about 6 kilometers you'll reach a fork; the trail to the right (south) will take you down to the Grizzly Cabin and campground. There's room for one tent here, but the cabin—not intended for public use—is filled with mouse droppings; avoid it.

Follow the main trail for another 300 meters to cross Grizzly Creek on a suspension bridge. From here the trail goes left (southeast) through an alpine meadow and will be heavily overgrown for about 100 meters. At about 6.6 kilometers you'll reenter the woods on a well-maintained trail. At about 7.7 kilometers you'll gain a bit of a view across the valley as you cross over a small stream; you'll notice that the climb intensifies here as you begin a short switchback section.

At about 11 kilometers you'll gain a glimpse of an unnamed peak through the trees; about 500 meters farther down the trail, you'll see an avalanche path off to your left (east). After hiking 13.4 kilometers uphill you'll finally come out of the trees into Copperstain Creek Valley. High above you to the right (west) sits the Copperstain warden's cabin, and you'll see Copperstain Mountain (2,606 m) straight ahead (southeast). You'll also notice that you're standing in the midst of an old burn. The lodgpole pine left standing throughout the valley are all charred.

Once you reach the campsite at Copperstain Pass, you'll have a good view of Copperstain Mountain to the east and Bald Mountain (2,326 m), its range, and the alpine meadows that seem to go on forever to the west. The views here are different from many of the others in Glacier National Park; the more subdued Purcell Mountains that sit off to your left (east) are in stark contrast to the crags of the Selkirk Ranges that sit to your right (west). While the marked trail ends here, you can explore the alpine meadows and continue south for about 7 kilometers to Caribou Pass and the Beaver Valley trail.

As you're leaving the campsite the views will be much nicer than those afforded on the way in; you can see the Purcells as well as the Dogtooth Range off to the right (east) as you make your way back to the parking area.

60 Bear Creek Falls

Highlights:	This short walk through the forest will take you to the base of Bear Falls.
Type of hike:	Short walk; out-and-back.
Total distance:	2 kilometers.
Difficulty:	Easy.
Hiking time:	30 minutes–1 hour.
Elevation at trailhead:	975 meters.
Elevation loss:	Minimal.
Topo maps:	Rogers Pass (Glacier National Park, The Adventure Map); Blaeberry, 82 N/6.

Finding the trailhead: Follow TransCanada Highway 1 approximately 13 kilometers west of Glacier National Park's east boundary or 10 kilometers southeast of Rogers Pass Centre; turn south, following the secondary road down to an unmarked trailhead. There is no signage for this trail anywhere. There is, however, a sign on the highway that reads VIEWPOINT 200M, and at the trailhead there is the standard hiking symbol. You'll only meet a BEAR FALLS sign once you reach the base of the waterfall.

Key points:
0.0 Trailhead at the west end of the parking area.
1.0 Bear Falls.
2.0 Parking area.

The hike: This short, steep walk through a forest of hemlock and Douglas fir is quite rewarding. You'll see plenty of wildflowers along the way, including dwarf dogwood, one-leafed foamflower, white clover, pearly everlasting, queen's cup, and oxeye daily in abundance. Toward the end of the trail you'll reach a wooden footbridge that crosses Connaught Creek, an excellent viewpoint for the waterfall, which is really quite spectacular. Continue along the straight trail heading up the stairs to the base of the falls. Here you'll inevitably be sprayed, but you will spot a few dancing arnicas.

Bear Creek Falls

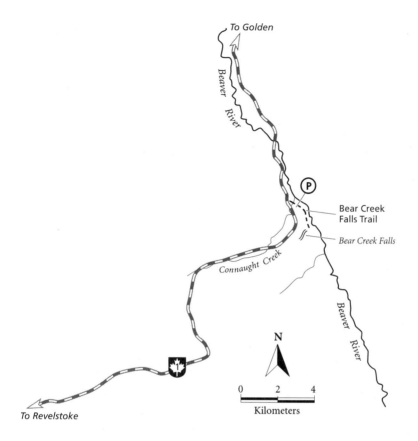

61 Hermit Trail

Highlights:	This short but incredibly steep hike offers fantastic views of Mount Tupper, the Swiss Glacier, Tupper Glacier, the Hermit, and Rogers Peak.
Type of hike:	Day hike; out and back.
Total distance:	5.6 kilometers.
Difficulty:	Strenuous.
Hiking time:	3½–4½ hours.
Elevation at trailhead:	1,290 meters.
Elevation gain:	770 meters.
Topo maps:	Rogers Pass (The Adventure Map); Blaeberry, 82 N/6.

Finding the trailhead: The Hermit trailhead is located on the north side of TransCanada Highway 1, approximately 23 kilometers west of Glacier National Park's east gate and just 1.6 kilometers east of Rogers Pass Centre. Parking and an outhouse are located at the trailhead.

Key points:

0.0	Trailhead.
0.5	Creek crossing.
1.4	Creek crossing.
2.0	Creek crossing.
2.2	Waterfall.
2.8	Trail ends.
5.6	Back at trailhead.

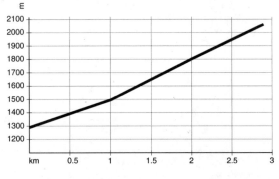

The hike: This trail is a natural stairmaster; you'll gain 750 meters of elevation in just 2.8 kilometers. But on a clear-blue day, the scenery from the top, as well as from several viewpoints along the way, more than compensates for the strenuous climb. If it's cloudy or foggy, skip this hike; you'll miss all the prime views.

The trail begins in a damp, mossy forest of western red cedar, Douglas fir, and western hemlock. You'll start climbing immediately through a series of switchbacks. Just 500 meters into the trail you'll cross a tributary of Connaught Creek and traverse a short, rocky slide area. At 900 meters look to your right (southwest) for the first of several great views of the avalanche slopes across the valley on Mount McDonald (2,878 m) and Avalanche Mountain (2,850 m).

At 1.3 kilometers you'll enjoy one of the best views on this trail; look to your right (east) for a fantastic vista of Mount Tupper (2,728 m) and the Hermit (3,094 m). You'll cross additional tributaries of Connaught Creek at approximately 1.4 and 2 kilometers.

At 2.1 kilometers to your right (southeast), you'll enjoy impressive views of the avalanche slopes on Mount McDonald and Avalanche Mountain. Just 100 meters later, don't miss the tumbling waterfall on the Hermit to your

Hermit Trail

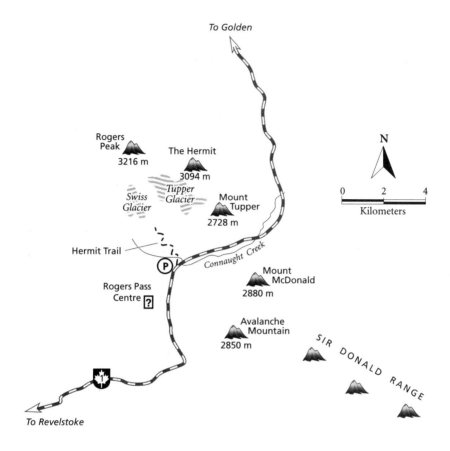

right (east), as well as the views behind you (south) of the Sir Donald Range. The last 200 meters of the trail involve a painfully steep scramble, which rewards you with excellent views to your north and northeast of Mount Tupper, the Tupper Glacier, the Hermit, Rogers Peak (3,216 m), and the Swiss Glacier.

62 Balu Pass

Highlights:	After 1.0 kilometer through the forest, the trail enters an alpine valley, traversing many old avalanche passes as you climb to Balu Pass.
Type of hike:	Day hike; out-and-back.
Total distance:	5 kilometers.
Difficulty:	Moderate.
Hiking time:	3–4 hours.
Elevation at trailhead:	1,330 meters.
Elevation gain:	712 meters.
Topo maps:	Rogers Pass (Glacier National Park, The Adventure Map); Glacier, 82 N/5.

Finding the trailhead: Follow TransCanada Highway 1 approximately 23.4 kilometers west of Glacier National Park's east boundary or 21.6 kilometers southeast of the west boundary to the Rogers Pass Centre on the north side of the highway. You can begin the trail at the north end of the parking area. The trailhead is well marked. There are washrooms at the Rogers Pass Centre.

Key points:

0.0	Trailhead at the west side of Rogers Pass Centre.
1.1	Enter the alpine valley to Balu Pass.
2.5	Waterfalls off Grizzly Mountain.
2.6	Footbridge over Connaught Creek.
3.7	Enter the alpine meadow below Balu Pass.
5.0	Top of Balu Pass.
10.0	Parking area.

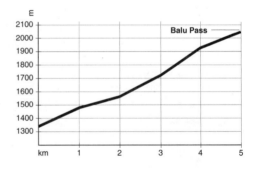

The hike: Balu means bear, and as you pass through the forest and into the alpine valley filled with old avalanche paths, you will feel the trail has been aptly named. This type of habitat provides the perfect feeding opportunity for bears, which in addition to digging through the chutes for a menu of grasses, glacier lilies, and a favorite, cow parsnip, will dig out marmots and seek ground squirrels for their high fat content. As we walked up this path yelling "Hello, bears; coming through," we saw four marmots—and thankfully, no signs of bears.

This hike, which allows for fantastic views after just a 1-kilometer trek, is well worth the trip. After leaving the trailhead you'll climb a root-filled path through a forest filled with hemlock and Douglas fir before dropping down into the kelly-green valley of Balu Pass. Here at the 1-kilometer point, you'll be surrounded by thick ferns and alders; you will see Grizzly Moun-

Balu Pass

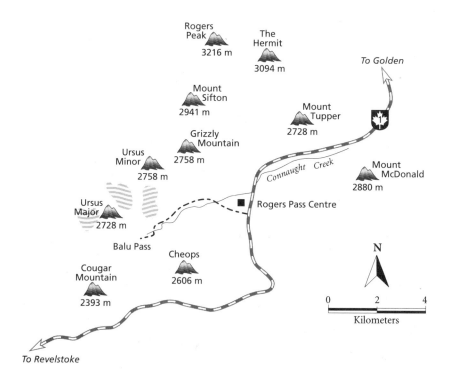

tain (2,758 m) off to your right (north) as well as Connaught Creek. If you look behind you on the trail, you'll see Mount Macdonald (2,880 m).

At 1.5 kilometers you'll cross a small bridge where your views of Grizzly Mountain will improve; just to the west is Ursus Minor (2,758 m). If you're lucky and it's full bloom, you'll see bright-yellow goosefoot violets, white mountain heather, and valerian—the common subalpine wildflower that's the original source of the muscle relaxant and tranquilizer diazepam, known commercially as Valium.

Continue along and at 2.5 kilometers you'll come to a beautiful triple waterfall that slides effortlessly down the slopes of Grizzly Mountain. Hike another 100 meters to cross another small footbridge over Connaught Creek. At 2.8 kilometers Cheops Mountain (2,606 m) is now visible to your left (south); you may even see a few folks scrambling up it.

As you walk into the alpine meadow just below Balu Pass, Ursus Major and its glaciers sit to your right (north), and Cougar Mountain (2,393 m) sits to your left (south). The ascent from this point is a little more difficult as you gain your final 140 meters of elevation. The trip up is well worth the short climb; from the top of the pass, the view of the unbelievably lush valley you just hiked through is spectacular.

63 Abandoned Rails

Highlights:	A short interpretive trail from the Rogers Pass Centre to the Summit Monument along the old rail route that once traveled this course through Rogers Pass. This trail is suitable for both wheelchairs and strollers.
Type of hike:	Shuttle or out-and-back walk.
Total distance:	1.2 kilometers as a shuttle; 2.4 kilometers out-and-back.
Difficulty:	Easy.
Hiking time:	30 minutes–1 hour.
Elevation at trailhead:	1,312 meters.
Elevation gain:	None.
Topo maps:	Rogers Pass (Glacier National Park, The Adventure Map); Glacier, 82 N/5.

Finding the trailhead: Follow TransCanada Highway Highway 1 approximately 23.4 kilometers west of Glacier National Park's east boundary or 21.6 kilometers southeast of the west boundary to the Rogers' Pass Centre. You can begin the trail behind, or just west of, the Centre or at the Rogers' Pass Summit Monument, just 1.5 kilometers further down the highway. The trailhead is well marked. There are washrooms at the Rogers' Pass Centre.

Key points:
- 0.0   Trailhead at the west side of Rogers Pass Centre.
- 1.2   Rogers Pass Summit Monument or Rogers Pass Centre.

The hike: You'll learn a little about the history of Rogers Pass on this short, flat trail that takes you along the rail grade that was abandoned in 1916. The new rail spans the most treacherous 8 kilometers of this pass through an underground tunnel far below your feet. If you're a bit of a train buff or are interested in learning more about the construction of the Canadian Pacific Railway, you may also want to hike Yoho's A Walk in the Past Trail (Hike 20).

You can begin this hike from the Rogers Pass Summit Monument or from the Rogers Pass Centre. The Centre, which looks much like an old snow shed, sits on the only sizable ground safe from avalanches in this entire area. In 1899 an avalanche destroyed the first Rogers Pass railway station, which was located just a few kilometers north of this point. From the Centre head left (west) along the lush, forested trail lined by yellow goosefoot violets, Indian hellebore, alpine forget-me-nots, and trees typical of the Columbia forest. You will see the Asulkan Glacier ahead of you before you come across the remains of shed number 16, one of the thirty-one snow sheds that were built in the most vulnerable spots along the pass to protect the line from avalanches.

At 1.2 kilometers you'll reach the end of the trail and the monument. From here you can see the ranges to the north and south. To the north you'll see Mount Tupper (2,778 m), The Old Man and His Dog, Hermit Mountain (3,110 m),

This nice flat trail spans the rail grade that ran through Rogers Pass before it was abandoned in 1916. Now it's known as the Abandoned Rails Trail.

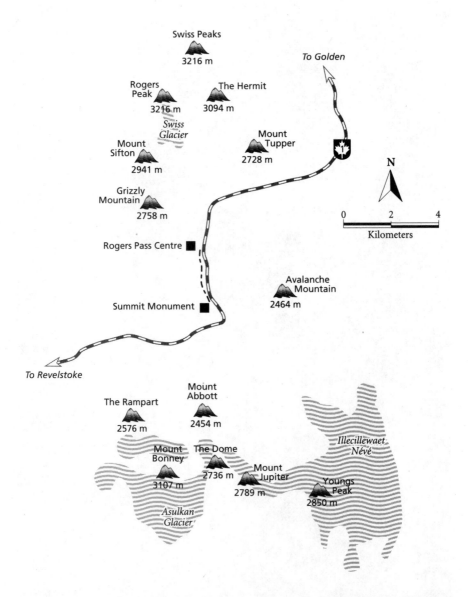

the Swiss Glacier, Truda Peaks (3,117 m), Swiss Peak (3,208 m), Fleming Peak (3,164 m), Grant Peak (3,117 m), Rogers Peak (3,214 m), and Grizzly (2,765 m). To the south you can see the Illecillewaet Glacier, Glacier Crest, the Asulkan Glacier, Mount Abbott (2,465m), the Rampart (2,574 m), and the Dome (2,736 m).

64 Abbott Ridge

Highlights:	An uphill hike to the top of Abbott Ridge. Before gaining extraordinary views of the entire park, you'll pass by Marion Lake and the Abbott Observatory.
Type of hike:	Day hike or loop; out-and-back.
Total distance:	11.8 kilometers.
Difficulty:	Strenuous.
Hiking time:	5–6 hours.
Elevation at trailhead:	1,250 meters.
Elevation gain:	1,040 meters.
Topo maps:	Rogers Pass (Glacier National Park, The Adventure Map); Blaeberry, 82 N/6; Glacier, 82 N/5; Illecillewaet, 82 N/4.

Finding the trailhead: Follow TransCanada Highway 1 approximately 26.3 kilometers south of the park's eastern boundary to the Illecillewaet Campground turnoff on the south side of the highway. Follow the road toward the campground, pass by the welcome station, and head toward the second parking lot. From here you'll see a gravel secondary road just beyond the parking lot. Walk up it approximately 100 meters and head right (west), crossing over the Illecillewaet River. The trailhead will be easy to spot ahead of you beside the Glacier House monument.

Key points:
- 0.0 Glacier House/trailhead.
- 0.1 Trail junction; right (west) to Abbott Ridge.
- 1.0 Bench.
- 1.3 Bench.
- 1.9 Bench.
- 2.5 Marion Lake.
- 3.0 Trail junction; turn right (west) to take the shortcut to Abbott Ridge.
- 4.5 Abbott Observatory.
- 5.0 Abbott Ridge.
- 5.8 Fork in the trail; continue on straight ahead (south) to complete lower loop.
- 8.8 Trail junction; continue straight ahead (north).
- 9.3 Marion Lake.
- 11.8 End of trail.

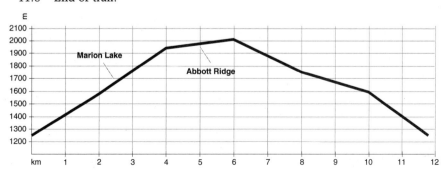

Abbott Ridge • Marion Lake

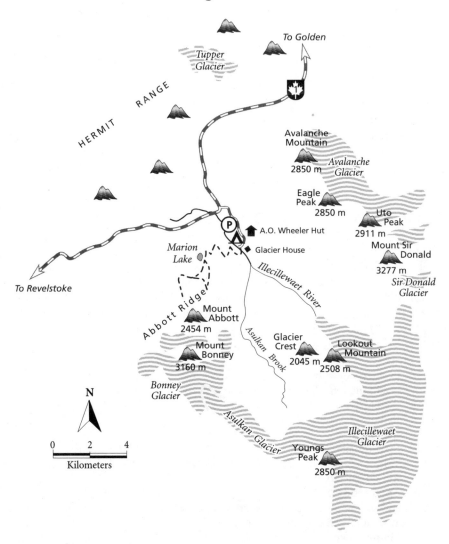

The hike: You'll hike this steep trail in anxious anticipation of what's ahead. The views through the trees are pretty good, but you won't truly be rewarded until you reach the alpine tundra on the lower ridge. And once you're there you'll be tempted to bellow out the *Sound of Music* as you twirl around to soak in the view.

Once you've passed by the Glacier House ruins, you'll reach a trail junction; take a steep right (west) and head up the trail. You'll be met by an abundance of ferns and lush green undergrowth, while surrounded by western red cedar, huge hemlocks, and a sprinkling of valerian, one-leafed foamflower, dwarf dogwood, queen's cup, and arnica. After climbing for 1.0 kilometer you'll reach a well-placed bench; off through the trees you'll have a great view of the waterfall that spills down from Avalanche Crest. Walk on for 100 meters, and you'll gain nice views of Avalanche Mountain (2861m), Eagle Peak (2846m), Uto Peak (2,927 m, and Mount Sir Donald (3,284 m) through the trees to your left (east). At 1.3 kilometers you'll reach another bench.

Continue on; at 1.7 kilometers you'll have a view of the Hermit Range across the highway (north) and the Tupper Glacier to the northwest, which you can see directly above the emerald-green roof of the Best Western at Rogers Pass. At about 2 kilometers you can see the grassy slopes of Avalanche Mountain (2,861 m), which look perfectly manicured thanks to the years of avalanches that have fallen down its northern flank. You may notice a lot of lichens in the trees; the green lichen is known as witch's hair and the black as old man's beard.

At 2.5 kilometers you'll reach Marion Lake. It's somewhat anticlimactic— a bit of a disappointment, really, given the amount of effort it takes to get here. Continue on; at 2.9 kilometers the Illecillewaet Glacier becomes visible through the trees to your left (east).

At 3.1 kilometers the false summit of Abbott Ridge sits in front of you. From here you leave the trees and ascend through the charcoal-gray rock that will lead you to the Abbott Observatory. There are a few short trees around, but you'll be quite exposed at this point, which can only mean one thing—great views. You'll see the Hermit Range, Avalanche Mountain, Eagle Peak, Uto Peak and Mount Sir Donald, the Illecillewaet Glacier, including Lookout Mountain and the huge green Asulkan Valley. From 3.3 kilometers on, we climbed through patches of snow at the end of July.

At about 4.2 kilometers, you'll be standing beside a white tower that contains weather-monitoring equipment. Look up to see the Abbott Observatory, an emergency shelter for the snow research and avalanche personnel who travel up here at least once a week all winter. You'll also see the spectacular snowfields of the Asulkan Glacier for the first time to the south. Follow the trail through the tundra, climbing the ridge with fantastic views all around you. You may see western anemones popping up as well as the occasional alpine buttercup. Once you've reached the observatory, follow the trail to the base of the cliffs, where the trail will switchback to the ridge top. From this windy peak you'll be overwhelmed by the 360-degree views, including Mount Bonney (3,100 m) and its glacier to the west and the Hermit Range across the pass (north). From this vantage point you can see nearly all of Glacier National Park.

Descend the same way you came; about 300 meters below the conservatory, you'll reach an unmarked fork in the trail. If you wish to complete the lower loop of the Abbott Ridge Trail, otherwise known as the "long way," you should follow the trail that leads east toward the Illecillewaet Glacier to your right. This will mean a more gradual descent; you'll avoid picking your way back down through the rocks you've just climbed up, and we're sure your knees will be grateful. Descend through the trees and you'll reach an old rockfall where you'll likely spot a few pikas and some lovely partridgefoot before walking along the bowl of Mount Abbott. You'll follow the

The Abbott Conservatory sits in the alpine tundra.

path back into the forest with a fantastic view of the valley beneath you; if you look closely you can even spot the terra-cotta colored Asulkan Valley Trail. Trees gnarled by the intense weather conditions await you as you reenter the forested trail that will lead you back to the lower loop junction. From here continue straight (north) along the path you followed up here, passing Marion Lake once again on the way down.

65 Marion Lake

See Map on Page 192

Highlights:	An uphill hike through Columbia forest to the cool waters of Marion Lake.
Type of hike:	Day hike; out-and-back.
Total distance:	5 kilometers.
Difficulty:	Moderate.
Hiking time:	3 hours.
Elevation at trailhead:	1,250 meters.
Elevation gain:	425 meters.
Topo maps:	Rogers Pass (Glacier National Park, The Adventure Map); Blaeberry, 82 N/6; Glacier 82 N/5.

Finding the trailhead: Follow TransCanada Highway 1 approximately 26.3 kilometers south of the park's eastern boundary to the Illecillewaet Campground turnoff on the south side of the highway. Follow the road toward the campground, pass by the welcome station, and head toward the second parking lot. From here you'll see a gravel secondary road just beyond the parking lot. Walk up it approximately 100 meters, and head right (west), crossing over the Illecillewaet River. The trailhead will be easy to spot ahead of you beside the Glacier House monument.

Key points:

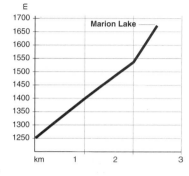

0.0	Glacier House/trailhead.
0.1	Trail junction; right (west) to Abbott Ridge.
1.0	Bench.
1.3	Bench.
1.9	Bench.
2.5	Marion Lake.
5.0	End of trail.

The hike: Two explorers, the Reverend Swanzy and the Reverend William Spotswood Green, put Glacier National Park on the map for nineteenth-century climbers. Marion Lake is named after Green's daughter.

Lakes are very uncommon in the central Columbia Mountains. This one sits in a basin gouged by glaciers during the last ice age. Its water is clear but looks gray-green, like the rocks that line its floor. And it's a tough climb for very little reward, as the lake is difficult to see through the trees. You will, however, have some nice views as you climb along this trail.

Once you've passed by the Glacier House ruins, you'll reach a trail junction; take a steep right (west) and head up the trail. You'll be met by the splendor of this wet montane forest filled with ferns, shrubs, western red cedar, huge hemlocks, and a variety of wildflowers, including valerian, one-leafed foamflower, dwarf dogwood, queen's cup and arnica. After climbing for 1.0 kilometer, you'll reach a well-placed bench; off through the trees you'll have a great view of the waterfall that spills down from Avalanche Crest. Walk on for 100 meters and you'll gain nice views of Avalanche Mountain (2,861 m), Eagle Peak (2,846 m), Uto Peak (2,927 m), and Mount Sir Donald (3,284 m) through the trees to your left (east). At 1.3 kilometers you'll reach another bench.

Continue on; at 1.7 kilometers you'll have a view of the Hermit Range across the highway (north) and the Tupper Glacier to the northwest. You'll reach Marion Lake at 2.5 kilometers. Unfortunately, the trip may be a bit of a disappointment given the amount of effort it takes to get here and the fact that the view of the lake isn't that great.

If you're looking for a nice day hike with the highlight of a glacial blue lake, consider heading to Mount Revelstoke National Park, where you can head out on the Eva/Miller/Jade Lakes Trail. (See Hike 84 for a full description.)

66 Asulkan Valley

Highlights: A pleasant walk through a valley with mountain scenery and waterfalls before you climb into spectacular views of the Asulkan Glacier and its amazing snowfield.
Type of hike: Day hike; out-and-back.
Total distance: 13 kilometers.
Difficulty: Strenuous.
Hiking time: 5–6 hours.
Elevation at trailhead: 1,250 meters.
Elevation gain: 800 meters.
Topo maps: Rogers Pass (Glacier National Park, The Adventure Map); Blaeberry, 82 N/6; Mount Wheeler, 82 N/3.

Finding the trailhead: Follow TransCanada Highway 1 approximately 26.3 kilometers south of the park's eastern boundary to the Illecillewaet Campground turnoff on the south side of the highway. Follow the road toward the campground, pass by the welcome station, and head toward the second parking lot. From here you'll see a gravel secondary road just beyond the parking lot. Walk up it approximately 100 meters, and head right, crossing over the Illecillewaet River. The trailhead will be easy to spot ahead of you beside the Glacier House monument.

Key points:

0.0   Glacier House/trailhead.
0.2   Trail junction; straight ahead (south) for Asulkan Valley.
0.6   Trail junction; straight ahead (south).
1.2   Cross a wooden footbridge over Asulkan Brook.
1.3   Trail junction; straight ahead (south) for Asulkan Valley.
4.1   Creek crossing, no bridge.
5.4   Cross a steel footbridge over Asulkan Brook.
6.5   End of trail.

The hike: At every turn, this feels like a different hike. You start out in the Columbia forest, then you walk through the Asulkan Valley alongside its brook, with fabulous mountain scenery and waterfalls along the way. You then hike through a subalpine meadow and into the interior subalpine, but not before gaining spectacular views of the Asulkan Glacier (south). From here you journey out along a rocky spine that will lead you to the toe of the glacier and its endless snowfields. Outstanding.

Asulkan Valley

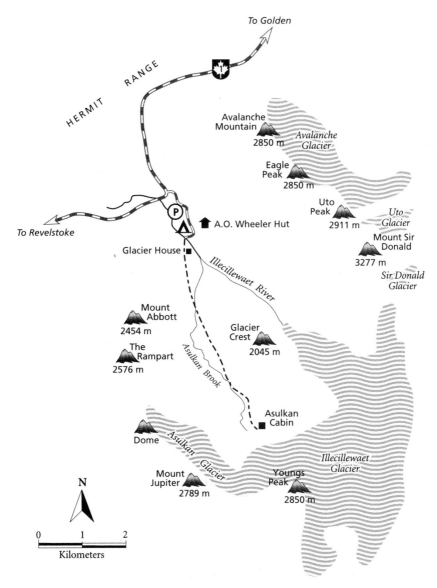

To Golden

HERMIT RANGE

Avalanche Mountain
2850 m

Avalanche Glacier

Eagle Peak
2850 m

Uto Peak
2911 m

Uto Glacier

Mount Sir Donald
3277 m

Sir Donald Glacier

To Revelstoke

P

A.O. Wheeler Hut

Glacier House

Illecillewaet River

Mount Abbott
2454 m

The Rampart
2576 m

Asulkan Brook

Glacier Crest
2045 m

Asulkan Cabin

Dome

Asulkan Glacier

Mount Jupiter
2789 m

Youngs Peak
2850 m

Illecillewaet Glacier

N

0   1   2
Kilometers

The Asulkan Valley Trail starts out on a relatively flat, wide trail with lots of apple-green fern, horsetail, and moss. This is the transition area between the Columbia forest and the interior subalpine. Both mountain and western hemlock grow side by side along this trail, which is also scattered with valerian, alpine buttercups, alpine forget-me-nots, Indian hellebore, and lots of dwarf dogwood. Hike about 200 meters before reaching a trail junction;

A hiker climbs the ridge leading up the Asulkan Valley as it drops off behind him.

continue straight ahead (south) with the Asulkan Brook's thundering sound off to your left (west). At 0.6 kilometer you'll reach another trail junction; continue straight ahead (south).

At 1.2 kilometers you'll have your first really nice view of the Asulkan Glacier ahead of you (south) as you cross the wooden footbridge over Asulkan Brook. Arnica, bouncing in the wet spray cast off by the brook, should meet you at the other side before you pass back into the woods. Just beyond the bridge you'll reach another trail junction; continue straight ahead (south).

As you walk along the valley bottom with the raging brook to your right (west), you'll spot hundreds of beautiful bright-pink monkeyflowers in late July, as well as pearly everlasting and a precious few yellow monkeyflowers that may be visible closer to the brook—but look closely. Here you'll also see a fantastic waterfall spilling off the Rampart (2,574 m), which is just to your right (west) across the valley. Glacier Crest is visible to the left (east); a few hundred meters farther along you'll see another waterfall.

Beyond 4 kilometers the ascent becomes much more challenging, but the view of the glacier makes it worthwhile. Another 100 meters down the trail, you'll have to do a little rock hopping to make it over a rushing creek; on the other side you'll see some Alaska saxifrage, which is commonly found alongside streambanks in these transition areas. At about 4.6 kilometers the trail changes from dirt track and becomes a little more rocky; we spotted a marmot basking in the sun on this section. From here you'll climb a short switchback section through a subalpine meadow that takes you to the end of the valley. I thought this was the end of the trail and was secretly celebrating until I looked off to the right; you'll gain a view of the trail climbing a silt-covered spine—and, yes, that is the trail you'll have to climb.

At 5.4 kilometers you'll cross Asulkan Brook on a stable steel footbridge. As you continue your hike you may notice some iron-rich, rust-colored clay in some of the streams as you pass by. Heading west now you'll have a fantastic view of the Hermit Range (north) as well as the valley you just walked through. Climbing up the spine you spotted earlier, a fellow hiker said it best: "They keep moving the finish line." As you head up this steep trail you'll see a ridge above you, and you'll likely think it will be the beloved end of the trail. No such luck. As you climb over it, you'll see yet another ridge; you'll also see a waterfall, and if you glimpse it quickly enough you'd swear it was an avalanche, as running water seems highly out of place above the huge snowfield that now lies beneath you for as far as you can see. The awesome glacier is off to your left (east) now.

At 6.5 kilometers you'll finally reach the finish line—an end-of-trail sign that rests just beyond a rock cairn and makes the perfect photo backdrop. About 500 meters ahead of you (east) sits the Asulkan Cabin, which Parks Canada owns but the Alpine Club of Canada runs. Apparently this hut was built without permission by a park superintendent, and it's become quite the bone of contention for backcountry skiers, as folks stay at the hut and ski in the bowl all day. By the time the day-trippers get to this part of the trail, there's no fresh snow left, which can make the trip very anticlimactic.

The day we hiked this trail it was 30 degrees Celsius; however, once we reached this point, the temperature dropped by at least 10 degrees, and the wind could knock you over. From our conversations with other hikers, we learned that this point is always particularly windy, so it doesn't make for the greatest lunch spot. Although there is an outhouse, just be careful the wind doesn't catch you off guard on your way out; it's an ugly 1-meter drop off the platform. (Yes, the wind caught me; no, I didn't fall.)

67 Avalanche Crest

Highlights:	This impressive but strenuous hike offers stunning views of the Hermit Range, the Illecillewaet Glacier, the Bonney Glacier, and Rogers Pass.
Type of hike:	Day hike; out and back.
Total distance:	8.4 kilometers.
Difficulty:	Strenuous.
Hiking time:	4–5 hours.
Elevation at trailhead:	1,250 meters.
Elevation gain:	795 meters.
Topo maps:	Rogers Pass (Glacier National Park, The Adventure Map); Blaeberry, 82 N/6; Glacier, 82 N/5; Illecillewaet, 82 N/4.

Finding the trailhead: The Avalanche Crest trailhead is located at Illecillewaet Campground on the south side of TransCanada Highway 1, approximately 18 kilometers west of Glacier National Park's east gate. Turn south off the highway and follow the Illecillewaet Campground road southeast past the welcome station to the end of the road. Park in the small lot on your right (west), and walk 100 meters up the dirt road to your south. The trailhead is located at the top of the road on your right (west). You'll find washrooms at the campground.

Key points:

0.0   Trailhead.
1.8   Scenic viewpoint trail junction; to view the waterfall, turn left (east).
2.6   Asulkan Brook crossing.
4.2   Trail ends on Avalanche Mountain.
8.4r Back at trailhead.

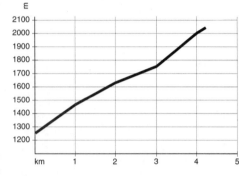

The hike: If you're looking for both fantastic views and a healthy workout, this hike's for you. You can trek for miles in the backcountry and never see the myriad glaciers and mountain peaks you'll see from the top of Avalanche Crest. But don't let the short distance fool you. With its steep incline, this hike will keep you occupied at least half a day.

The initial part of the trail leads you through a lush forest of Douglas fir, hemlock, and western red cedar. Alpine forget-me-nots, dwarf dogwood, bead lilies, and arnica add a spatter of color. There's no easing into this trail; the monstrous climb starts immediately with a series of switchbacks, and the high humidity makes it seem like you're trudging through a tropical rain forest.

Just after the trailhead you'll encounter a fork in the trail; stay to your left (east). At 170 meters you'll catch a glimpse of the Asulkan Brook beneath you to your right (west). At 1.8 kilometers you'll pass a sign for a viewpoint off to your left (east). It's well worth the 1.8-kilometer stroll to either the upper or lower viewpoint to soak in views of the bubbling waterfall. From here you'll also gain a fantastic view of the entire Illecillewaet River Valley to your left (northwest).

At 2.6 kilometers you'll cross the Asulkan Brook. Starting at 3.7 kilometers you'll enjoy impressive views of the Hermit Range behind you to your left (northwest), the Illecillewaet Glacier to your right (south), and the Bonney Glacier behind you to your right (southwest). At this point you'll climb through a brief rocky section before following a series of switchbacks up Avalanche Mountain (2,861 m) to arrive at a small meadow, where the trail ends. From here you'll enjoy tremendous panoramic views of the Asulkan Valley behind you (southwest). You'll also gaze upon Avalanche Mountain and Eagle Peak (2,846 m) straight ahead (north and northeast), Uto Peak

Avalanche Crest

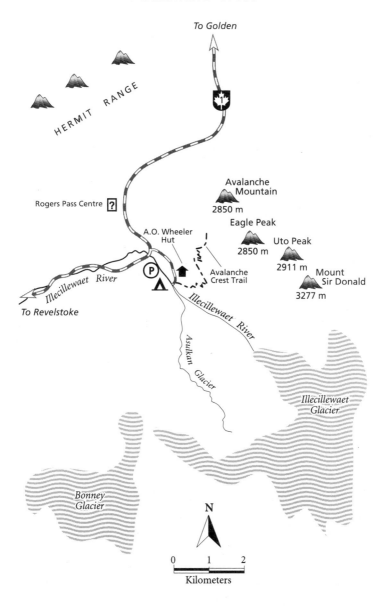

To Golden

HERMIT RANGE

Rogers Pass Centre ?

Avalanche
Mountain
2850 m

Eagle Peak

A.O. Wheeler
Hut

Avalanche
Crest Trail

Uto Peak
2850 m

2911 m

Mount
Sir Donald
3277 m

Illecillewaet River

To Revelstoke

Illecillewaet River

Asulkan Glacier

Illecillewaet
Glacier

Bonney
Glacier

N

0   1   2
Kilometers

(2,927 m) and Mount Sir Donald (3,284 m) to your right (southeast), and Rogers Pass (1,314 m) to your left (northwest), along with continued views of the Illecillewaet and Bonney Glaciers and the Hermit Range.

68 Glacier Crest

<table>
<tr><td>Highlights:</td><td>A nice hike up Glacier Crest with panoramic views, including an up-close look at the Asulkan Glacier.</td></tr>
<tr><td>Type of hike:</td><td>Day hike; out-and-back.</td></tr>
<tr><td>Total distance:</td><td>9.6 kilometers.</td></tr>
<tr><td>Difficulty:</td><td>Moderate.</td></tr>
<tr><td>Hiking time:</td><td>3–5 hours.</td></tr>
<tr><td>Elevation at trailhead:</td><td>1,250 meters.</td></tr>
<tr><td>Elevation gain:</td><td>795 meters (1,005 meters if you scramble to the top of the crest).</td></tr>
<tr><td>Topo maps:</td><td>Rogers Pass (Glacier National Park, The Adventure Map); Blaeberry, 82 N/6; Mount Wheeler, 82 N/3.</td></tr>
</table>

Finding the trailhead: Follow TransCanada Highway 1 approximately 26.3 kilometers south of the park's eastern boundary to the Illecillewaet Campground turnoff on the south side of the highway. Follow the road toward the campground, pass by the welcome station, and head toward the second parking lot. From here you'll see a gravel secondary road just beyond the parking lot. Walk up it approximately 100 meters and head right (west), crossing over the Illecillewaet River. The trailhead will be easy to spot ahead of you beside the Glacier House monument.

Key points:

0.0	Glacier House/trailhead.
0.5	Trail junction; continue straight ahead (south).
0.8	Trail junction; continue straight ahead (south).
1.2	Cross Asulkan Brook.
1.3	Trail junction; head left (southeast).
4.8	Top of Glacier Crest.
9.6	End of trail.

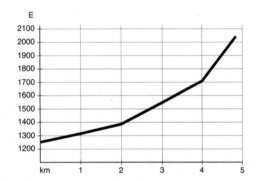

The hike: You won't even notice if you're short of breath after completing the 795-meter ascent to the top of this trail. The scenery is absolutely breathtaking.

At the trailhead for this hike, you'll come across the ruins of Glacier House. After the main line through Rogers Pass was moved underground in 1916, the house no longer attracted explorers. Glacier House was burned in 1929, and here lie its ruins.

Walk alongside the ruins while enjoying the view of the Illecillewaet Glacier straight ahead (southeast). Enter the trees following a wide, dirt trail until you reach the junction for Meeting of the Waters at 0.5 kilometer (see Hike 69), and continue straight ahead (south) to Glacier Crest. At 0.8 kilometer you'll reach another trail junction; continue straight ahead. Cross the rag-

Glacier Crest

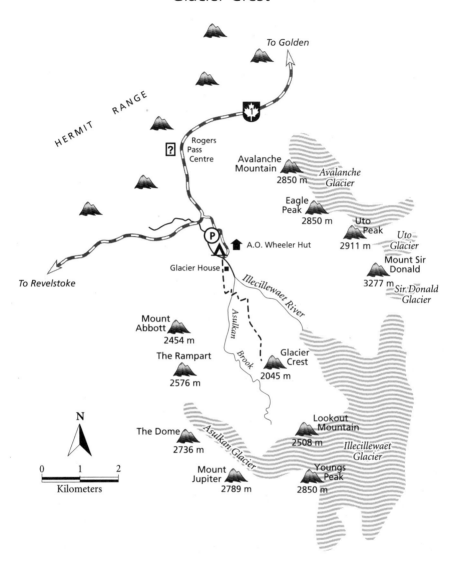

ing Asulkan Brook and you'll immediately reach another trail junction; head left (southeast).

At about 2.6 kilometers you'll see another trail heading off to the left; ignore it and continue along the well-beaten path leading up the switchbacks to your right (south). If it's a hot day this section of trail offers some nice shade, as well as glimpses of cobwebs shining under the sun's rays. Through the trees you'll see Mount Abbott (2,465 m) and the Rampart (2,574 m) off to the right (west). After gaining a few hundred meters you'll be able to look

This hiker is taking a rest at the top of Glacier Crest. Behind him is Mount Sir Donald (right), Avalanche Mountain (left), and Hermit Ridge (across the valley).

north to see Rogers' Pass Centre, the Hermit Range, and Avalanche Mountain (2,861 m).

After the 4-kilometer point you'll leave the trees behind, gaining great views every way you look as you walk through the gray rocks leading up the crest. Looming above you to the southeast is Lookout Mountain (2,508 m), and as you gain a little more elevation you'll see Young's Peak (2,815 m) straight ahead (south). Below it to the right (south) is the Asulkan Pass (2,341 m), then Mount Jupiter and its peaks, with The Dome (2,736 m) beside it to the southwest. Below you lies the Asulkan Valley, and straight across from you (south) is the Asulkan Glacier.

The trail ends with jaw-dropping views at 4.8 kilometers. Find a nice flat rock, and enjoy your lunch here. If the conditions are just right, you can carefully pick your way through the rock to reach the summit of the crest (2,255 m). The panoramic views from this alpine spine are breathtaking.

69 Meeting of the Waters

Highlights:	A nice short walk past the ruins of Glacier House to the confluence of the Illecillewaet River and Asulkan Brook. Perfect for a picnic and afternoon stroll.
Type of hike:	A short loop.
Total distance:	1.0 kilometer.
Difficulty:	Easy.
Hiking time:	30 minutes.
Elevation at trailhead:	1,250 meters.
Elevation gain:	Minimal.
Topo maps:	Rogers Pass (Glacier National Park, The Adventure Map); Blaeberry, 82 N/6.

Finding the trailhead: Follow TransCanada Highway 1 approximately 26.3 kilometers south of the park's eastern boundary to the Illecillewaet Campground turnoff on the south side of the highway. Follow the road toward the campground, pass by the welcome station, and head toward the second parking lot. From here you'll see a gravel secondary road just beyond the parking lot. Walk up this road approximately 100 meters, and follow it to the right (west) as you cross a bridge over the Illecillewaet River. The trailhead will be easy to spot ahead of you beside the Glacier House monument.

Key points:
    0.0   Glacier House/trailhead.
    0.7   Meeting of the Waters.
    1.0   End of trail; follow the secondary road straight ahead (south) to the parking/campground area.

The hike: At the trailhead for this short stroll, you'll meet up with a bit of history—the ruins of Glacier House. Traveling across Canada by train in 1886 was a hungry business, and the Canadian Pacific Railway preferred not to haul their heavy dining cars through the treacherous Rogers' Pass. Instead they stationed a dining car here, on the old route of the railway, so that weary passengers could stretch their legs and eat lunch while enjoying the view of the Illecillewaet Glacier (southeast).

The aptly named Glacier House, a collection of Swiss-style buildings, replaced the dining car in 1887. Until it was shut down in 1925, it hosted nearly 4,000 hungry guests each summer. After the main line through Rogers Pass was moved underground in 1916, the House no longer attracted explorers. Glacier House burned in 1929, and here lie its ruins.

Continue along past the meadows where Glacier House sat while enjoying the view of the Illecillewaet Glacier straight ahead (southeast). Enter the trees following the wide dirt trail until you reach the junction for Meeting of the Waters at 0.5 kilometer. Turn left (east) and walk 200 meters to the confluence of the Illecillewaet River and Asulkan Brook. There's a bench here if you care to stop and take a break; otherwise walk onto the bridge

Meeting of the Waters

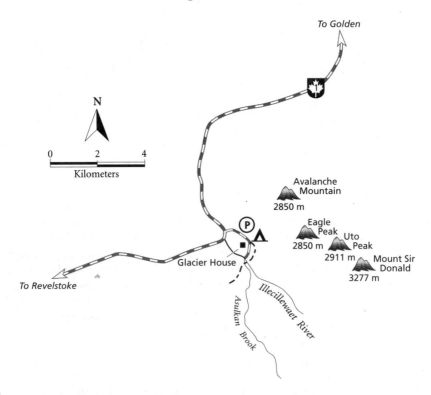

for a better view of the milky-blue water filled with glacial silt. Cross to the other side of the bridge, and follow the trail left (north) back toward the campground.

70 Perley Rock

Highlights:	A challenging hike to the base of Perley Rock.
Type of hike:	Day hike; out-and-back.
Total distance:	11.2 kilometers.
Difficulty:	Strenuous.
Hiking time:	4–5 hours.
Elevation at trailhead:	1,250 meters.
Elevation gain:	897 meters.
Topo maps:	Rogers' Pass (Glacier National Park, The Adventure Map); Blaeberry, 82 N/6.

Finding the trailhead: Follow TransCanada Highway 1 approximately 26.3 kilometers south of the park's eastern boundary to the Illecillewaet Camp-

Here is the black beaded Perley Rock.

ground turnoff on the south side of the highway. Follow the road toward the campground, pass by the welcome station, and head toward the second parking lot. From here you'll see a gravel secondary road just beyond the parking lot. Walk up it approximately 100 meters, passing by the A. O. Wheeler hut, which is tucked away in the woods; you'll see the Perley Rock trailhead right in front of you (south).

Key points:
- 0.0 Trailhead.
- 0.02 Trail junction; continue straight ahead (south).
- 0.9 Illecillewaet River crossing.
- 2.7 Creek crossing.
- 2.8 Creek crossing.
- 3.2 Trail junction; head right (east).
- 5.6 Base of Perley Rock.
- 8.0 Trail junction; head left (southeast).
- 11.2 End of trail.

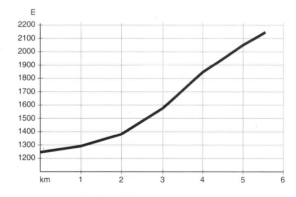

The hike: Many a guest of the Glacier House trekked this historic route to the summit of Perley Rock upon the recommendation of the hotel manager, H. A. Perley. This peak was named on his behalf.

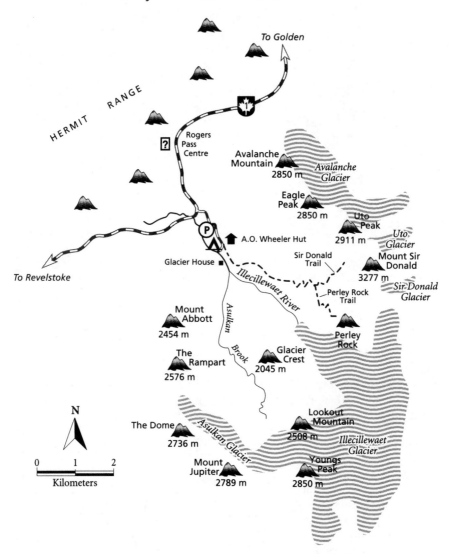

To Golden

HERMIT RANGE

Rogers Pass Centre

Avalanche Mountain
2850 m

Avalanche Glacier

Eagle Peak
2850 m

Uto Peak
2911 m

Uto Glacier

A.O. Wheeler Hut

Sir Donald Trail

Mount Sir Donald
3277 m

Glacier House

Illecillewaet River

Sir Donald Glacier

Perley Rock Trail

To Revelstoke

Mount Abbott
2454 m

Asulkan Brook

Perley Rock

The Rampart
2576 m

Glacier Crest
2045 m

N

The Dome
2736 m

Asulkan Glacier

Lookout Mountain
2508 m

Illecillewaet Glacier

0   1   2
Kilometers

Mount Jupiter
2789 m

Youngs Peak
2850 m

Follow the hike as described for the Sir Donald Trail (Hike 71); at 3.2 kilometers, you'll reach the junction where the trails for Sir Donald and Perley Rock branch off in different directions. Head right (east), following the switchback route along the wooded dirt and pine-needle-packed trail. Within 300 meters you'll venture back out of the trees alongside an old rockfall. From here soak in the views of the Illecillewaet Glacier and Glacier Crest to the left (south), Mount Abbott (2,465 m) to the right (west), and the Hermit Range on the north side of the TransCanada Highway. Lookout Mountain (2,508 m) is also in clear view looming to the right (west) above the glacier.

You'll pass some gorgeous cliffs as well as some large, dead, gnarled trees that could have easily been plucked from the set of *Alice in Wonderland*. From here the trail becomes more rocky as you climb a few switchbacks before coming back out alongside the charcoal-gray rockfall. If you look back down the valley you can see the beginnings of an alluvial fan forming as the streams deposit their glacial silt on their travels. You'll quickly gain views of the top of the Asulkan Glacier and Leda Peak (2,701 m) to the right (south) as you pass through a beautiful heath filled with white, pink, and yellow mountain heather as well as shrubby purple penstemon and the occasional arnica and red Indian paintbrush. Across the valley to the right (southwest) you'll have great views of Mount Abbott, The Rampart (2,574 m), The Dome (2,736 m), Sapphire Col (2,581 m), Castor Peak (2,777 m), and Leda Peak; on a clear day you can even see Mount Jupiter off in the distance to the southwest. Follow the switchbacks under an overhang of black and beige rock as you admire the pink-and-white-spotted heath that surrounds you.

Climbing on, you'll gain great glimpses of the black-beaded Perley Rock. Lookout Mountain and Glacier Crest sit off to the right (west), as you watch Terminal peak growing larger to your left (north). Once you've climbed the last switchback to the base of Perley Rock, stop to admire the phenomenal vista beneath you. If you have a lot of leftover energy after completing this ambitious climb, you can continue along the boulder-filled path to the summit of Perley Rock (2,412 m), where you'll gain an incredible view of the Illecillewaet Glacier. Do not walk out onto the ice without mountaineering gear, and be sure to register with the park warden service before you set out.

71 Sir Donald Trail

See Map on Page 208

Highlights:	What begins as a gentle uphill hike turns into a steep switchback trail to reach the basin of Mount Sir Donald and the Vaux Glacier. Well worth the effort, it's a great hike for a sunny day.
Type of hike:	Day hike; out-and-back.
Total distance:	8 kilometers.
Difficulty:	Strenuous.
Hiking time:	3–5 hours.
Elevation at trailhead:	1,250 meters.
Elevation gain:	705 meters.
Topo maps:	Rogers Pass (Glacier National Park, The Adventure Map); Blaeberry, 82 N/6.

Finding the trailhead: Follow TransCanada Highway 1 approximately 26.3 kilometers south of the park's eastern boundary to the Illecillewaet Campground turnoff on the south side of the highway. Follow the road toward the campground, pass by the welcome station, and head toward the second parking lot. From here you'll see a gravel secondary road just beyond the parking lot. Walk up it approximately 100 meters, passing by the A. O. Wheeler hut, which is tucked away in the woods; you'll see the Sir Donald trailhead right in front of you (south).

Key points:

0.0 Trailhead.

0.02 Trail junction; continue straight ahead (south).

0.9 Illecillewaet River crossing.

2.7 Creek crossing.

2.8 Creek crossing.

3.2 Trail junction; continue straight ahead (east).

4.0 Basin of Mount Sir Donald.

8.0 End of trail.

The hike: If you're hemming and hawing over your decision between hiking Perley Rock or Sir Donald at the shared trail junction, choose Sir Donald. The remaining 800-meter route to its base is relentless, but the trip to the basin and the toe of the Vaux Glacier is definitely worth the steep climb (Perley Rock climbs to a higher elevation; it just does it over 2.4 kilometers).

About 2 meters into this wooded trail you'll reach your first trail junction; continue straight ahead (south) along the softly climbing trail. Once you've walked nearly a kilometer, you'll cross a wooden footbridge over the Illecillewaet River before heading back into the lush, fern-filled forest of western and mountain hemlock. If it's a sunny day you'll walk through rays of sunshine that fall through the thick woods, lighting up the shimmering spider webs and foliage as you pass along this wide dirt trail. In late July we spotted quite a few wildflowers on this route, including tiny purple alpine forget-me-nots, white valerian, and pink monkeyflowers.

Just beyond the 1.0-kilometer point, there will be huge mossy boulders in the woods—one of which has two trees growing out of it. Continue on, and cross over a small brook as you enter a subalpine meadow; you'll have a great view of the river beside you (south). From here the smooth trail changes and has a few roots and rocks mysteriously placed. Look left (east) through the trees to gain your first view of Sir Donald (2,284 m).The vista straight ahead (southeast) is spectacular as you see all the glacial runoff rolling down the lush valley toward you. The Illecillewaet Glacier is off to your right (south), and you'll see Lookout Mountain (2,508 m), Terminal Peak (2,997 m), Sir Donald, and Uto Peak (2,927 m) straight ahead (east).

At about 2 kilometers the trail begins to narrow, and you may see some shrubby penstemon as you continue through the big rocks surrounded by alders. You'll also gain views of the misty falls ahead of you. At 2.7 kilometers you'll come to a small creek crossing that is perfect for dunking your head on a hot summer day (highly recommended). After gaining another 100 meters, you'll come to the base of three roaring waterfalls; pick your way across the creek as you notice three more falls off to your right (southeast). Cross a steel bridge at about 3 kilometers; you can look back to see the valley of Rogers Pass to the north. Enter back into the trees, where you'll likely see some white mountain rhododendron bushes among the alders.

At 3.2 kilometers you'll reach the trail junction for Sir Donald and Perley Rock; continue straight ahead (east), climbing steep switchbacks that pass through an old rockfall. Continue up the spine toward the basin as a waterfall rolls off the cliffs ahead of you.

This trail, like many others in this area, was originally built by the Canadian Pacific Railway as an access route for climbers. Named after Sir Donald A. Smith, the famous railway director who drove the last spike on the CPR in 1885, this mountain's north face is coveted by climbers. Once you reach the basin, their rock-walled bivy site makes the perfect lunch spot. The gray and sand-colored rock of Sir Donald looms above you (east), with Uto Peak (2,927 m) sitting just to its left (north). The view of the Vaux Glacier is quite awesome; however, you may want to keep your distance, as rock and ice often fall from its toe. If you turn around you'll also have phenomenal views of the Asulkan Valley below and Mount Abbott (2,465 m) (southwest), as well as the entire Hermit Range that guards the pass on the north side of the highway.

You could easily spend an afternoon up here scrambling around; from the basin you can see the climbers' route that spans across the green moraine to the north. Another option is to head back down to the trail junction and climb the remaining 2.4 kilometers to the base of Perley Rock. (For a full description see Hike 70.)

72 Loop Brook

Highlights:	This interpretive hike follows a section of the original railway that once looped through Rogers Pass. You'll also gain a spectacular view of the north face of Mount Bonney and its glacier.
Type of hike:	Short walk; loop.
Total distance:	1.6 kilometers.
Difficulty:	Easy.
Hiking time:	1 hour.
Elevation at trailhead:	1,190 meters.
Elevation gain:	Minimal.
Topo maps:	Rogers Pass (Glacier National Park, The Adventure Map); Glacier, 82 N/5.

Loop Brook

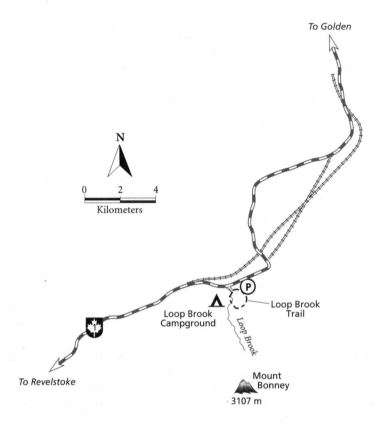

Finding the trailhead: Follow TransCanada Highway 1 approximately 6.6 kilometers south of the Rogers Pass Centre, or 15 kilometers north of the western boundary of Glacier National Park, to an unmarked parking area on the south side of the highway. This is where the Loop Brook Trail officially begins; however, you can also start this trail from Loop Brook Campground. There is an outhouse beside the parking area.

Key points:
- 0.0 Trailhead.
- 1.0 Loop Brook Campground.
- 1.6 Loop Brook parking area.

The hike: Between the valley bottom and summit of Rogers Pass, the original Canadian Pacific Railway line made many continuous loops to soften the grade and avoid the worst avalanche slopes. The total curvature of these loops actually equaled seven complete circles. This short interpretive hike takes you along one of these loops through the dense woods along the old

Orange-flowered false dandelions greet you on the Loop Brook Trail.

track and up to a fantastic view of Mount Bonney (3,100 m) and its studded glacier (south).

Construction of the railway through the mountains was a constant struggle, particularly through the pass where the steep grade of the valley and intricate rivers made the route treacherous. Loop Brook was first bridged at two points in 1885—about 25 meters into the trail and again at the same point where you cross the footbridge to the campground. In 1908 the original wooden trestles were replaced with the stone pillars you see as you immediately enter the trail. A few years after their installation, the CPR abandoned this part of the line; these stone pillars were left as a monument to the pioneers who built them.

From the trailhead you'll pass up a few short switchbacks through a forest filled with hemlock, western red cedar, and ferns as well as beautiful white wildflowers, including queen's cup, pearly everlasting, wild roses, and dwarf dogwood. You'll hear the rumble of the modern railway as you walk, which creates a nice ambience as you think back to what those early railway days must have been like. Follow the old route of the line westward. Look closely at the ground; you can see the original railway ties beneath the raised moss. Before you cross Loop Brook you'll encounter the ruins of an old snow shed as you walk into a fantastic view of Mount Bonney, to your left (south). This type of view is seldom found on a short interpretive trail.

Cross the bridge to the campground, and follow the directional arrows that will lead you back north toward the highway. Red Indian paintbrush, orange-flowered hawkweed, and lupine will greet you before you cross the small wooden bridge under the highway and head back to the parking area.

73 Rock Garden Trail

Highlights:	This short walk loops around a rocky moraine with occasional views of nearby mountain peaks.
Type of hike:	Short walk; loop.
Total distance:	700 meters.
Difficulty:	Easy.
Hiking time:	30 minutes.
Elevation at trailhead:	1,260 meters.
Elevation gain:	Minimal.
Topo maps:	Rogers Pass (Glacier National Park, The Adventure Map); Mount Revelstoke, 82M/1.

Finding the trailhead: Follow TransCanada Highway 1 approximately 37 kilometers west of Glacier National Park's east entrance, or 8.2 kilometers east of the park's west entrance. Turn north off Highway 1 and park in the small lot alongside the road. The trailhead is in the northeast corner of the parking lot. You'll find an outhouse in the parking lot.

Key points:
- 0.0 Trailhead.
- 0.1 Directional arrow.
- 0.5 Viewpoint.
- 0.7 End of trail.

The hike: If you need to stretch your legs on a long car trip, this trail is a perfect choice. Wear hiking boots or runners, as the trail winds through rough, uneven terrain. The trail starts on a boardwalk, which leads you through a

Rock Garden Trail

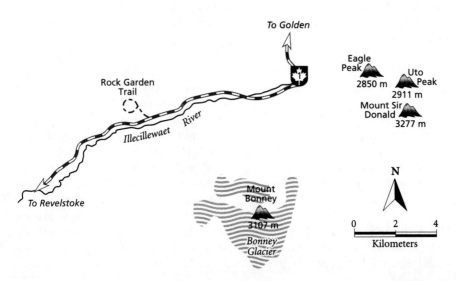

forest filled with hemlock and Douglas fir to a directional arrow. Head right (north) at the arrow through the wet montane forest. You'll pass through a rocky section, eventually climb up and over the large boulders, and briefly overlook the highway before looping back to the directional arrow. At 500 meters you'll enjoy a great view to your right (south) of Mount Bonney (3,107 m) and the Bonney Glacier as well as Eagle Mountain (2,850 m), Mount Uto (2,911 m), and Mount Sir Donald (3,277 m) straight ahead (east).

74 Hemlock Grove Trail

Highlights:	A short interpretive trail along a boardwalk through an old-growth forest. This trail is suitable for both wheelchairs and strollers, as well as the visually impaired.
Type of hike:	Day hike; loop.
Total distance:	400 meters.
Difficulty:	Easy.
Hiking time:	10–30 minutes.
Elevation at trailhead:	910 meters.
Elevation gain:	Minimal.
Topo maps:	Rogers Pass (Glacier National Park, The Adventure Map); Glacier, 82 N/5.

Finding the trailhead: Follow TransCanada Highway 1 approximately 38.7 kilometers west of Glacier National Park's east boundary, or 6.3 kilometers southeast of the west boundary, and turn north into the Hemlock Grove parking area. The trailhead is well marked. There are outhouses and picnic tables at the parking area.

Hemlock Grove Trail

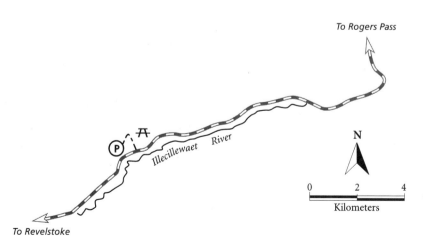

Key points:
   0.0   Trailhead.
   0.4   End of trail.

The hike: Rainy day? Hemlock Grove is perfect—no mud, and the density of the forest will keep you quite dry, even in a downpour. This 400-meter boardwalk is Glacier's most accessible trail. It takes you through an old-growth stand of massive western red cedar and western hemlock, including some trees more than 350 years old. Once you enter the trail you'll be overcome by the size of the trees and the thickness of this rain forest's lush green undergrowth.

    Because two-thirds of the park is made up of rock, ice, avalanche track, or alpine meadow, this type of old-growth forest is extremely rare; it thrives in the cool, moist air of the Columbia Mountains. This short trail is well worth the stop; if you're lucky you may spot a few chickadees, red crossbills, or pileated woodpeckers. If you're looking to spend more time hiking through a forest like this, consider Hike 75, the Bostock Creek Trail.

75 Bostock Creek

Highlights:	An uphill hike through the wet montane forest of the Columbia Mountains to Bostock Pass, where you'll gain views of Fidelity Mountain and Corbin Peak.
Type of hike:	Day hike; out-and-back.
Total distance:	14.4 kilometers.
Difficulty:	Moderate.
Hiking time:	4–6 hours.
Elevation at trailhead:	1,021 metrs.
Elevation gain:	732 meters.
Topo maps:	Rogers Pass (Glacier National Park, The Adventure Map); Illecillewaet, 82 N/4; Glacier 82, N/5.

Finding the trailhead: Follow TransCanada Highway 1 approximately 40.8 kilometers south of the park's eastern boundary and 4 kilometers east of the western boundary to the turnoff on the north side of the highway. There is a sign with a hiking symbol about 1.0 kilometer before the parking area on either side of the highway; however, the Bostock Creek sign

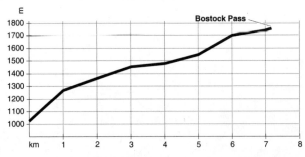

appears only at the entrance to the parking area. The trail leaves the parking area alongside the highway heading northeast.

Bostock Creek

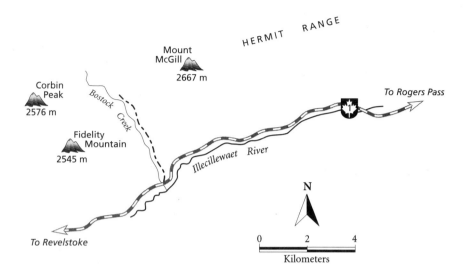

There is an outhouse in the parking area.

Key points:
- 0.0   Bostock Creek parking area/trailhead.
- 1.5   Stream crossing.
- 2.7   Stream crossing.
- 3.3   Several small stream crossings.
- 3.5   Creek crossing over a wooden footbridge.
- 3.8   Creek crossing over a wooden footbridge.
- 4.8   Creek crossing over a wooden footbridge.
- 5.0   Creek crossing.
- 7.2   Bostock Pass.

The hike: If you've spent a few days in the Illecillewaet area, this trail encourages a nice change of scenery. Unlike the ever-present glacial landscape of the Asulkan and Illecillewaet, Bostock is a pleasant, seldom-traveled trail that winds through a wet montane forest up the valley to Bostock Pass, where you gain great views of Fidelity Mountain (2,545 m) and snow-capped Corbin Peak (2,576 m). These peaks of the Selkirk Mountains have sedimentary rock covering the older metamorphic rock. The limestone and shales give these rock faces a distinctly different appearance from the other mountains in the park; they shine like freshly laid tarmac.

Leaving the parking area, you descend a gravel trail to cross Bostock Creek. In late July we spotted an abundance of wildflowers here, including orange-flowered hawkweed, lupine, crimson-colored Indian paintbrush, mauve fleabane, and one-leafed foamflower, which will follow you for the rest of the day. After crossing the creek you'll immediately ascend through a fern-filled old-growth forest overflowing with western hemlock and western red cedar, as well as an assortment of shrubs. It's similar to the Hemlock Grove Trail, without the wooden boardwalk. As you begin to climb through switchbacks, the path will change from gravel to dirt. Even on a sunny day you'll be in darkness with lots of shade as you pass by the huge hemlocks that line the trail.

Occasionally you'll see white wild roses and tiny, pink twinflowers as you pass through this damp, humid forest. As you climb along the trail, the creek will drop farther below you and the grade alongside the trail will become much steeper. Even though you're in a thick forest, you can see quite a distance around you. You'll come to a few tiny creek crossings as the water comes down off the Hermit Range to feed Bostock Creek. At this point you'll also be able to see Christiana Ridge (2,332 m) through the trees across the valley to the left (west). Caribou once thrived in this valley, thus the creek's original name, Caribou Creek. Unfortunately, caribou are no longer abundant anywhere in Glacier National Park. In 1896 the name was changed to honor Senator Hewitt Bostock, an early rancher and member of the Alpine Club of Canada.

Continue along, making several small creek crossings, where you'll likely spot some pink monkeyflowers. At about 2.5 kilometers the trail is quite overgrown in places; the trail is easy to see, but it's best to wear pants to avoid a needless lashing by aggressive shrubs. At 2.7 kilometers you'll cross another small stream filled with deadfall. If you look through the opening in the trees, you'll see the snow-covered peak of Fidelity Mountain to your left (west). If you look closely you'll see the hut of the Christiana snow research station on the ridge running east from Fidelity Mountain. As I scoured the slope I saw an odd-shaped spruce tree that looked as though it had snow on top of it. Since the snow had already melted, I took a better look with the binoculars and realized I was actually looking at the station.

At 3.3 kilometers you'll encounter several small wooden footbridges over trickling streams filled with deadfall and rock. You'll then hike through a wet subalpine meadow, where you'll be able to see Corbin Peak to the left (northwest) in the distance. Mount McGill (2,667 m) is also visible now off to the right (east). From here the trail descends to a creek crossing over a wooden footbridge. You'll then climb through another large meadow—where we would recommend you alert any wildlife of your presence—before crossing another creek over a wooden footbridge. As you hike into another overgrown meadow, you'll gain a fantastic view of Fidelity Mountain to your left (west) and the bench below it. Corbin Peak sits off to your left (northwest) in the distance.

At about 4.5 kilometers you'll head back into a forest before crossing another creek. Looking through the trees you'll have beautiful views of the lush green flanks of the range across the valley. At 5.2 kilometers you'll reach another small creek crossing; if you look back down the valley to the south, you'll have a great view of the mountains across the highway. Along the trail you may see some sharp-tooth angelica.

At 5.6 kilometers the trail takes a sharp right (east) as you gain fantastic views of Corbin Peak. Climb through the forest into another alpine meadow,

As you hike toward Bostock Pass, you'll be greeted by this great view of the snowcapped Corbin Peak.

where you'll spot a few goosefoot violets, arnica, Indian paintbrush, and Indian hellebore as you go. At about 7.2 kilometers you'll reach the pass, where two small footbridges cross trickling streams in a small meadow. This is a great spot to stop for lunch as you admire the mountain scenery across the valley.

From the pass you can hike west up the ridge, where awesome mountain views will reward you, or you can continue along this unmaintained 18-kilometer trail, crossing Casualty Creek twice to reach Avalanche and Carson cabins, which are closed to the public.

Mount Revelstoke National Park
Trail Locator Map

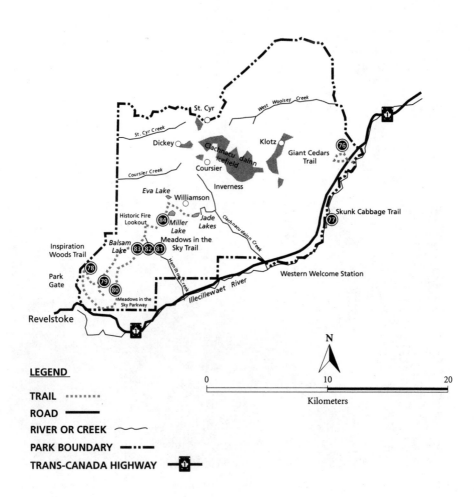

LEGEND

TRAIL ········

ROAD ▬▬▬

RIVER OR CREEK ⌇

PARK BOUNDARY ▬ ·· ▬

TRANS-CANADA HIGHWAY

N

| 0 | 10 | 20 |

Kilometers

Mount Revelstoke National Park

Mount Revelstoke National Park, Glacier's much smaller neighbor, located 24 kilometers to the west, was established in 1914 after much lobbying by local residents. Located less than 1 kilometer north of the City of Revelstoke, B.C., in the Selkirk Mountains, the park offers eleven hiking trails and covers 260 square kilometers.

Mount Revelstoke National Park is accessible by car or bus via two highways: The most common route, TransCanada Highway 1, runs along the southeast perimeter of the park. Provincial Highway 23 North runs across the park's west boundary.

Mount Revelstoke offers the only opportunity in the Canadian national parks to reach the summit of a mountain by private vehicle. The 26-kilometer Meadows in the Sky Parkway, which ends just 2 kilometers from the summit of Mount Revelstoke, is accessible from the TransCanada Highway. You can either walk to the summit or take the free shuttle bus to the summit (operates midmorning to late afternoon, usually from early July through late September).

In 1908 City of Revelstoke residents built the first trail to the summit of Mount Revelstoke and later broke trails to some of the area's alpine lakes. Mount Revelstoke also served as one of Canada's first ski hills, and its ski jump was the site of numerous world records before 1930.

The Columbia Mountains, in which both Glacier and Mount Revelstoke National Parks are located, boast the world's only temperate inland rain forest, caused by plentiful snowmelt at the beginning of the growing season and high precipitation during the middle of the growing season. Expect plenty of moisture when hiking in these parks, and be sure you're dressed appropriately for the wet, rainy conditions.

The unique climate in Revelstoke helps protect the habitats of threatened and endangered wildlife, such as the mountain caribou and grizzly bear. All 2,500 of the mountain caribou in the world are in southeastern British Columbia and frequently travel through Glacier and Revelstoke National Parks. Black bears and grizzly bears are typically seen along the highway, as are mountain goats. Anywhere from 6,000 to 12,000 grizzlies live in Mount Revelstoke and Glacier—roughly half the remaining population in Canada. So pack your bear spray and bear bangers, and be sure you know what to do should you encounter a bear. (See Preparing for the Backcountry.)

SEASONS AND WEATHER

Located in the Columbia Mountain region of British Columbia's interior wet belt, Mount Revelstoke's climate is characterized by high precipitation, heavy snowfall, and moderate winter temperatures. Generally, summer

(July through August) and winter (December through February) are the best times to enjoy park trails—for hiking, cross-country skiing, or snowshoeing. Snow season is mid-October through mid-June, but snow can fall anytime at higher elevations, so it's a good idea to carry a good weatherproof jacket and to dress in layers—regardless of the weather at the trailhead.

Regular weather reports, including fire danger and lightning forecasts, are available at the Rogers Pass Centre or on-line (see Appendix A). You may also want to pick up a copy of Falcon's *Reading Weather* at your local bookstore.

BASIC SERVICES

The City of Revelstoke, located less than 1.0 kilometer south of the Meadows-in-the-Sky Parkway, offers full services including gas stations, restaurants, grocery stores, a hospital and a variety of accommodations ranging from bed and breakfasts to motel chains. The nearest commercial airports are at Kamloops and Kelowna, British Columbia, and Calgary, Alberta.

FRONTCOUNTRY CAMPGROUNDS

There are no road-accessible campgrounds in Mount Revelstoke National Park. However, there are two provincial campgrounds, Martha Creek and Blanket Creek, available within twenty minutes of the park. There are also several commercial campgrounds available in the City of Revelstoke. Ask at Rogers Pass Centre or at the staffed entrance to the Meadows in the Sky Parkway in Revelstoke National Park for more information. Campground information is also available at the Parks Canada office in downtown Revelstoke and at the City of Revelstoke Information Centre, which is located on the north side of TransCanada Highway 1 just before the turnoff for the Revelstoke City Centre.

BACKCOUNTRY CAMPGROUNDS

A Wilderness Pass is required for all backcountry camping in Mount Revelstoke National Park. Available from the Rogers Pass Centre, passes cost CDN $6.00 per person per night or CDN $42.00 for an annual pass.

76 Giant Cedars Trail

Highlights:	A short interpretive stroll through a rain forest of giant western red cedar and hemlock.
Type of hike:	Short walk; loop.
Total distance:	0.5 kilometer.
Difficulty:	Easy.
Hiking time:	15–30 minutes.
Elevation at trailhead:	700 meters.
Elevation gain:	Minimal.
Topo maps:	Mount Revelstoke (The Adventure Map); Illecillewaet, 82 N/4.

Finding the trailhead: Follow TransCanada Highway 1 approximately 1.2 kilometers west of Mount Revelstoke National Park's eastern boundary, or 32.0 kilometers east from the Revelstoke city center. The well-marked trail is located on the north side of the highway. There are outhouses, picnic tables, and a picnic shelter at the parking area.

Giant Cedars Trail

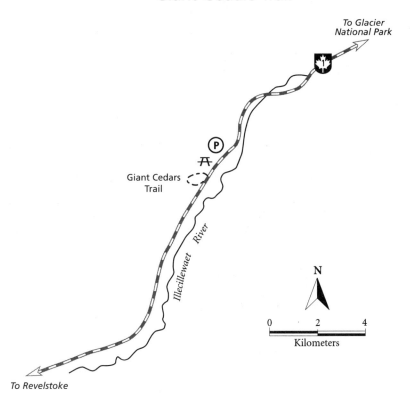

A group of German tourists walk along this boardwalk in awe of the giant western red cedar and hemlock in this old-growth forest.

Key points:
    0.0   Trailhead.
    0.5   End of trail.

The hike: The Pacific winds carry moisture across the Columbia Mountains. When the winds cool they drop rain in the summer and snow in winter, nourishing this rain forest of western hemlock and western red cedar. The smell and the sounds alone make this stroll worthwhile, and you'll be moved by both before you even enter the trail.

Ascend the steps, where you'll be met by interpretive signs identifying the major plant and animal species that thrive here—including the long-eared bat. A creek sits off to your left (south), and you can hear it trickling throughout your walk.

If you're looking for a similar, barrier-free trail, try Hemlock Grove in Glacier National Park. (See Hike 74 for more information on this hike.)

77 Skunk Cabbage Trail

            Highlights: A short interpretive stroll through the swamplands of
                            the Columbia Valley.
          Type of hike: Short walk; loop.
       Total distance: 1.2 kilometers.
            Difficulty: Easy.
          Hiking time: 20–30 minutes.
 Elevation at trailhead: 610 meters.
       Elevation gain: Minimal.
             Topo maps: Mount Revelstoke (The Adventure Map); Illecillewaet,
                            82 N/4.

Finding the trailhead: Follow TransCanada Highway 1 approximately 4 kilometers southwest of Mount Revelstoke National Park's eastern boundary, or 8.7 kilometers northeast of the west welcome station. The well-marked trail is located on the south side of the highway. There are picnic tables, a picnic shelter, and washrooms at this rest area.

Key points:
    0.0   Trailhead.
    1.2   End of trail.

The hike: If you're driving through Mount Revelstoke National Park from April to mid-May, you must stop and explore the Skunk Cabbage Trail. At this time of year the trailside is lined by the plant's full-blooming bright-yellow flowers. These valley-bottom wetlands along the Illecillewaet River are rich in animal and plant life; May and June are ideal for bird-watching.

Skunk Cabbage Trail

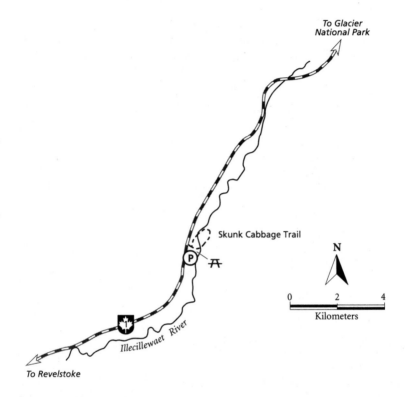

This is an excellent place to stop for lunch; the picnic tables are nicely spaced out, and the gentle sound of the nearby Illecillewaet River nearly drowns out the rushing highway.

78 Inspiration Woods Trail

Highlights:	A short walk through a forest filled with Douglas fir, western hemlock, and western white pine.
Type of hike:	Loop, day hike.
Total distance:	3 kilometers.
Difficulty:	Easy.
Hiking time:	30 minutes–1 hour.
Elevation at trailhead:	610 meters.
Elevation gain:	Minimal.
Topo maps:	Mount Revelstoke (The Adventure Map); Mount Revelstoke, 82M/1.

Finding the trailhead: Follow TransCanada Highway 1 approximately 17 kilometers west of Mount Revelstoke National Park's west welcome station, or 3.4 kilometers east from the city center. Turn north off the highway toward the Meadows in the Sky Parkway. Follow the parkway approximately 7.6 km to its first switchback; the trailhead is on the left-hand (west) side of the road in the corner. There's room for two cars to park on the road at the trailhead, and there's one more gravel spot on the right-hand (east) side of the road just after you complete the turn.

Key points:
0.0	Trailhead.
0.7	Creek crossing.
0.9	Unmarked trail junction; turn left (west).
1.0	Creek crossing.
1.7	Creek crossing.
1.9	Back at the unmarked junction; continue straight ahead (south).
2.1	Creek crossing.
3.0	Mount Revelstoke Summit Road.

The hike: If you're interested in taking a short walk through a Columbia forest, this hike is ideal—as long as you aren't expecting any mountain views.

You'll likely notice that the trailhead sign reads 5 KM LOOP ; however, we found the trail to be 3 kilometers, as stated on the Revelstoke Hiking Trail Map and in the brochure. Once on this trail you'll immediately spot some red clover and sweet vetch as well as mauve fleabane, depending on the time of year. You'll begin a short ascent through a forest of Douglas fir, western hemlock, and western white pine before coming across a small creek on the left. After about ten minutes (0.9 km) you'll reach an unmarked junction; turn left (west) and enter the 1.0-kilometer loop, which will bring you back to this point. Follow the trail south back to the road.

Inspiration Woods Trail

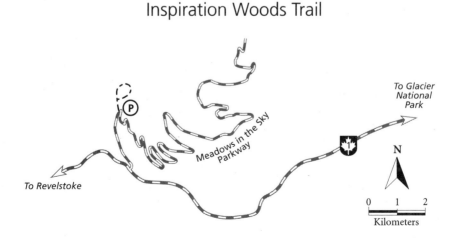

79 Lindmark Trail

Highlights:	This pleasant forested hike leads you through a variety of vegetation and offers views of Lake Revelstoke and the City of Revelstoke.
Type of hike:	Day hike; shuttle.
Total distance:	8 kilometers.
Difficulty:	Easy (strenuous if you climb from the Monashee Lookout to Balsam Lake).
Hiking time:	2–3½ hours.
Elevation at trailhead:	875 meters.
Elevation loss:	955 meters.
Topo maps:	Mount Revelstoke (The Adventure Map); Mount Revelstoke, 82M/1.

Finding the trailhead: Follow TransCanada Highway 1 approximately 17 kilometers west of Mount Revelstoke National Park's east welcome station, or 3.4 kilometers east from Revelstoke's city center. Turn north off the highway on the Meadows in the Sky Parkway.

You can start this hike in one of two places: directly across the road (north) from the Monashee Lookout and Picnic Area or at Balsam Lake. The Monashee Lookout is located 7.6 kilometers from the base of Mount Revelstoke. From here you can expect a challenging climb to Balsam Lake. Balsam Lake is located approximately 26 kilometers from the base of Mount Revelstoke on the left (west) side of the Meadows in the Sky Parkway. The trailhead is located 100 meters from the parking lot on the west side of Balsam Lake. We chose the Balsam Lake option—after all, why go up when you can go down?

Note: This is a shuttle hike. To avoid the monotony of following the trail down and then back up again to your car, leave a car at both trailheads if possible.

Key points:

0.0	Trailhead.
1.6	Fork in trail.
5.0	Stream crossing.
6.0	Directional signage.
6.5	Revelstoke/Lake Revelstoke viewpoint.
8.0	Monashee Lookout and Picnic Area.

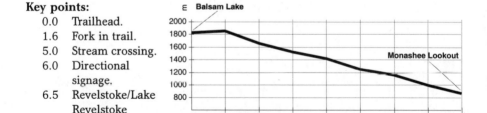

The hike: You're unlikely to see another hiker on this peaceful walk in the woods—and for good reason. While the variety of vegetation in itself is interesting, the Lindmark Trail lacks the beautiful alpine vistas of other hikes in the area. It's also not well maintained—undoubtedly because the other, more popular trails take priority with the trail crew. We found ourselves climb-

228

Lindmark Trail

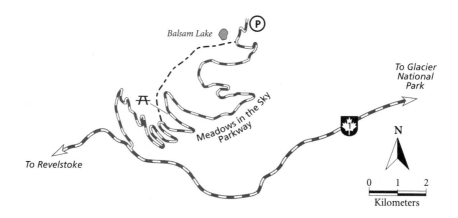

ing over countless downed trees as we hustled to complete this seemingly never-ending trail. But if you're looking for a cool, shady walk on a sweltering day, this hike may be an option.

Starting on the west side of Balsam Lake, follow the single-file dirt trail with scattered roots, rocks, and pinecones into the forest of subalpine fir. Just 500 meters into the trail, you'll skirt a small swampy lake to your right (east). If you haven't slathered on the mosquito spray, you'll serve as the prime attraction for the swarm of bugs living near the lake at this point. At 1.0 kilometer you'll catch a glimpse through the trees of the Monashee Mountains just to the west of the City of Revelstoke.

Just 600 meters later you'll reach a fork in the road; stay to your right (southwest) here. You'll see a small red handwritten sign pointing you in the right direction. At 2.1 kilometers you'll walk next to a small unnamed stream to your right (north). At approximately 3 kilometers the fir and spruce on the trail give way to hemlock and western red cedar. You may also spot a few king bolete mushrooms and baldhip rose on the trail.

At 5.2 kilometers you'll pass a field of huge boulders to your left (east). At this point you'll start to hear traffic buzzing by on the Meadows in the Sky Parkway. You'll reach a trail junction with a sign pointing to Balsam Lake at 6 kilometers. Just 500 meters later you'll pass the best view on the trail; look to your right (west) to see Lake Revelstoke and the City of Revelstoke far beneath you. The trail gets wider as you descend and ends across from the Monashee Lookout and Picnic Area at 8 kilometers.

80 Summit Trail

Highlights:	This challenging climb through the forest travels from the base of Mount Revelstoke to Balsam Lake.
Type of hike:	Day hike; shuttle.
Total distance:	10 kilometers.
Difficulty:	Strenuous.
Hiking time:	2½–4 hours.
Elevation at trailhead:	600 meters.
Elevation gain:	1,230 meters.
Topo maps:	Mount Revelstoke (The Adventure Map); Revelstoke, 82M/1.

Finding the trailhead: Follow TransCanada Highway 1 approximately 17 kilometers west of Mount Revelstoke National Park's west welcome station, or 3.4 kilometers east from Revelstoke's city center. Turn north off the highway onto the Meadows in the Sky Parkway.

You can start this hike at one of two trailheads: at the Nels Nelson Historic Area (the option we chose) or at the motor home parking lot at Balsam Lake. The Nels Nelson Historic Area is located near the base of Mount Revelstoke on the right (east) side of the Meadows in the Sky Parkway. Follow the signs to the trailhead. The motor home parking lot at Balsam Lake is located on the right (west) side of the Meadows in the Sky Parkway, approximately 25.5 kilometers from the base of Mount Revelstoke. The trailhead is located in the southwest corner of the parking lot.

This is a shuttle hike. To avoid the monotony of following the trail up and then down again, leave a car at both trailheads if possible. For a bit of extra fun, leave a car at the Balsam Lake parking lot and ride your bike down the 26-kilometer Meadows in the Sky Parkway to the Nels Nelson Historic Area, then climb the trail back to your car.

Key points:
- 0.0 Trailhead.
- 1.5 Trail crosses road.
- 2.1 Trail crosses road.
- 2.4 Trail crosses road.
- 2.9 Trail crosses road.
- 3.6 Trail crosses road.

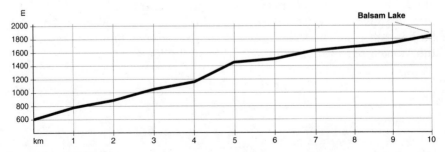

Summit Trail

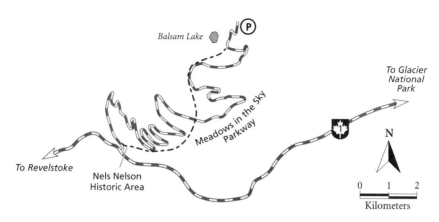

4.6   Trail crosses road.
7.4   Trail junction; head right (northeast) along the road.
9.5   Balsam Lake motor home parking lot.
10.0 Balsam Lake parking lot.

The hike: This is one heck of a steep climb, and you'll actually enjoy better views from the Meadows in the Sky Parkway than you will from the trail itself. We wouldn't recommend it unless you're looking for some heavy-duty exercise and don't mind the fact that you're always in the trees or crossing the road that everyone else drives up.

From the Nels Nelson Historic Area, follow the mountain bike trail to your left (north) rather than the hiking trail straight ahead (east) for the most direct route. (The hiking trail simply loops back to the mountain bike trail a short distance later.) If you're hiking this trail in mid- to late-August, you'll likely spot a tempting buffet of wild blueberries, raspberries, and huckleberries on the initial part of the trail. But remember, you're not allowed to pick up any souvenirs—even if you eat them immediately—in a national park.

You're unlikely to see any other hikers on this wide trail lined with lodgepole pine, poplar, Douglas fir, and western red cedar. This trail crosses the Meadows in the Sky Parkway and continues on the other side of the road at 1.5, 2.1, 2.4, 2.9, 3.6, and 4.6 kilometers, respectively. Wildflowers, including honeysuckle, mountain avens, valerian, and Indian paintbrush, add a splash of color along the way.

At 7.4 kilometers you'll arrive at a scratched-out trail junction sign that you won't be able to read. Look for the wooden arrows in the same area pointing you toward either Balsam Lake straight ahead (north) or the Summit Trail to your right (northeast). To continue on the Summit Trail, you'll walk along the road more than 1.0 kilometer before heading back into the trees to your left (west) at an unmarked trail junction. No matter which option you choose, you'll be a happy hiker when you arrive at the Balsam Lake parking lot after this challenging, relatively viewless trail.

81 Meadows in the Sky Trail

Highlights:	A short walk.
Type of hike:	Loop.
Total distance:	1.0 kilometer.
Difficulty:	Easy.
Hiking time:	30 minutes.
Elevation at trailhead:	1,920 meters.
Elevation gain:	Minimal.
Topo maps:	Mount Revelstoke (The Adventure Map); Mount Revelstoke, 82M/1.

Finding the trailhead: Follow TransCanada Highway 1 approximately 17 kilometers west of Mount Revelstoke National Park's west welcome station, or 3.4 kilometers east from the Revelstoke city center. Turn north off Highway 1 toward the Meadows in the Sky Parkway. Follow the parkway approximately 26 kilometers to the Balsam Lake parking area (the second parking lot). From here you can take the free shuttle bus to the summit or hike 1.0 kilometer along the Upper Summit Trail (located at the southeast end of the parking lot) to the trailhead.

Key points:
- 0.0   Trailhead.
- 0.3   Bench.
- 0.5   The "Icebox."
- 0.6   Bench.
- 1.0   End of trail.

The hike: Perhaps the most popular of hikes on the summit of Mount Revelstoke, this short loop takes you through subalpine meadows and forests filled with gnarled trees—typical of the summit of Mount Revelstoke.

Before Parks Canada reclaimed this area about ten years ago, towns folk used to drive to the summit of Mount Revelstoke on a gravel road and park right beside Heather Lake. They would picnic, pick wildflowers, and travel wherever they liked, not realizing the impact this would have on this fragile mountain environment. Well known for its abundance of wildflowers, the parkway is surrounded by purple lupines, yellow arnica, red and pink Indian paintbrush, valerian, and masses of mauve fleabane. Once you arrive at the summit you'll notice there's not nearly the amount of wildflowers there were on the way up. Nonetheless, depending on the time of year, you may also see glacier lily and the tiny white heads of the western spring beauty. And the view, which is why so many people travel to this point, is breathtaking.

You'll see the trailhead once you arrive at the summit; from here follow the paved trail and take the first fork off to your right (southeast). As you pass through the subalpine meadow filled with tiny pools of water from the snow melt, you'll have fantastic mountain views to the northwest, south to

The Icebox on the Meadows in the Sky Trail is filled with snow that will never melt.

Meadows in the Sky Trail • Heather Lake Loop • Balsam Lake Loop

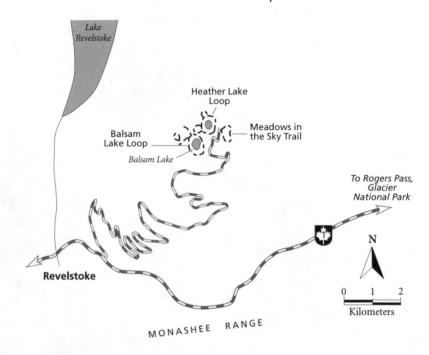

the Monashee Range, and northeast as far as you can see. In fact, every way you look on this trail, you'll see snow-capped mountains with grassy-green slopes. After walking about 300 meters, you'll come across a nicely placed bench. Continue on, and climb a few rocky steps before you see the Icebox; even on the warmest days of summer the shade of the rockwall keeps the snow from melting. At 0.6 kilometer you'll come across a few more benches, where you'll have awesome mountain views to the northeast. From here follow the loop back to the trailhead.

82 Heather Lake Loop

<blockquote>
Highlights: A short walk around Heather Lake to gain views of the Columbia Valley. From here you can walk to the historic fire tower on the true summit of Mount Revelstoke or head back along the west shore of Heather Lake. Constant mountain views.

<blockquote>
See Map on Page 234
</blockquote>

Type of hike: Loop.

Total distance: 600 meters (1.5 kilometers if you continue on to the Parapets viewpoint and the Fire Tower Trail).

Difficulty: Easy.

Hiking time: 10–30 minutes.

Elevation at trailhead: 1,920 meters.

Elevation gain: Minimal.

Topo maps: Mount Revelstoke (The Adventure Map); Mount Revelstoke, 82M/1.
</blockquote>

Finding the trailhead: Follow TransCanada Highway 1 approximately 12.7 kilometers west of Mount Revelstoke National Park's west welcome station, or 3.4 kilometers east from the Revelstoke city center. Turn north off the highway toward the Meadows in the Sky Parkway. Follow the parkway approximately 26 kilometers to the Balsam Lake parking area (the second parking lot). From here you can take the free shuttle bus or hike 1.0 kilometer along the Upper Summit Trail at the southeast end of the parking area to the Eva/Miller/Jade Lakes trailhead.

Key points:
- 0.0 Trailhead.
- 0.1 Fork in the trail, head left (northwest).
- 0.2 Trail junction; head right (north) to North Summit Loop Trail.
- 0.9 Parapets Viewpoint (bench).
- 1.1 Fire tower.
- 1.5 End of trail.

The hike: Where else can you hike around the top of a mountain in your sandals? The trails are so well maintained you'll have no fear of vicious undergrowth grabbing at your ankles. You will, however, be swarmed by horseflies and mosquitoes, so bring your bug spray and a swatter if you have one (or better yet, a complete bug suit).

Begin by passing by the clear waters of Heather Lake to your left (west). Follow the trail 100 meters with nice views of the range to the north, and take a right (north) toward the unmarked North Summit Loop Trail. You'll pass a lot of mountain heather, globeflowers, valerian, western spring beauty, and glacier lilies before meeting an unmarked junction; head right (east) to complete the loop. You'll quickly reach a fork in the trail; it doesn't matter which way you go, because you'll come to a bench either way. In August, once the snow has cleared, you'll likely spot white mountain rhododendron, pink mountain heather, and purple lupines along the way.

From the viewpoint you'll have a great view of Lake Revelstoke. You'll also notice all the logging roads and clear-cuts across the deep green Columbia Valley. Follow the loop back toward the lake and you'll see the historic fire tower on the summit of Mount Revelstoke (southwest). From here you can either head back along the west side of Heather Lake to complete the hike, or you can continue along straight ahead, passing the stone walls of the Parapets viewpoints and the low-lying woolly pussytoes before you climb the final 200 meters to the fire lookout, which was declared a Federal Heritage building in 1988. From the summit the panoramic views are beautiful—to the northeast, the Selkirks; to the west, Mount Dickey (2,525 m) and Mount Cyr (2,527 m); to the northeast, Mount Coursier (2,646 m), Mount Williamson (2,37 3m), and the Inverness Peaks. Eagle Pass lies to the southwest, and Ghost Peak (2,469 m) and Mount Mackenzie (2,461 m) loom to the southeast. To the west sits Mount Copeland (2,582 m). Follow the flowers and the steep trail back toward the shores of Heather Lake.

83 Balsam Lake Loop

Highlights: Take this short walk around Balsam Lake, then follow the Eagle Knoll Trail for great views of Lake Revelstoke and its surrounding valley.

See Map on Page 234

Type of hike: Loop.
Total distance: 400 meters (2 kilometers if you complete the Eagle Knoll Loop and the lookout).
Difficulty: Easy.
Hiking time: 10–45 minutes.
Elevation at trailhead: 1,830 meters.
Elevation gain: Minimal.
Topo maps: Mount Revelstoke (The Adventure Map); Mount Revelstoke, 82 M/1.

Finding the trailhead: Follow TransCanada Highway 1 approximately 12.7 kilometers west of Mount Revelstoke National Park's west welcome station, or 3.4 kilometers east from the Revelstoke city center. Turn north off the highway toward the Meadows in the Sky Parkway. Follow the parkway approximately 26 kilometers to the parking area at Balsam Lake (the second parking lot). The trail begins at the lakeshore. There are outhouses, picnic tables, and a picnic shelter near the parking area.

Key points:
  0.0   Trail sign.
  0.2   Trail junction for the Lindmark Trail; continue straight ahead (north).
  0.25   Trail junction for the (unmarked) Eagle Knoll Loop; head left (west).

Beautiful purple lupines line the Eagle Knoll Trail at Balsam Lake.

0.5	Eagle Knoll viewpoint.
1.2	Balsam Lake.
1.3	Unmarked trail junction; head left (north) to the lookout.
1.6	Lookout.
1.9	Balsam Lakeshore.
2.0	Parking area.

The hike: There are several short hikes around the summit of Mount Revelstoke if you're looking for a leisurely afternoon adventure. If you plan to take a short stroll around Balsam Lake, be sure to take in the Eagle Knoll Trail as well; the views are spectacular.

Follow the trail south along the east shore of Balsam Lake. At the end of July there are plenty of western spring beauty, Indian paintbrush, and glacier lilies lining the clear watered lakeside. You'll reach the Lindmark Trail junction on the northwest shore; pass this trail and take your next left (west) to follow the Eagle Knoll Trail through a short section of a subalpine fir forest before meeting a fork in the trail. Either direction will lead you back to this spot, so take your pick; you'll meet one more fork where once again you can hike in either direction.

Walking up a small hill to the lookout, you'll likely see a lot of valerian, lupines, and white mountain rhododendron before you gain a spectacular view of Lake Revelstoke and the snow-capped mountain landscape off to the left (west). You can also see all the mountains to your right (east), including Mount Dickey (2,525 m) and Mount Coursier (2,646 m). There are a few benches that make nice rest spots along this short trail.

Once you've walked back to Balsam Lake, head east back toward the parking area, and turn left (north) on the next unmarked trail to go to another lookout. Continue along past short, gnarled trees for about 300 meters; you'll reach a bench that looks out over Lake Revelstoke and its surrounding green valley to the west. You'll also have mountain views for as far as you can see.

Reach the lake once again and follow the trail left (east) past the picnic shelter and back to the parking area.

To make the most of this short adventure, bring along some bug spray; you'll meet a lot of horseflies and mosquitoes, as this area can be quite wet.

84 Eva Lake/Miller Lake/ Jade Lakes Trail

Highlights:	A rolling hike from the summit of Mount Revelstoke to the glass-blue glacial waters of Miller Lake or the clear waters of Eva Lake. Climb onto the spectacular Jade Pass and look out over the green waters of upper and lower Jade Lakes.
Type of hike:	Day hike or backpack trip; out-and-back. (Both Eva and Jade Lakes have backcountry campsites, and each lake has an outhouse).
Total distance:	11-kilometer round trip to Miller Lake, 12.6-kilometer round-trip to Eva Lake, 18-kilometer round-trip to Jade Lakes (15-kilometer round-trip to Jade Pass).
Difficulty:	Easy (Jade Pass and Jade Lakes Trail would be considered moderate).
Hiking time:	4–9 hours.
Elevation at trailhead:	1,920 meters.
Elevation gain:	From 90 to 785 meters.
Topo maps:	Mount Revelstoke (The Adventure Map); Mount Revelstoke, 82M/1.

Finding the trailhead: Follow TransCanada Highway 1 approximately 12.7 kilometers west of Mount Revelstoke National Park's west welcome station, or 3.4 kilometers east from the Revelstoke city center. Turn north off the highway toward the Meadows in the Sky Parkway. Follow the parkway approximately 26 kilometers to the Balsam Lake parking area (the second parking lot). From here you can either take the free shuttle bus or hike 1.0 kilometer along the Upper Summit Trail at the southeast end of the parking area to the Eva/Miller/Jade Lakes trailhead.

Key points:
- 0.0   Trailhead.
- 0.1   Fork in the trail; head right (northeast).
- 1.8   Stream crossings.

2.5	Bench.
2.9	Stream crossing.
4.2	Stream crossing.
5.0	Stream crossing, small waterfall.
5.5	Trail junction; right (southeast) 400 meters to Miller Lake.
5.6	Trail junction; right (east) for Jade Lake, straight ahead (north) for Eva Lake (700 meters).
7.5	Jade Pass (2160m).
9.0	Upper Jade Lake.
10.5	Jade Pass.
12.4	Trail Junction; left (southwest) to summit of Mount Revelstoke.
18.0	End of trail.

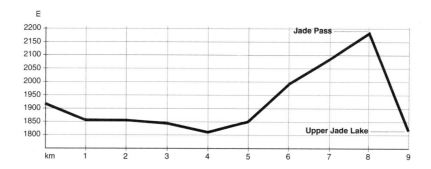

The hike: If you look at a map or read a brochure about this hike, it can be a bit deceiving. The lakes appear to be at a lower altitude than that at the trailhead—with the exception of Eva, which is 13 meters higher than the summit of Mount Revelstoke.

So there you are, set to start out on a nice flat trail, but what the brochures neglect to mention is that this rolling trail climbs and falls. To get to Jade Lakes, you have to first ascend the 360 meters from Miller Lake to Jade Pass, where you can then descend 335 meters to the lakeshore—only to climb right back over the pass again for the hike home.

Our advice? Any of these three destinations will be highly rewarding; however, we strongly recommend the climb to Jade Pass. You can stay there to enjoy the panoramic mountain landscape, where snow-capped peaks lie all around you for as far as you can see. It's absolutely breathtaking, and what's even better is that even in high season (August), you'll likely have the pass all to yourself. You can admire the jade-green waters from this perfectly peaceful spot. It will make for one memorable day.

Begin this rolling trail as you skirt the east side of Heather Lake to your left (west). You'll immediately meet a junction, where you will head right (northeast) along a dirt trail surrounded by grassy views of the mountainous crests to the north. You can easily spot western anemones, glacier lilies, western spring beauty, and Indian hellebore along the trail, which is scattered with the occasional rock or root. After walking downhill for about 500 meters, you'll spot Lake Revelstoke and the Columbia Valley ahead of you

Eva Lake/Miller Lake/Jade Lakes Trail

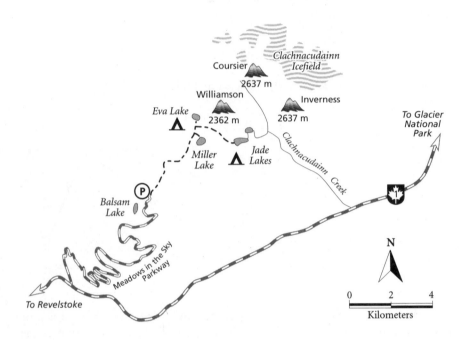

in the distance. Here the trail is quite open and crosses several meadows as you pass in and out of the subalpine forest. After hiking approximately 1.0 kilometer, you'll glimpse the unnamed peak that sits above Jade Pass. If you look off to the left (west), you'll notice the variant greens caused by clear-cutting in the Columbia Valley.

Continue along, and at about 3.6 kilometers you'll come across an old rock slide. Halfway through it you'll begin to hear the gentle sound of rushing water before you enter the forest filled with mountain hemlock and Engelmann spruce once more. At 4.4 kilometers you'll walk through another rocky area where you may see the tiny white-flowered Alaska saxifrage as well as some white mountain rhododendron bushes.

At the 5-kilometer point you'll cross a wooden footbridge over a small waterfall (the one you've been hearing for a while). At 5.5 kilometers you'll reach the trail junction for Miller lake (1,900 m); it's just a ten-minute walk to the right (southeast). Named after a turn-of-the-century school inspector, A. E. Miller, who spent much time exploring and writing about this area, the lake sits below a snow-capped peak covered by contrasting grassy slopes. During the last ice age, a glacier once sat in this basin. Today the clear waters are reminiscent of its past; they are a fantastic glacial blue. There are some rocky outcrops from the lakeshore that make for a perfect lunch spot if this is your final destination.

If you're forging on to Eva Lake, pass by the trail junction, continuing straight ahead (north). You'll walk through another rocky pass, where you may see the yellow partridgefoot before you come to the lake, which was named after an early explorer and member of the Revelstoke Mountaineering club, Eva Hobbs. Looking out over the lake it almost seems as though it's just hanging in this valley, and in fact it is. If you take a few minutes to walk around it, you'll gain a spectacular view of the Coursier Creek Valley, which drops off below the north side of the lake. There is a small cabin open to the public (offering a momentary respite from the mosquitoes and black flies); overnight camping is allowed here.

If you're heading for Jade Lakes, turn right (east) at the trail junction. You'll immediately head into the subalpine forest, which offers some nice shade on a sunny day. Continue for about 400 meters before you walk across the rocky flanks of Mount Williamson (2,373 m), gaining a fantastic view of deep-blue Miller Lake sparkling in the sun beneath you (south). From this elevation you can see many of the large boulders on the lake bottom. You'll soon pass a few small pools of meltwater, spots of white mountain heather, and a stream that's spilling down the slope to your right (east) as you begin the steep rocky switchback section that will lead you to the pass. Even in mid-August, you may see the occasional patch covered in watermelon snow.

You'll gain a great view of Mount Williamson to your left (north) as you pass a grassy section dotted with western anemones and alpine buttercups. If you look back the way you came (west), you'll have a great view of Miller

The clear waters of Eva Lake are the highlight of this mountain basin.

Lake and the golf course–green valley you just climbed through. Hiking over the pass, you'll be immediately rewarded by overwhelming panoramic views of snow-capped mountains and the jade-green waters of the icy lake below. The Inverness Peaks lie straight ahead of you (east), Mount Williamson is to your left (north), and an unnamed peak looms above Jade Lake (southeast). This is a special place to stop and enjoy the view, which you could do in quiet for hours if you wished. The scenery reminded us of the coveted Lake O'Hara area in Yoho National Park; the only thing missing was the many other hikers drawn by its beauty.

From here strong hikers can descend the steep trail, which skirts the shale slope to your left, to Jade Lakes. You can camp overnight or turn around and climb back up to Jade Pass and down toward Miller Lake, before meeting the junction that will lead you back to the summit of Mount Revelstoke.

Appendix A: For More Information

Visit Parks Canada on-line: www.worldweb.com/parkscanada.

YOHO NATIONAL PARK

Yoho National Park
P.O. Box 99
Field, B.C. V0A 1G0
(250) 343-6783
E-mail: yoho_info@pch.gc.ca

Superintendant
P.O. Box 99
Field, B.C. V0A 1G0
(350) 343-6324

The Friends of Yoho
P.O. Box 100
Field, B.C. V0A 1G0
(250) 343-6393

The Yoho–Burgess Shale Foundation
P.O. Box 148
Field, B.C. V0A 1G0
E-mail: burgshal@rockies.net

The Lake O'Hara Trails Club
Box 98
Lake Louise, AB T0L 1E0

KOOTENAY NATIONAL PARK

Kootenay National Park
P.O. Box 220
Radium Hotsprings, B.C. V0A 1M0
(250) 347-9615
E-mail: kootenay_reception@pch.gc.ca

The Friends of Kootenay
P.O. Box 215
Radium Hotsprings, B.C. V0A 1M0
(250) 347-6525

East Kootenay Environmental Society
Box 8
Kimberley, B.C. V1A 2Y5
(250) 427-2535

Superintendent
Kootenay National Park
P.O. Box 220
Radium Hot Springs, B.C. V0A 1M0
(250) 347-9615
E-mail: kootenay_reception@pch.gc.ca

GLACIER AND MT. REVELSTOKE NATIONAL PARKS

Glacier and Mt. Revelstoke National Park
P.O. Box 350
Revelstoke, B.C. V0E 2S0
(250) 837-7500
E-mail: revglacier_reception@pch.gc.ca

The Friends of Mt. Revelstoke & Glacier
Box 2992
Revelstoke, B.C. V0E 2S0
(250) 837-2010

GENERAL

The Alpine Club of Canada
Box 8040 Indian Flats Road
Canmore, AB T1W 2T8
(403) 678-3200

The Canadian Avalanche Association
P.O. Box 2759
Revelstoke, BC V0E 2S0
(250) 837-2437
voice bulletins: (800) 667-1105
E-mail: geninq.canav@avalanche.ca
Web site: www.avalanche.ca

WHERE TO GET MAPS:

- Most outdoor adventure stores (e.g. Mountain Equipment Co-op) or Map Town in Edmonton or Calgary
- The GemTrek Publishing Web site at www.gemtrek.com
- Glacier Circle Bookstore, located at Rogers Pass Centre
- The Friends of Yoho shop in the Field Information Centre

WHERE TO GET WEATHER INFORMATION:

All parks:	Environment Canada's Meteorological Service: www.weatheroffice.com
Yoho and Kootenay:	(403) 762-1460 (recorded information).
Road Conditions:	(403) 762-1450

Avalanche Hazards:
Kootenay and Yoho: (403) 762-1460
Rogers Pass: (250) 837-6867
Canadian Avalanche Association voice bulletins: (800) 667-1105

Weather information is also available at park information centers (see phone numbers above) and is often posted at campgrounds.

IN CASE OF EMERGENCY:

Yoho National Park
Ambulance: (250) 344-6226
Fire: (250) 343-6028
R.C.M.P: (250) 344-2221
Wardens: (403) 762-4506 (24 hours)

Kootenay National Park
Ambulance: (250) 342-2055
Fire: (250) 347-9333
R.C.M.P: (250) 347-9393
Wardens: (250) 347-9361
After hours call (403) 762-4506

Mount Revelstoke and Glacier National Parks
Ambulance: (250) 837-5885
Fire: (250) 837-5123
R.C.M.P: (250) 837-5255

Wardens: Rogers Pass, (250) 841-5202; Revelstoke, (250) 837-7500

Appendix B: Further Reading

PLANTS AND WILDLIFE

Bear Attacks: Their Causes and Avoidance, Herero, McClelland & Stewart.
Birds of the Rocky Mountains, Fisher, Lone Pine.
The Canadian Rockies Guide to Wildlife Watching: The Best Places to See and Appreciate Animals in Their Natural Habitat, Kerr, Fifth House.
Handbook of the Canadian Rockies, Gadd, Corax Press.
Plants of Southern Interior British Columbia, Parish, Coupe & Lloyd, Lone Pine.
The Pocket Guide to Wild Flowers of North America, Forey, Sino Publishing House.
Rocky Mountain Nature Guide, Bezener and Kershaw, Lone Pine.
Wild Animals of Western Canada, Van Tighen, Altitude Press.

LOCAL HISTORY

Canadian Pacific Railroad and the Development of Western Canada, 1896–1914, Eagle, McGill-Queen's University Press.
Canadian Rockies Placenames, Porter, Luminous Compositions.
Park Prisoners: The Untold Story of Western Canada's National Parks, 1915–1946, Waiser, Fifth House Publishers.

WILDERNESS TRAVEL

Basic Mountain Safety A-Z, Johnson, Altitude Publishing.
Leave No Trace, Harmon, Falcon.
Reading Weather, Falcon.
Wilderness First Aid, Preston, Falcon.
Wilderness Navigation, Burns, The Mountaineers.

OTHER

A Hiker's Guide to Art of the Canadian Rockies, Christensen, Canada Council for the Arts.
Kootenay National Park, Hahn, Rocky Mountain Books.
The Sacred Balance: Rediscovering Our Place in Nature, Suzuki, Greystone Books.

Appendix C: Top Ten Hikes Based on Best Overall Views

1. Alpine Loop, Yoho National Park (Hike 14)
2. Iceline Trail/Little Yoho/Yoho Valley Loop, Yoho National Park (Hike 17)
3. Avalanche Crest, Glacier National Park (Hike 67)
4. Niles Meadows, Yoho National Park (Hike 4)
5. The Rockwall, Kootenay National Park (Hike 40)
6. Asulkan Valley, Glacier National Park (Hike 66)
7. Eva Lake/Miller Lake/Jade Lakes Trail, Mt. Revelstoke National Park (Hike 84)
8. Emerald Triangle, Yoho National Park (Hike 24)
9. Odaray Highline (Grandview) Trail, Yoho National Park (Hike 10)
10. Stanley Glacier, Kootenay National Park (Hike 36)

The glacial blue waters of Miller Lake provide the perfect spot to take a quick dip after lunch.

Appendix D: Trail Finder Table

	Easy	Moderate	Strenuous
Lakes	**Yoho** 1. Ross Lake 3. Sherbrooke Lake 6. Lake O'Hara Shoreline 7. Lake Oesa 9. Lake McArthur/Big Larches Loop 11. Linda Lake Circuit & Morning Glory Lakes 18. Yoho Lake 21. Emerald Lake Circuit	**Yoho** 4. Niles Meadows 12. Cathedral Basin 14. Alpine Loop 17. Iceline (Celeste Lake option) 24. Emerald Triangle	**Yoho** 22. Hamilton Lake
	Kootenay 37. Kaufmann Lake 50. Dog Lake 51. Cobb Lake	**Kootenay** 40. The Rockwall	**Kootenay** N/A
	Glacier/Mt. Revelstoke 79. Lindmark Trail 82. Heather Lake Loop 83. Balsam Lake Loop	**Glacier/Mt. Revelstoke** 65. Marion Lake 84. Eva/Miller/Jade Lakes	**Glacier/Mt. Revelstoke** 64. Abbott Ridge
Waterfalls	**Yoho** 6. Lake O'Hara Shoreline 7. Lake Oesa 15. Takakkaw Falls 16. Laughing Falls 22. Hamilton Falls 33. Wapta Falls	**Yoho** 4. Niles Meadows 8. Opabin Circuit/Highline	**Yoho** N/A
	Kootenay 55. Juniper	**Kootenay** 40. The Rockwall 41. Hawk Creek - Ball Pass	**Kootenay** N/A
	Glacier/Mt. Revelstoke 60. Bear Creek Falls	**Glacier/Mt. Revelstoke** 62. Balu Pass	**Glacier/Mt. Revelstoke** 61. Hermit Trail 66. Asulkan Valley 67. Avalanche Crest 70. Perley Rock 71. Sir Donald
Glacier Views	**Yoho** 6. Lake O'Hara Shoreline 7. Lake Oesa 9. Lake McArthur/Big Arches Loop 11. Linda Lake Circuit & Morning Glory Lakes 16. Point Lace, Laughing & Twin Falls (Yoho Glacier option) 21. Emerald Lake Circuit	**Yoho** 4. Niles Meadows 8. Opabin Circuit/Highline 10. Odaray Highline 12. Cathedral Basin 14. Alpine Loop 17. Iceline Trail 23. Emerald Basin 24. Emerald Triangle	**Yoho** N/A

	Easy	Moderate	Strenuous
Glacier Views (contd.)	**Kootenay** 36. Stanley Glacier	**Kootenay** 40. The Rockwall 41. Hawk Creek - Ball Pass	**Kootenay** N/A
	Glacier/Mt. Revelstoke 63. Abandoned Rails 69. Meeting of the Waters 72. Loop Brook 73. Rock Garden	**Glacier/Mt. Revelstoke** 62. Balu Pass 65. Marion Lake	**Glacier/Mt. Revelstoke** 61. Hermit 64. Abbott Ridge 66. Asulkan Valley 67. Avalanche Crest 68. Glacier Crest 70. Perley Rock 71. Sir Donald
Lookouts and Mountain Tops	**Yoho** N/A	**Yoho** 2. Paget Peak 4. Niles Meadows 10. Odaray Highline 14. Alpine Loop 26. Burgess Pass 34. Mt. Hunter Lookout	**Yoho** N/A
	Kootenay N/A	**Kootenay** 40. The Rockwall 41. Hawk Creek to Ball Pass 43. Honeymoon Pass 52. Kindersley Pass/ Sinclair Creek Loop	**Kootenay** N/A
	Glacier/Mt. Revelstoke 79. Lindmark Trail 81. Meadows in the Sky 82. Heather Lake Loop 84. Eva/Miller/Jade Lakes Trail	**Glacier/Mt. Revelstoke** 62. Balu Pass 68. Glacier Crest	**Glacier/Mt. Revelstoke** 64. Abbott Ridge 66. Asulkan Valley 70. Perley Rock 71. Sir Donald Trail 80. Summit Trail
Backpacking Trips	**Yoho** 27. Amiskwi 29. Otterhead 30. Ottertail 32. Ice River	**Yoho** 17. Iceline/Little Yoho Valley	**Yoho** N/A
	Kootenay 37. Kaufmann Lake	**Kootenay** 40. Rockwall 43. Honeymoon Pass	**Kootenay** N/A
	Glacier/Mt. Revelstoke 84. Eva/Miller/Jade Lakes Trail	**Glacier/Mt. Revelstoke** 59. Copperstain Trail	**Glacier/Mt. Revelstoke** N/A
Interpretive Trails	**Yoho** 20. A Walk in the Past 21. Emerald Lake Circuit	**Yoho** N/A	**Yoho** N/A

	Easy	Moderate	Strenuous
Interpretive Trails (contd.)	**Kootenay** 35. Fireweed Trail 38. Marble Canyon 39. Paint Pots 55. Juniper Trail 58. Valley View Trail	**Kootenay** N/A	**Kootenay** N/A
	Glacier/Mt. Revelstoke 64. Abandoned Rails 72. Loop Brook Trail 74. Hemlock Grove Trail 76. Giant Cedars Trail 77. Skunk Cabbage Trail 81. Meadows in the Sky 82. Heather Lake/Lookout Loop	**Glacier/Mt. Revelstoke** N/A	**Glacier/Mt. Revelstoke** N/A
Short Walks	**Yoho** 6. Lake O'Hara Shoreline 15. Takkakaw Falls 19. Centennial Loop 20. A Walk in the Pas 21. Emerald Lake Circuit 22. Hamilton Falls 33. Wapta Falls	**Yoho** N/A	**Yoho** N/A
	Kootenay 35. Fireweed Trail 38. Marble Canyon 39. Paint Pots 55. Juniper Trail 56. Redstreak Campground/ Sinclair Canyon Trail 57. Redstreak Campground Loop 58. Valley View Trail	**Kootenay** N/A	**Kootenay** N/A
	Glacier/Mt. Revelstoke 60. Bear Falls 63. Abandoned Rails 70. Meeting of the Waters 72. Loop Brook 73. Rockgarden Trail 74. Hemlock Grove Trail 76. Giant Cedars Trail 77. Skunk Cabbage 78. Inspiration Woods 81. Meadows in the Sky 82. Heather Lake/Lookout Loop 83. Balsam Lake/Lookout Loop	**Glacier/Mt. Revelstoke** N/A	**Glacier/Mt. Revelstoke** N/A

Appendix E: Hiker's Checklist

Always make and check your own checklist!

If you've ever hiked into the backcountry and discovered that you've forgotten an essential, you know that it's a good idea to make a checklist and check the items off as you pack so that you won't forget the things you want and need. Here are some ideas:

Clothing
- [ ] Dependable rain parka
- [ ] Rain pants
- [ ] Windbreaker
- [ ] Thermal underwear
- [ ] Shorts
- [ ] Long pants or sweatpants
- [ ] Wool cap or balaclava
- [ ] Hat
- [ ] Wool shirt or sweater
- [ ] Jacket or parka
- [ ] Extra socks
- [ ] Underwear
- [ ] Lightweight shirts
- [ ] T-shirts
- [ ] Bandannas(s)
- [ ] Mittens or gloves
- [ ] Belt

Footwear
- [ ] Sturdy, comfortable boots
- [ ] Lightweight camp shoes

Bedding
- [ ] Sleeping bag
- [ ] Foam pad or air mattress
- [ ] Ground sheet (plastic or nylon)
- [ ] Dependable tent

Hauling
- [ ] Backpack and/or day pack

Cooking
- [ ] 1-quart container (plastic)
- [ ] 1-gallon water container for camp use (collapsible)
- [ ] Backpack stove and extra fuel
- [ ] Funnel
- [ ] Aluminum foil
- [ ] Cooking pots
- [ ] Bowl/plates
- [ ] Utensils (spoons, forks, small spatula, knife)
- [ ] Pot scrubber
- [ ] Matches in waterproof container

Food and Drink
- [ ] Cereal
- [ ] Bread
- [ ] Crackers
- [ ] Cheese
- [ ] Trail mix
- [ ] Margarine
- [ ] Powdered soups
- [ ] Salt-pepper
- [ ] Main course meals
- [ ] Snacks
- [ ] Hot chocolate
- [ ] Tea
- [ ] Powdered milk
- [ ] Drink mixes

Photography
- [ ] Camera and film
- [ ] Filters
- [ ] Lens brush/paper

Miscellaneous
- [ ] Sunglasses
- [ ] Map and a compass
- [ ] Toilet paper
- [ ] Pocket knife
- [ ] Sunscreen
- [ ] Good insect repellent
- [ ] Lip balm
- [ ] Flashlight with good batteries and a spare bulb
- [ ] Candle(s)
- [ ] First-aid kit
- [ ] Your FalconGuide
- [ ] Survival kit
- [ ] Small garden trowel or shovel
- [ ] Walter filter or purification tablets
- [ ] Plastic bags (for trash)
- [ ] Soap
- [ ] Towel
- [ ] Toothbrush
- [ ] Fishing license
- [ ] Fishing rod, reel, lures, flies, etc.
- [ ] Binoculars
- [ ] Waterproof covering for pack
- [ ] Watch
- [ ] Sewing kit

About the Authors

Wherever there's an adventure to be had, you'll find Michelle Gurney and Kathy Howe—whether it's climbing Mount Kilimanjaro, riding elephants in Thailand, or trekking through the Canadian Rockies, hoping not to spot any bears. Both professional writers, Michelle and Kathy have collaborated on numerous projects, although this is their first hiking guide. They left their corporate jobs behind to pursue life and their dream of completing this book.

In the three months they spent researching and writing the book, while based in Golden, British Columbia, they drew on their knowledge of years of hiking and backpacking all over the world. Along the way, they hiked more than 1,200 kilometers, encountered the most curious of grizzly bears (and spotted thirty-five in total), forded icy-cold creeks, and experienced the full gamut of weather conditions—including a Fourth of July blizzard.

When she's not exploring the great outdoors, Michelle works as a communications strategist in Edmonton, Alberta. Kathy, who has called Alberta home for the past seven years, now lives in Phoenix, Arizona, where she's enjoying the novelty of hiking year-round.

Meet the authors, Kathy Howe and Michelle Gurney.